SCHOOLS AND POLITICS:
THE KAUM MUDA MOVEMENT
IN WEST SUMATRA (1927-1933)

Taufik Abdullah

SCHOOLS AND POLITICS: THE KAUM MUDA MOVEMENT IN WEST SUMATRA (1927-1933)

EQUINOX PUBLISHING (ASIA) PTE LTD
No 3. Shenton Way
#10-05 Shenton House
Singapore 068805

www.EquinoxPublishing.com

Schools and Politics:
The Kaum Muda Movement in West Sumatra (1927-1933)
by Taufik Abdullah

ISBN 978-602-8397-50-6

First Equinox Edition 2009

Copyright © 1971 by Cornell Southeast Asia Program Publications; renewed 2009. This edition is authorized by the original publisher, Cornell Southeast Asia Program Publications.

Printed in the United States

1 3 5 7 9 10 8 6 4 2

All rights reserved. No part of this publication may be reproduced, stored in a retrieval system, or transmitted in any form or by any means, electronic, mechanical, photocopying, recording or otherwise without the prior permission of Equinox Publishing.

TABLE OF CONTENTS

	Page
INTRODUCTION	7

Chapter

I.	THE MINANGKABAU WORLD: ALAM AND RANTAU	11
II.	OPPOSITION AND REBELLION	33
III.	THE GRADUATES OF THE KAUM MUDA SCHOOLS AND THEIR LEADERS	57
IV.	MUHAMMADIJAH AND LOCAL POLITICS	85
V.	SCHOOLS AND THE FORMATION OF POLITICAL PARTIES	129
VI.	POLITICIANS AND EDUCATORS	159
VII.	THE SEARCH FOR AN IDEOLOGY	177
VIII.	THE POLITICS OF RADICALISM	199
IX.	PRIVATE SCHOOLS AND POLITICS	235

IN RETROSPECT	257
GLOSSARY	265
SELECTED BIBLIOGRAPHY	277

INTRODUCTION

The continuing process of Islamization and the introduction of new ideas by Minangkabau people returning from abroad form two paramount themes in the history of West Sumatra. The desire to maintain the validity of existing values and assumptions and the need to cope with the new elements resulted in social conflict and in an incessant effort to reformulate the concept of the Minangkabau world. The traditional world view, as expressed in numerous adat-sayings and illustrated in historical traditions (*tambo*) and epics (*kaba*), stresses the continuing worth of ancient wisdom, but, at the same time, it recognizes the importance of change. Both are thought necessary for the attainment of a perfect society, one in which social and cosmic harmony prevail. The strength of this traditional view is reflected both in the conservatism of the Minangkabau social system and in the dynamic attitude often displayed by its individual members.

The driving force of Minangkabau history arises from the struggle to build a balanced social order on a convergence of seemingly contradictory social and cultural aspects. From the time when Islam was conceived as a pillar of the Minangkabau world, the history of Minangkabau has been dominated by an effort to attain an acceptable equilibrium between the doctrine of a universal religion and the wisdom and ideals of the pre-existing pillar, the indigenous element or *adat*. The idea that Islam is an inseparable part of Minangkabau has generated constant internal struggle. A traditional notion that ideas which came from the outside world (the *rantau*) might endanger the foundation of Minangkabau or stimulate disturbing potentialities already inherent in it resulted in ambivalence toward Western-oriented modernization.

In the beginning of the 1900's, the Islamic modernist movement began spreading its influence in West Sumatra. Launched by religious scholars (*ulama*) who had been influenced by new intellectual trends in the Middle East, the movement was directed at the purification of prevailing religious practices and also at using Islam as a basis for social change. In the process, the movement generated religious and social conflicts which lasted for almost two decades. The Islamic modernist scholars, known as the *Kaum Muda* ulama, eventually dominated Minangkabau social and political movements. The religious and educational activities of the Kaum Muda ulama and their students and followers brought about an expansion and modernization of religious schools. By using Islam as the basis of their programs, the Islamic modernists could claim religious sanction for their activities.

The purposes of the study which follows are to trace the development of the Kaum Muda movement and to inquire into its intellectual and social impact on Minangkabau. The principal actors were actually from the second generation of Islamic modernists, the students of the Kaum Muda ulama. We will examine the way they confronted their social and political environment; the path they followed in carrying out their various programs; their encounter with the Dutch government; and their relationship with the adat authorities. We will seek to determine the impact of the activities and intellectual development of these young Islamic modernists upon their own group and upon their relationship with their former mentors, the Kaum Muda ulama. For this reason, the study concentrates on the period beginning in early 1927 and ending with the third quarter of 1933.

On New Year's Eve of 1927, a rebellion broke out in Silung-kang, a village in West Sumatra. It precipitated extensive and repressive government action throughout the Residency. This so-called "communist" rebellion delivered a major psychological shock to the Minangkabau. The post-rebellion period witnessed continuous attempts by the Islamic modernists, whose followers were some of the most important promoters of the Islamic-communist movement, to recover from this traumatic event and to find new channels for their activities. Though rejecting rebellion as a suitable means for achieving their political goals, the second generation of the Islamic modernists continued their anti-government political activities, emphasizing the importance of an enlarged concept of unity. They wanted the Minangkabau people to view their own traditional ideas about legitimate power, thought to be based on popular consensus, in the light of the actual political situation. With the cooperation of the Western-educated intellectuals and under the leadership of recent returnees from Cairo, they developed new private schools and intensified the modernization process in existing religious schools. In August 1933, provoked by the renewed political radicalism on the part of Islamic parties, the government instituted regulations which paralyzed political activity. This was followed by the arrest of several important leaders of the Islamic movement. Many Kaum Muda educators were forbidden to teach and some of their schools were closed down.

The six years from 1927 to 1933 comprised a period in which various political and social aspects of Minangkabau life were intensified and erupted into open conflict. It was a time when the Islamic modernists politicized Minangkabau and extensively spread the new ideas of "progress" and "modernization."

CHAPTER ONE
THE MINANGKABAU WORLD: ALAM AND RANTAU

In the beginning, according to Minangkabau historical tradition, there was only *Nur Muhammad* (The Light of Mohammad) through which God created the universe and the first human being.[1] Within this transcendental and universal unity existed the Minangkabau world, one of three known worlds (the other two are China and "Ruhum"). The Minangkabau world, or *alam Minang kabau*, began with the landing of the first ancestors on Mount Merapi, which was then surrounded by water. The history of Minangkabau thus began before the water subsided, before the face of the earth increased in extent, before its inhabitants multiplied. As the water receded, new settlements were established, and finally the "region of the three *luhak*,"[2] which were to become the heartland of Minangkabau, was populated.

The Minangkabau people continued their geographical explorations and established new settlements beyond the heartland. These new territories were called rantau. Geographically, therefore, the rantau was constantly extended in accordance with the expansion of the Minangkabau people. Both the static heartland and the ever-expanding rantau, however, belonged to the alam Minangkabau.

Though a world in itself, the alam Minangkabau is at the same time a conglomeration of smaller worlds, the *nagari*, each forming an "independent" political community with its council hall (*balai*), mosque,

---

1 One example of a Minangkabau traditional history is Datuk Sangguno Diradjo, *Mustiko Adat Alam Minangkabau* (Djakarta: Kementerian P.P.ӃK., 1955).
2 The three *luhak* referred to in the text are the three major regions of the heartland: Tanah Datar, Agam and the Lima Puluh Kota, called collectively the *luhak nan tigo*.

roads and public bathing place. In Minangkabau adat theory, a nagari is considered the most developed type of settlement; it has a definite boundary and its own recognized satellite territories.[3] All nagari share common adat ideals and adat assumptions, but, at the same time, a nagari is a smaller alam and regards its neighbors as its rantau, and hence regions to be explored. Within this context, merantau, going to the rantau, can simply mean leaving one's own nagari.

The Minangkabau world view includes an indigenous political tradition of *penghulu* and of kings.[4] The penghulu acts as the head of several matrilineal families, and his position is based on the consensus of his own people. The king provided a sacral mediating influence among the "independent" nagari. This dichotomy in the political system was bridged by the co-existence in the heartland of the Koto Piliang and Bodi Tjaniago traditions. The former recognized a hierarchical ranking of the penghulu whereas the latter considered all penghulu as equal. Unlike the heartland, the rantau nagari were ruled by *radja*, representatives of the king who himself lived in the heartland. The rantau's most important function however was not as a dependency for the royal family but as a gate to and from the outside world.

Minangkabau history constantly demonstrates the role of the rantau as the provider of outside influences which are incorporated into the existing alam. Such influences, however, were most significant when they coincided with potentials already contained in the alam itself. The incorporation of kingship into an indigenous world which was based on penghuluship was facilitated by a pre-existing tradition of hierarchy in certain political structures; thus the new element could easily meld with the existing system. The absorption of Islam into the Minangkabau system of belief and social structure did not displace the adat but rather enriched the alam Minangkabau. Through continuing exploration, the alam's potentialities unfolded, and outside elements were incorporated. But original elements remained identifiable; it was not a featureless synthesis in which the old ways were completely submerged.

---

3 A. M. Dt. Maruhum Batuah and Dt. Bagindo Tanameh, *Hukum Adat dan Adat Minangkabau* (Djakarta: Pusaka Aseli, 1956), pp. 58-60.

4 P. E. de Josselin de Jong, *Minangkabau and Negri Sembilan: Socio-Political Structure in Indonesia* (Djakarta: Bhratara, 1960), pp. 97-116.

Within the context of tradition, a new element can only be accepted after it has met certain requirements. It must be introduced through the established pattern of social hierarchy, which culminates in the *mufakat* (consensus) of the penghulu.[5] This will ensure that the new element will not cause a change in the basic adat foundation. The innovation moreover should be logically possible (*mungkin*) and morally proper (*patut*).[6] If it cannot meet these qualifications, the new element might disrupt social harmony and the alam might deviate from its correct course of development.

The acceptance of Islam is an illustration of the absorption of new elements, for the alam Minangkabau has come to be seen as a harmonious world containing both Islam and adat. This harmony was expressed in the concept of the three kings of Minangkabau—the King of Adat, the King of Religion, and the King of the World. On the nagari level as well, religious func-tionaries were included in the adat hierarchy. This harmony is usually characterized by the adat aphorism (*pepatah adat*) that "adat is based on *sjarak* (religious law), sjarak is based on adat." Adat should maintain the harmony of society, while sjarak works to achieve harmony between self and the cosmic order. The unity of the nagari is symbolized by the existence of one balai and one mosque. The former represents adat, the latter religion.[7]

Nineteenth-Century Crises in Minangkabau

The traditional conception of alam as a harmony among contradictions faced a major challenge at the turn of the nineteenth century from an orthodox religious reform movement, the Padri. Launched by three Minangkabau *hadji*, who had been influenced by the Wahabists in Arabia, the movement rejected the idea of a balance between adat and Islam. Rather than "purity of heart," the Padri stressed the outward manifestation of religiously correct behavior. Instead of harmony, the Padri aimed at the

---

5 Datuk Sangguno, *Mustiko Adat*, Chapters 1-4.
6 For example: It is possible to make a ricefield in someone else's yard, but is it proper (*patut*)? It is proper to make a ricefield on top of a mountain, but is it possible (*mungkin*)?
7 See my article, "Adat and Islam: An Examination of Conflict in Minangkabau," *Indonesia*, No. 2 (October 1966), pp. 1-14.

predominance of religious law (sjarak) over other rules and standards. This militant, religious movement condemned traditional practices as against the sjarak. It thereby threatened the whole concept of alam and caused a major civil war. The fierce struggle was not just a conflict between fanatical religious believers and the custodians of the old order; it was also one between a totalistic and a relative view of the world.

In spite of the social polarization which existed during the fierce conflict, Minangkabau gradually recovered from this crisis. The increase in the Padri's following resulted in a dilution of its earlier elan and a willingness to seek accommodation.[8] This process was accelerated in 1821 by Dutch intervention. In the meantime, the external stimulus was waning because the Wahabists in Arabia had lost the offensive and had begun to retreat.

When the war ended in 1837, it was clear that the Padri had not substantially changed Minangkabau political and social structure, though the movement had strengthened the force of religion and enlarged its scope throughout the social system. A new adat formulation was introduced which emphasized the contrast between *adat djahilijah*, syncretic and unenlightened adat, and *adat islamijah*, adat in accord with religious law. The highest adat category, "adat which is truly adat," was now interpreted as the Quran and the Hadith (Prophetic Tradition). A new aphorism on the relation between adat and religion was also introduced: "adat is based on sjarak; sjarak is based on Kitabullah [The Book of God]." The subordination of adat to religious law was expressed as "sjarak designs, adat applies." Ideally, then, adat was the correct manifestation of the religious law. In addition to this new formulation, which was still to be contested, another consequence of the Padri war was the strengthened position of religious teachers and an expanded network of religious schools.

The end of the internal war, however, had resulted from the conquest of the alam Minangkabau by the Dutch. The sacral royalty, formerly the mediating influence among the nagari, was replaced by a powerful Dutch governor, and a functional supranagari organization was introduced. The nagari council theoretically remained the power

---

8 Sophia Raffles, *Memoirs of the Life and Public Services, with Some of the Correspondence, of Sir Thomas Stamford Raffles* (London: John Murray, 1830), pp. 347-350; Ph. S. van Ronkel, "Inlandsche Getuigenissen Aangaande de Padri-Oorlog," *IG*, 17 (NS), No. 2 (1915), p. 1259.

center in the individual nagari, but above it was placed the office of the *tuanku laras*, who acted as the adat and administrative head of a nagari federation. In-stead of the balai, it was now the tuanku laras who made binding decisions in adat as well as administrative matters.[9] In the 1870's, a further encroachment on the penghulu tradition occurred; the introduction of Western criminal law deprived the balai of its punitive powers as the upholder of nagari law. The erosion of the balai's authority and the decline of the penghulu's prestige were intensified by the unprecedented duties imposed on the penghulu as the supervisors of the *rodi kompeni* (government corvee).

The conquest of Minangkabau weakened the traditional political system and led to a crisis of self-confidence. The decline of penghuluship was seen as a reflection of weakening social ties and deviations from the Minangkabau paradigm, from the alam, The Dutch coffee purchase monopoly and the corvee system, both of which were introduced soon after the end of the Padri war, served as symbols of the intolerable situation. Minangkabau referred to the time as a period in which rodi not adat prevailed.

In this period, another pillar of alam, religion, also experienced a crisis. In the 1850's, an orthodoxly-oriented mystical brotherhood (*tarekat*), the Naqsjabandijah,[10] began denouncing older tarekat, particularly the Sjatariah, as heretical. Naqsjabandijah belief was based on the notion of cognitive unity with God, in contrast to the existential unity preached by other schools, and on the prime importance of outward religious behavior. At the turn of the twentieth century, another religious movement began. Sjech Achmad Chatib,[11] a Minangkabau ulama and an *imam* ("head") of the Shafiite school in the Mosque of Haram (Mecca), attacked the prevalent

---

9 L. C. Westenenk, "De Inlandsche Bestuurshoofden ter Sumatra's Westkust," *KT*, 2 (1913), pp. 673-693.

10 The first ulama to bring the Naqsjabandijah ideas to Minangkabau was presumably Sjech Ismail of Simabur. B. Schrieke, "Bijdrage tot de Bibliografie van Huidige Godsdienstige Beweging ter Sumatra's Westkust," *TBG*, 59 (1920), pp. 262-269.

11 Achmad Chatib (1860-1916) was born in Kota Gedang (near Bukittinggi). A son of Abdul Latif Chatib, the first "Malay" teacher at the teachers' training school in Bukittinggi, he went to Mecca while still young. He studied and taught there and married into the family of an influential, rich Arab merchant. Through his father-in-law's influence, Achmad Chatib was appointed imam. He was one of the most influential teachers among the Indonesian and Malayan community (the *Jawah*) in Mecca. He wrote some forty-nine books. "Sjech Achmad Chatib bin Abdul Latif Al-Minangkabawi," *Pedoman Masjarakat* (1941), pp. 307-323.

religious doctrines and the adat matrilineal inheritance law. The attack on the inheritance law, which he considered in contradiction with religious law, has remained until today at the heart of an unending social and legal issue.[12] Achmad Chatib's denunciation of the mystical brotherhoods,[13] particularly the Naqsjabandijah, as unorthodox signalled the beginning of more than two decades of religious conflict in Minangkabau.

By the beginning of the twentieth century, the foundation of the Minangkabau world was being attacked from all sides. Externally, it faced the strengthening grip of Dutch political and economic power and internally the onslaught of a new religious reform movement. People began to question the capability of alam assumptions to deal with the new and complicated forces. The period was dominated by a feeling that the old order had been disrupted.

During this critical situation, the government introduced a new, monetary tax, in 1908. A decrease in coffee production dating from the last quarter of the nineteenth century caused the government to abolish the coffee monopoly and replace it with revenue from taxation.[14] From a purely economic point of view, the new policy was advantageous to the people, because they could now sell their coffee on the open market for considerably higher prices. But this proved irrelevant, for the people felt that they were being cheated and humiliated by the new regulation. In their eyes, the Dutch government had now bluntly proclaimed itself the "ruler," not just the "protector" of Minangkabau. The provisions of the Plakat Pandjang (Long Declaration), issued by the Dutch during the Padri war, had promised that no direct tax would ever be levied on the Minangkabau.[15] Led by the penghulu, who were irritated by the encroachment on their power, and by the tarekat leaders, who were angered by the attack on

---

12 Jan Prins, "Rondom de Oude Strijdvraag van Minangkabau," *Indonesië*, 7 (1960-1961), pp. 117-129.

13 Sjech Achmad Chatib bin Abdul Latif, *Fatwa Tentang Tharikat Naqsjabandij* ah, translated by A. Mn. Arief (Medan: Islamijah,1965). On the debates over the tarekat schools, see Schrieke, "Bijdrage," pp. 249-325.

14 The tax system was part of a new aggressive policy in the so-called Outer Possessions (Buitenbezittingen) which began after the Dutch-Atjeh War. F. Heckler, "Memorie van Over-gave Betreffend den Toestand van het Gouvernement Sumatra's Westkust (1905-1910)," *Mailrapport* 387/'10 and *Verbaal* April 21, 1911, No. 8.

15 For the full text of the Plakat Pandjang (Lange Verklaring), see H. J. J. L. Ridder de Stuers, *De Vestiging en Uitbreiding der Nederlanders ter Westkust van Sumatra* (Amsterdam: P. N. van Kampen, 1849/1850), II, pp. 8-14.

religious doctrine, an initially passive resistance to the new regulations erupted into rural revolt. The tarekat teachers provided a religious foundation for the scattered uprisings. The government's legitimacy was questioned because it was not based on the consensus of the people (*sakato alam*). The government itself was condemned as a *kafir* (infidel) institution which humiliated religion.

The scattered rural uprisings, however, were mostly a defensive reaction meant to prevent any further breakdown of the old order. They were directed against the unintelligible forces that increasingly dominated people's lives. By employing strong repressive measures the government suppressed the unrest and imposed the taxation program.[16]

The Idea of Kemadjuan

The tragic events of 1908 marked the beginning of a new era in Minangkabau, a period of economic change and of the increasing predominance of urban influences in the nagari. The rapid penetration of the money economy into the nagari began to break down the traditional notion of the nagari as a more or less self-sufficient community. Following the introduction of the monetary tax system, the government removed some of the obstacles to economic growth by abolishing the ban on rice export and other controls over rice production. At the same time, the traditional eastern outlet via the Straits of Malacca was reopened.[17] In 1911, the government introduced the People's Credit System, a network of village banks under the jurisdiction of adat authorities; by 1916 banks were located throughout the greater part of Minangkabau.[18]

The positive response of the Minangkabau to the new economic opportunities was facilitated by the rotating market system. Since the end of the nineteenth century, in every subdistrict a nagari held its own market days once or twice a week. On its market day, the nagari became the economic center for the surrounding area. This rotating market system was repeated on the district level, so that each district administrative

---

16 Heckler, "Memorie van Overgave,"p. 7.
17 B. Schrieke, "The Causes and Effects of Communism on the Westcoast of Sumatra," in his *Indonesian Sociological Studies* (The Hague: W. van Hoeve, 1955), I, pp. 95-106.

center once a week became the focal point where people from the several sub-districts conducted their business.[19]

Unlike the nagari, which resulted from gradual expansion of an old settlement, interior towns, such as Padang Pandjang, Bukittinggi (Fort de Kock), Batu Sangkar (Fort van der Capellen), and Pajakumbuh, were created by the Dutch to serve specific purposes. Established originally as military fortresses during the Padri war, these towns later became depots for coffee deliveries and general administrative and economic centers of the districts. The towns in the interior could be considered as a rantau in terms of the people from surrounding nagari who were attracted to them. Town dwellers who were not natives of the town itself were called *perantau* and were under the jurisdiction of the *penghulu dagang* (literally, the penghulu for foreigners) who served as a temporary head for their quasi-adat community. The perantau were traditionally people who left their home nagari and traveled to the rantau. But unlike the case in the past, they now commonly settled in the rantau and established households there. In spite of the powerful pull of the matrilineal family, based on its communal house and lands, a trend placing greater importance on the nuclear family developed among the urban perantau. This process tended to weaken the matrilineal uncle-to-nephew relationship and was an important aspect of Minangkabau social development in the twentieth century. In the rantau nuclear family, the father gradually began to assume many of the functions formerly exercised by his wife's brother (the *mamak*), who was the traditional guardian of the children.[20]

It was also in these towns that the first slow progress toward accommodation with the new situation began. Since the second half of the nineteenth century, the Dutch government had operated a school system designed to train lower government officials and, to a lesser extent, to combat illiteracy. In the district capitals, the government established

---

19 *Ibid.*, pp. 98-100. On the markets, see H. W. Stap, "De Nagari-Ordonnantie ter Sumatra's Westkust," *TBB*, 53 (1917), pp. 754-760.
20 This is somewhat exaggerated. In spite of the stronger authority which the father now has over his children, the *mamak* is still highly respected, and he remains a person to be consulted. In this, I agree with Umar Junus' criticism ["Some Remarks on Minangkabau Social Structure," *BKI*, 120, No. 3 (1964), pp. 293-320] of Maretin's models of The Minangkabau family system ["Disappearance of Matriclan Survivals in Minangkabau Family and Marriage Relations," *BKI*, 117 (1961), pp. 168-196].

five year vernacular schools, the so-called second class schools. In Padang and Bukittinggi, the two largest towns, "European schools" were founded. A *kweekschool*, a teachers' training institute, had opened in Bukittinggi in the mid-1850's. By the end of the nineteenth century, this school, popularly referred to as Sekolah Radja (School of the Kings) was the most important educational institution in the territory. Many of the early Minangkabau modernizers graduated from it. Throughout the latter part of the nineteenth and the first decade of the twentieth century, the government school system in the rural areas developed very slowly. Popular suspicions about the intention of the kafir government plus the fact that establishment of schools was entirely dependent upon the initiative of nagari heads and the tuanku laras combined to hinder early development in education. But in the early 1910's, the educational system expanded rapidly after the introduction of the so-called *volksschool* (people's schools). These were three year elementary schools directly under government control but financed by the nagari community. By 1913, there were 111 such volksschool and by 1915 the number had increased to 358.[21] Some nagari, particularly Kota Gedang (near Bukittinggi), produced large numbers of school teachers and government officials. In 1911, Kota Gedang through its own locally-financed Study Fund managed to send two students to Holland for advanced education, and by 1914 the nagari had its own Dutch-Native School (Hollandsch-Inlandsche School, HIS).[22]

The conscious drive to create new conditions in West Sumatra originated in Padang, the capital of the province. In the latter part of the nineteenth century, the coastal aristocrats and the native officials had' begun adopting a new style of life, characterized by Dutch-style clubs and newspapers.[23] They propagated notions of *kemadjuan* (progress and modernity). *Insoelinde*, which began publication in 1901 as a journal for teachers and native officials, represented the first important mouthpiece of the drive for kemadjuan. It had correspondents throughout the archipelago, and it contained articles urging the "Indies" as a whole to become progressive (*mendjadi madju*). "Look at Japan," one writer stated,

---

21 Ballot, "Memorie van Overgave," pp. 81-82.
22 K. A. James, "De Nagari Kota Gedang," *TBB*, 49 (1915), p.185.
23 Insoelinde, 1, No. 1 (1902), p. 13.

"for thirty years the nation has been rapidly developing, the country is now rich and the people are well educated."[24] The early generation of Western-educated teachers, who formed the principal writers for the journal, believed that the way to achieve progress was through development of a modern school system. They insisted that education should no longer be based on the outdated religious schools and that teachers should not be misled by the still-influential religious teachers.[25]

The notion of kemadjuan was reinterpreted beginning in 1904, after Abdul Rivai, a Minangkabau medical student in Holland, became the Malay editor of *Bintang Hindia* (The Star of the Indies), the journal most influential among educated Indonesians. He suggested that a sense of "national pride" should form the basic driving force toward kemadjuan. He stressed the need for a "catch-up" psychology, so that the "Indies" would be able to participate in the modern world.[26] Joining the world of progress, Rivai argued, should not be seen as the elimination of one's own identity or nation. Because the modern world involved an incessant competition between nations, "The Indies would remain the Indies, no matter how developed or how high their status might become."[27] Rivai's interests were perhaps politically rather than culturally oriented, but his appeal raised an important question which became the central issue for future debates over the course of progress.

In Minangkabau the idea of kemadjuan was at the heart of intellectual conflicts on such diverse subjects as adat and religion. The rhetoric of the first two decades of the twentieth century contrasted "young" (*muda*), defined as the symbol of progress, with "old" (*tua*), seen as backward and conservative. "Young" was also used to mean "rootless" while "old" was exalted as the representative of "the glory (*kernegahan*) of Mount Merapi," the nexus of the Minangkabau world. In secular terms the con-flict was defined as that between progressive and conservative groups. In religious

---

24 Bagindo tan Emas, "Pengharapan pada Kota Padang," *Insulinde*, 2, No. 2 (1903), pp. 518-519. Japan was the most popular example cited by the writers in *Insoelinde*. The victory of Japan over Russia in 1905 confirmed japan's role as a model to be emulated.
25 One writer put it: "We should not follow [the guidance] of the Quranic teachers [*guru mengadji*] because their objectives are different from that of the school teachers. Their objectives are to make the children believe in them and to follow their orders." *Insoelinde*, 1, No. 2 (1901), pp. 22-23.
26 *Bintang Hindia*, 4, No. 3 (1904), p. 38.
27 *Bintang Hindia*, 4, No. 12 (1904), pp. 153-155.

terms, it was the struggle between modernist and traditionalist ulama.

The first overt response to the problems of progress and modernity arose in 1906 among the so-called "Young Malay" group under the leadership of Datuk Sutan Maharadja. It began in Padang as a political-cultural movement of perantau in opposition to the coastal aristocratic class and particularly the office of the Regent. They argued that progress should be the elaboration and articulation of ideas and ideals inherent in the genuine Minangkabau adat, and they denounced existing coastal political institutions as deviations from the alam Minangkabau.[28]

According to its leader, the movement was intended to return Padang to the fold of the alam and to eliminate the gulf between the rulers (the so-called "first class human beings") and the ruled.[29] Influenced by the "Young Turks" movement in the Middle East, he called his group the Kaum Muda (Group of the Young, or Progressives) and labeled his opponents the Kaum Kuno (Group of the Old, or Conservatives).

Datuk Sutan Maharadja also championed the cause of women's education. In 1909 he established the first weaving school in Padang; by 1912 there were about twelve such schools in the town. His program was based on the idea that progress and "women's welfare" could be attained by reviving the Minangkabau legacy. Education for girls was a means for realizing the high status of women prescribed in the adat. As part of his campaign, in 1911 Datuk Sutan Maharadja organized the first feminist newspaper, *Soenting Melaju* (Malay Ornament). Edited by his daughter, Ratna Djuita, then by Rohana Kudus, often called "the Kartini of Sumatra,"[30] the newspaper provided the first public forum for educated Minangkabau women.

By the mid-1910's, the adat oriented kemadjuan movement had to face an increasing challenge from the Islamic modernists. Students of Sjech Achmad Chatib had returned to propagate his ideas on orthodox reform in their home districts. Prominent among these were Sjech M. Djamil Djambek in Bukittinggi, Hadji Abdullah Ahmad in Padang and Padang

---

28 G. de Wal van Anckeveen, "Maleische Democratie en Padangsche Toestanden," *Adatrechtbundels*, 1 (1911), pp. 114-128.
29 Datuk Sutan Maharadja, "Kaoem Moeda Tahoen 1906," *Oetoesan Melajoe*, December 22, 1917.
30 Rohana Kudus was a sister of Sutan Sjahrir, the Indonesian nationalist leader and prime minister (1945-1947). On her life, see "Kartini Ketjil dari Minangkabau: Sitti Rohana," *Pandji Islam* (1940), pp. 9054-9080.

Pandjang, Hadji Rasul (also known as Sjech Abdul Karim Amrullah) in Manindjau and Padang Pandjang, and Sjech Thaib Umar in Batu Sangkar. They attacked the heterodoxy of the tarekat and opposed unauthorized innovation (*bid'ah*) in religious practices. Their purification movement was greatly influenced by the nineteenth-century Egyptian reformer, Sjech Muhammad Abduh. By the second decade of the twentieth century, these young religious scholars, also referred to as the Kaum Muda, had begun to denounce traditional religious experts for basing their own religious judgments solely on *naql*, that is to say, on the established authorities. The reformers argued that belief (*iman*) if based on *taqlid* (uncritical acceptance of textual authorities) was wrong, because the real sources of religious law were the Quran and the Hadith. Scholars should return to the original sources, according to the Kaum Muda ulama, and strive to attain truth by using their *akal* (reasoning), a process known as idjtihad.

> Man who does not use his akal is an inferior human being... He can be considered as one whose objective in life is only motivated by his desire to satisfy his appetites...[31]

Appeals for a rational attitude toward religion and for a return to Islamic orthodoxy would not only liberate Muslims from inhibiting traditions but also would recall Islam's inherent greatness for them. Kaum Muda ulama denounced the tarekat for their essentially escapist orientation. They refuted the notion prevalent in religious circles that religious knowledge for its own sake was the only thing of importance in the world. "Islam," one Kaum Muda spokesman stated, "is not just a religion for the world hereafter, but rather the guide for life in this world."[32] He criticized, in this regard, the attempts of the older genera-tion of religious teachers to prevent pupils from pursuing sciences based on reasoning (*akalijah*).

---

[31] Hadji Abdullah Ahmad, *Pemboeka Pintoe Sjoerga* (Padang: Al-Moenir, 1914/1915), p .47.
[32] *Ibid*. In one of his books, Sjech Muhammad Abduh asserted that in "Islam, life takes precedence over religion" and that "the health of the body takes precedence over the health of the religion." Instead of drawing a sharp distinction between material progress and spiritual growth, Abduh stressed the complementary nature of the two. In his words, "God reminds us that the Hereafter can be achieved while enjoying God's blessing in this world." Cited in Malcolm H. Kerr, *Islamic Reform: The Political and Legal Theories of Muhammad 'Abduh and Rashid Rida* (Berkeley: University of California Press, 1966), pp. 117-118.

In the past our people were trapped in the valley of suffering and destruction because of the corrupt teachers and traders of religion, who persuaded and tied our people to the religion of ignorance.[33]

The purification of religion and the rejection of taqlid were considered the first steps toward the rediscovery of the true ethics of Islam, which in the past had brought Muslims to the peak of civilization and temporal power. The reformers were not motivated by a desire to transform the theological foundations of Islam but rather by a wish to prepare the ground for social change which would create a religiously-based, rational society. Kemadjuan was regarded as a renaissance of Islam rather than as a transformation of it.

As part of the conflict with the traditionalist, Kaum Tua religious scholars, the modernists began to attack traditional religious practices, such as the way to celebrate the Prophet's birthday. In denouncing the prevailing practice, the Kaum Muda ulama attacked the dogmatic mentality of the Kaum Tua and at the same time undermined the position of adat religious functionaries, who officiated at religious rites incorporated into adat. A consequence of these controversies was a temporary polarization among the Muslims. For some years, for example, the central mosque of Padang, which was under adat jurisdiction, employed two imam, representing the Kaum Tua and Kaum Muda respectively. The end of the fasting month (*idulfitri*), theoretically a time for forgetting and forgiving past mistakes, was celebrated separately by the two groups. In the Minangkabau interior, where adat authorities were more powerful, religious conflict was even more intense. Religious issues often caused estrangements between father and son, husband and wife. The religious reformers however believed that *aqidah* (religious doctrine) was worth the risks of such polarization.

While facing the challenge of successive religious reform movements, from the Padri through the Naqsjabandijah to the Islamic modernists, adat changed from a collection of commonly accepted forms and traditions into a statement of regulations and philosophy. In response to the activities of the Islamic modernists, however, adat began to assume the

---

33 Hadji Abdullah Ahmad, *Ilmoe Sedjati* (Padang: Sjarikat Ilmoe, 1916), I, p. 75.

status of an ideology. Its ideas and institutions were being crystal—lized into a universal system. The social network characterized by the uncle-and-nephew relationship, for example, was interpreted as demonstrating the "socialist" character of Minangkabau adat, as opposed to a father-and-son relationship which would be "natural."[34] Adat proponents argued that religion came from God and adat came from the recognition of truth, but, in the last analysis, truth could not be separated from God. The correct kemadjuan, they said, was not simply a response to unavoidable circumstances but something imperative in the adat itself. Adat's ability to survive depended on its ability to maintain its form while gradually enlarging its content.[35] In the face of continuing attack by the Kaum Muda ulama, and often by the Western-educated intellectuals, the adat-oriented kema-djuan protagonists, such as Datuk Sutan Maharadja, had begun to call themselves Kaum Kuno by the end of the 1910's.

The suitability of adat for the changing times was seriously questioned by the Western-educated generation on the rantau. In 1918, a group of young Minangkabau intellectuals on Java formed their own organization, the Jong Sumatranen Bond (Young Sumatran's Union). They came mostly from the upper levels of colonial Minangkabau society and had grown up in the period of religious conflict and the debate over kemadjuan. They professed the desire to create a fatherland "whose population respects adat custom highly, but [which respect is based on] Western civilization and knowledge."[36] The "fatherland" was Sumatra, not Minangkabau, because they believed that a single ethnic group could not carry out the task of elevating the people from "their ignorance and indifference" by itself. Picturing themselves as "the builders of a new nation," these young intellectuals were convinced that progress could not be achieved simply by a new attitude toward the adat. Modernity was possible only by an incorporation of the "Western mind" into the adat.[37]

Although in the early stages of their movement these young

---

34 The writings of Datuk Sutan Maharadja in *Oetoesan Melajoe* and *Soenting Melajoe* are contained in "Artikelen van Datoek Soetan Maharadja in de *Oetoesan Melajoe*, 1911-1915," *Adatrechtbundels*, 27 (1928), pp. 291 ff.
35 Most Minangkabau adat theoreticians subscribe to this view. For example, M. Nasroen, *Dasar Falsafah Adat Minangkabau* (Djakarta: Pasaman, 1957).
36 *Jong Soematra*, 1, No. 6/7/8 (June/July/August 1918), pp. 120-121.
37 *Soeara Perempoean*, 1, No. 5 (September 1918), pp. 114 ff.

intellectuals worked closely with the older generation of the religious and secular Kaum Muda, later they became increasingly separated from their own alam. Rather than return to Minangkabau, as was expected by their society and tradition, a large number of them were absorbed into the rantau society permanently.

The secular and religious controversies between the Kaum Muda and Kaum Tua groups were discussed in their numerous publications and debated publicly. They formed the basis for a proliferation of voluntary associations. Every faction had its own organ and spokesmen. The second decade of the twentieth century, especially, was a time when voluntary associations sprang up like mushrooms all over Minangkabau.[38] In 1912, with the cooperation of traders and civil servants, the religious Kaum Muda of Padang established the Sarekat Usaha (Association of Endeavor), which in turn founded the first private Dutch-Native School (HIS) offering a religious education. They also formed the Sarekat Ilmu (Association for Knowledge), which published Kaum Muda-oriented religious texts. In 1920, the Minangkabau Kaum Muda ulama organized the Persatuan Guru Agama Islam (PGAI, Association of Islamic Religious Teachers). In 1921, the Kaum Tua ulama, who had refused to join the PGAI, established their own organization, the Ittihadul Ulama (Association of Ulama). In 1916, Datuk Sutan Maharadja, in an effort to counteract the Kaum Muda education and political movements, established the Sarekat Adat Alam Minangkabau (SAAM, Adat Association of the Minangkabau World).

> The voluntary association was now seen as the best method for achieving economic and educational progress. "Organization or association," as a writer of the Kaum Muda journal, Al-Moenir, put it, is an institution for channeling the spirit of reform..., to encourage enterprising vigor and to enhance the nobility of knowledge [*kemuliaan ilmu*]. It is a place to cultivate [brotherhood] among mankind and nations.[39]

The voluntary association was idealized as the best instrument through

---

38 See my "Minangkabau 1900-1927: Preliminary Studies in Social Development" (M.A. Thesis, Cornell University, 1967), pp. 98-120.
39 *Al-Moenir*, 2, No. 1 (May 1912).

which the objectives of its members could be advanced, and the success of organizations such as the Sarekat Usaha of Padang and the Study Fund of Kota Gedang provided supporting evidence for such views.

At the same time such organizations helped reduce controversy and conflict. Sometimes a conscious effort was made as in the case of the Kaum Tua organization which said that its members should abandon controversy and should only maintain their loyalties to the teachings of the Shafiite school of law (*mazhab*).[40] But more important, such organizations formed a kind of community, a place where the members could feel secure in their opinions; one might say that it functioned as a kind of "internal rantau" for its members. Whether formed within or outside the adat community, the organization had its own rules and assumptions which were not necessarily identical with those of the adat world. Some organizations were designed to support the existing order in the adat community and others to change it from within by developing the organization into a counter-institution.

The Role of the Rantau

The Minangkabau chronicles (tambo) demonstrate the essential part played by the rantau in the development of the alam. The institution of kingship and the Islamic religion are the two most important elements which came from the rantau but were subsequently incorporated into the alam. The successive series of religious reform movements, from the Padri to the modernists, were started by persons who had been to Islamic centers beyond Minangkabau. The drive toward Western concepts of progress received its major support from traders, civil servants and school teachers who had lived in the newly emerging towns. Educational and political development in twentieth-century Minangkabau were deeply influenced by perantau intellectuals, both Islamic- and Western-educated.

The important role of the rantau can be explained by examining its place in the Minangkabau conception of the world and in Minangkabau social structure. It was not just a gate through which new elements could

---

40 *Oetoesan Melajoe*, August 20 and September 1, 1921.

enter the alam but also one through which dissatisfied persons in the alam community could find an outlet. The rantau acted as a means for easing the internal tensions which arose from discrepancies between the Minangkabau conception of the relationship between the individual and society, on the one hand, and the demands of its matrilineal social structure, on the other.

The individual and society, according to adat ideals, though two entities, are yet inseparable. The relationship between them is determined by the cycles of authority and obligation, in which the object and the ultimate source of authority reside within the same locus. The *kemenakan* (nephew), who symbolizes the individual, should acknowledge the authority of his mamak (uncle), who in his turn relies on the penghulu. The latter should base his judgment on the mufakat which expresses society's wishes and communal wisdom. According to this hierarchical order of authority, the individual comes under the full control of his society. But the pepatah adat state that in fact the kemenakan is not merely the object, he is also the ultimate source of authority. Outwardly the penghulu is the master but in essence he acts only as a servant of his kemenakan. The penghulu's power is not based on his personal attributes but on the legitimacy invested in him by his nephews. A penghulu "is great [because] he is made great [by his kemenakan]." His authority is based on sakato alam, the consensus of his small world, his people.[41]

The foundations of the Minangkabau social system rest on a matrilineal uncle-and-nephew (mamak-kemenakan) network. It centers on the figure of the mother, who is the most important person with regard to the inherited communal house and the inalienable landed properties. As head of the family, the mamak, usually the oldest male, is responsible for the maintenance of the inherited property and for the welfare of his kemenakan; he also serves as the family's representative in *suku* (lineage) affairs. The kemenakan, in turn, must consider the mamak as his "king" (*baradjo kamamak*); he must "ask [his mamak] for permission whenever he leaves and inform him when he returns." In inter-lineage relationships a kemenakan relies on the mamak of the whole suku, that

---

41 For a discussion of this philosophical idea, see Nasroen, *Dasar Falsafah*, pp. 128-136.

is, the penghulu.⁴² A penghulu serves as the chief mamak for his own lineage and a recognized leader of the entire matrilineal political unit. He symbolizes the glory (kemegahan) and the harmony of the adat community under his jurisdiction.⁴³

The Minangkabau have always been fascinated by their adat ideals, and their lives are dominated by elaborate adat social networks and complex adat regulations. The adat functionaries act both as the holders of power and as the legitimate custodians of adat ideals.

In this adat-intensive situation, then, the concept of the rantau provides a philosophical outlet for tolerance of peripheral values. The nagari tacitly recognizes its own "internal rantau," that is, places where peripheral and deviant sets of values can be openly expressed. A typical example from Minangkabau is the *lapau*, the village coffee house, which traditionally has been a place where people may discuss and criticize the members of the balai and the ideas they represent. At its best, the lapau, which is also frequented by people from other nagari, can serve as a source for change within the nagari. At its worst, it is an arena where the Minangkabau can give free rein to their delight in sarcasm. The lapau thus provides a place where both cynics and advocates of active change find a common internal rantau. The various kinds of internal rantau sometimes were transformed into counter-institutions challenging the entire system. Counter-institutions could develop from a new *madrasah*, or other religious school, in the case of a religious reform movement or, in the modern period, from a voluntary association. Voluntary associations, in which adat assumptions and status were irrelevant, offered alternative institutions for advancing individual ideas and wishes. Membership and position depended not upon adat status but personal choice and actions. Voluntary associations provided their members with a sense of participation and satisfaction which they might not be able to find in the existing adat organization and its hierarchy. In the course of modern history voluntary associations often undermined the traditional nagari

---

42 For a fuller description of the obligations of the kemenakan, see, *Adatrechtbundels*, 11 (Sumatra, 1915), pp. 115-129.

43 A penghulu is usually selected from among the male members of the lineages of *urang usali* (original settlers). It sometimes happens that the newly-elected *penghulu* is still a minor in which case an adult pemangku (lit. "holder") is chosen to act in his stead. A pemangku may also be needed if the penghulu is residing outside the nagari.

council's power and sometimes captured the initiative from it.

"Going to the rantau," called merantau, is, according to adat philosophy, one way to fulfill that Principal Law which charges the individual to "subject himself to the largeness of the world."[44] By leaving the nagari, or the Minangkabau world, the youth learns about his own place in the alam and his relationship with other people. The urang siak (religious student) provides a typical and traditional example of a youth who goes to the rantau in search of knowledge. He would travel from one religious school to another seeking to perfect his studies. The *urang siak* maintained the ties between a madrasah and the nagari which surrounded it. The student and the community at large were bound to each other by mutual needs and obligations. The madrasah members distributed elementary religious knowledge and performed religious rites for the nagari people, but at the same time, by their travels, they also served as channels for inter-nagari communication. The community for its part generally supported the urang siak with food and other necessities. When he considered his religious training to be complete, an urang siak was expected to become a religious teacher in his home nagari.

Economic changes and improvements in the religious school system at the turn of the twentieth century also transformed the nature of the urang siak. He was no longer a peripatetic religious scholar living on community charity; he had become a student attached to a particular "modern" madrasah, and his study was financed by his family. The ideal of leaving the nagari in the search for knowledge persisted, however. The establishment of new kinds of schools abroad, such as secular government schools on Java, combined with the increased opportunity to go to the distant rantau, such as the Middle East, meant that the role of rantau as an educational center for the youth remained substantially unchanged.

Rantau is regarded as a strange land with which a Minangkabau young man must familiarize himself. Awareness of the outside world benefits the youth in his personal development as a mature member of the alam, but, at the same time, he is expected to act as an informant and teacher enabling his community to "adopt what is good [from the rantau] and discard what is bad [in the alam]." One reason for the uneven

---

44 *Adatrechtbundels*, 27 (1928), pp. 291 ff.

development between Minangkabau nagari resulted from the number of perantau commuting between a given nagari and the rantau. Economic factors were important determinants for the number of perantau. The more economically self-sufficient nagari had fewer perantau and were thus generally less affected by the money economy or by ideas which developed in the rantau. These nagari were thus relatively successful in maintaining traditional adat patterns of land ownership and social classification. The nagari which were economically more dependent on the rantau were often the first to be affected by new ideas brought by returning perantau, both by participants in Islamic modernist movements and through the increased numbers of children enrolled in the Western schools. Aside from problems associated with a money economy, economic influence could undermine the penghulu's power, by enlarging the numbers of the village elite.

In spite of its place in the Minangkabau world view, "going to the rantau" also represented some personal hardship. A youth often went to the rantau because he felt, or was made to feel, that he had as yet no place in his community, and he hoped that on return he would occupy a proper place in society. Responsibilities to his matrilineal family and to his wife and children might force an adult male to go to the rantau to earn a living. When he returned, he was expected to pay off the family's debts and to increase the family's kemegahan. Alam Minangkabau and the smaller world of the nagari should ideally benefit from the rantau. Money from the rantau would increase the prestige as well as the property of the nagari; perantau ideas would stimulate its philosophical growth. Thus the perantau should make sure the alam is the chief beneficiary of his experiences in the rantau. This accords with the historic tradition, for, according to the tambo, one of the legendary adat-givers gave Minangkabau its adat foundation after his return from adventures abroad.

Successive religious movements which forced a review of the cultural assumptions of the alam were launched by perantau who had been trained in the centers of the Islamic world. The notion of the superiority of Western models for progress prompted the actions of Western-educated perantau in their drive for kemadjuan in Minangkabau. Experience abroad and awareness of ideas developing there helped the perantau to formulate new and enlarged meanings for traditional conceptions about the alam Minangkabau. The perantau introduced the notion of a unity of ideas and faith and a unity of destiny with people outside Minangkabau. Despite differences in emphasis, successive

Islamic reform movements, political parties and educational organizations stressed the importance of realizing a greater Islamic brotherhood. By these conceptions of a greater unity, the perantau threatened to eliminate existing adat ideas about an ever-expanding alam in geographic terms and at the same time to weaken the traditionally centripetal nature of the alam Minangkabau.

CHAPTER TWO
OPPOSITION AND REBELLION

Concern about progress and the rise of Islamic modernism coincided with a period of economic change in Minangkabau. Though originating from different sources, both the intellectual and economic changes were urban phenomena and both had a profound influence on Minangkabau as a whole. During this period, the towns began to assume the leadership in conceptualizing nagari grievances about the corvee and taxes. The tax rebellion of 1908 had shown that traditional kinds of antigovernment actions were not adequate for coping with the new situation. Scattered rebellions fed by a belief in the invulnerability of those who fought against a kafir government clearly could end only in death or exile for the participants.

The emergence of the towns as leaders in political life was precipitated by the introduction of several government regulations. In 1914, the office of tuanku laras, the government-installed adat and administrative head of a nagari federation, was abolished, and the office of *demang*, a purely administrative position covering a larger territorial unit, was instituted. The nagari head, according to the Nagari Ordinance of 1914, had to be elected from among the so-called "core penghulu," those whose adat positions were recognized by the government; all other penghulu were ineligible. The government thus nullified the traditional right of every penghulu to assume membership in the nagari council.[1] The Agrarian

---

1 H. W. Stap, "De Nagari-Ordonnantie," pp. 699-765. Governor Ballot believed this was the best way to establish an organic political structure in the nagari and at the same time to secure a good relationship between the government and the people. Gov. Ballot, "Memorie van Overgave," *Verbaal* April 5, 1916, No. 15. Resident LeFebvre later changed the ordinance to allow village notables (the *urang patuik*) to participate in the nagari council if necessary. Ordinance of 1918, *Staatsblad* 1918, no. 677. Res. LeFebvre, "Memorie van Overgave," *Mailrapport* 2904/'19.

Regulation of 1915 declared that all unoccupied lands fell under government jurisdiction, thereby repudiating the adat concept of *tanah ulajat*, or reserved communal land. The Agrarian Regulation, according to Governor Ballot, proved "a bitter pill for the people."[2] The new statutes exacerbated the persisting antagonisms toward the government. Unlike the anti-tax rebellion, however, now the opposition was guided by urban leaders.

Into this situation was introduced an increasing influence from political activities in Java, particularly the formation of parties. The Sarekat Islam (SI, Islamic Association) soon emerged as the first political party in Minangkabau, largely as a result of its activities in other parts of Sumatra.[3] At the suggestion of a Minangkabau perantau, who had been an SI leader in Atjeh, Hadji Achmad, a Padang trader-ulama, and Sjech Chatib Ali, a Kaum Tua leader, founded the first branch of the party in Padang. The members were mainly the students and followers of the two men, most of whom worked as petty traders and farmers in the neighborhood of Padang.[4] Some Kaum Muda followers also joined. They were generally better-educated and had a more secure economic base as school teachers and government employees. As a result, the Kaum Muda group soon dominated the party's local board.

The first important activity of the Padang SI was its participation in the first national congress of the Central Sarekat Islam (CSI) in Bandung in 1916. At this congress Abdul Muis,[5] himself a Minangkabau perantau intellectual and vice-president of CSI, criticized the local administration and the government's policies for the West Coast of Sumatra. In his speech,

---

2 *Mailrapport* 640/'17.
3 In 1914 and 1915, most newspaper articles in Minangkabau were strongly anti-SI, particularly after alleged SI involvement in a rural rebellion in Djambi. Abdullah, "Minangkabau 1900-1927," pp. 114-115.
4 *Mailrapport* 29/'17.
5 Abdul Muis (1878-1956) was the son of the tuanku laras of Sungai Puar (Agam). He dropped out of the Indies Medical School (STOVIA) in 1903 and went to work as a clerk in the Department of Education in Batavia, leaving in 1905 when he became an assistant editor of *Bintang Hindia*. From 1907 until 1912, he worked in several government offices. In 1912, he became an editor of the *Preanger Bode* and in 1915 editor-in-chief of *Kaoem Moeda*. He joined the Sarekat Islam in 1915 and occupied several positions in the party before his election as vice-president. For a discussion of his political activities, see Robert Van Niel, *The Emergence of the Modern Indonesian Elite* (The Hague: W. van Hoeve, 1960), pp. 107 ff.; also Ruth T. McVey, *The Rise of Indonesian Communism* (Ithaca: Cornell University Press, 1965), esp. p. 23.

Muis described the situation after the anti-tax rebellion, recounting a story of death, destruction and the unjust enforcement of the hated tax. This speech marked the first time that Minangkabau grievances had been expressed this way in an open forum, and the results demonstrated the usefulness of public protest. Muis' address led to the passage of a resolution by the SI urging the government to inquire into the problems of tax collection in Minangkabau.[6] The central government responded by sending a special commission to investigate the situation in Minangkabau and Tapanuli at the end of 1916.[7]

The Padang SI, however, soon suffered an internal crisis, because, although the majority of the members were loyal followers of the two Kaum Tua founders, most of the board members were Kaum Muda. The conflict was exacerbated by a general lack of organizational and financial skills on the part of the founders. The newly established SI divided into two factions after a crisis which began three months after its founding. In August 1916, the Kaum Muda faction formed its own SI, most of whose members also belonged to the Kaum Muda organization, Sarekat Usaha.[8] The Kaum Muda SI was referred to as the White Card SI, while the Kaum Tua faction became the Red Card SI. The former was led by a teacher of a government Dutch-Native School and the latter remained under the leadership of Hadji Achmad and Sjech Chatib Ali.[9]

The party split also reflected different attitudes toward the government and toward kemadjuan. The Kaum Muda Sarekat Usaha had established in Padang a highly successful HIS-Adabijah which received a subsidy from the government. It was the first Kaum Muda secular school which used Dutch as its medium of instruction. Hadji Abdullah Ahmad, the most aggressively "modern" Kaum Muda ulama, and several Western-educated intellectuals and important Minangkabau traders, such as Abdullah Basa Bandaro, led the Kaum Muda group, and maintained good relations with Dutch officials in Padang. Kaum Tua leaders Sjech Chatib Ali and Hadji Achmad, however, were distrusted by the Resident and his

---

6 Kantoor voor Inlandsche Zaken, *Sarekat Islam Congres (le Nationaal Congres), 17-24 Juni 1916 te Bandoeng* (Behoort bij de geheime missieve van Wd. Adviseur voor Inlandsche Zaken, dd. 29 September 1916, No. 226) (Batavia: Landsdruk-kerij, 1916-1919), pp. 55-57.
7 Abdullah, "Minangkabau 1900-1927," pp. 148-149.
8 *Mailrapport* 2357/'16.
9 *Oetoesan Melajoe*, August 14 and 15, 1915.

subordinates.[10] In addition to their opposition to Islamic modernism, the Kaum Tua SI also distrusted the secular drive toward kemadjuan. The Kaum Tua had their power base in the nagari, and they acted as the urban counterparts of disgruntled rural tarekat leaders. The SI of the Kaum Tua ulama represented a first step toward a new means for opposing the government. They remained the spiritual leaders of anti-government sentiments.[11]

Soon after the SI split, Hadji Achmad requested and received recognition from the Central SI in Java for his faction as a separate SI branch.[12] Hadji Achmad successfully exploited this new status in his competition with the Kaum Muda, establishing several branches of the Kaum Tua SI in the interior. The SI presented itself as a new and more effective means for dealing with popular grievances. In some places its leaders even announced that those who joined would no longer be obliged to pay taxes.[13] Though effective, this approach also had its risks. Taxation had always been the most politically sensitive and potentially explosive issue, and consequently the spread of the Kaum Tua SI generated considerable concern in provincial government circles. In September 1916, the Resident forbade Kaum Tua SI leaders from propagandizing the party outside their respective districts without the permission of local authorities.[14] In Suliki, the Assistant Resident actively participated in a nagari council meeting called to discuss whether permission should be granted for the formation of an SI branch in the nagari. In Solok, Sjech Chatib Ali was confronted by the local Dutch authority in the nagari council. At such meetings, Dutch officials posed all but unanswerable challenges for the SI promoters. "Is Minangkabau adat already so decayed

---

10 Letter of Resident LeFebvre to the Governor-General, October 11, 1916 (secret), No. 175 in *Mailrapport* 2357/'16. W. A. C. Whitlaw, LeFebvre's successor, stated in his own "Memorie van Overgave" that Sjech Chatib Ali was an unreliable person and full of intrigues, Mailrapport 2488/'26.

11 *Mailrapport* 291/'17 and 2357/'17.

12 The recognition was granted on September 21, 1916. In October, Hadji Achmad and Sjech Chatib Ali were already busy propagating the SI in Padang, Painan, Manindjau and Ampat Angkat. Telegram of the Resident on October 7, 1916, in Mailrapport 2357/'16.

  The central government refused to acknowledge the legal right of the SI as a whole, but it did grant legal recognition to individual branches. Van Niel, *Emergence of the Modern Elite*, pp. 117-118.

13 *Oetoesan Melajoe*, September 2, 1916.

14 Koloniaal Verslag, September 1916, *Mailrapport* 2355/'16.

that it needs the SI's support?" or "Are the existing religious institutions no longer able to cope with the situation?"[15] These questions were intended to undercut the SI by implying that it had no legitimate role to play. Adat was already under the jurisdiction of local penghulu; religion could be protected by adat religious functionaries, the Friday Council of the nagari mosque, and the numerous religious teachers.

Nevertheless, the Kaum Tua SI, supported by tarekat leaders, continued to expand into several nagari. The development of the Kaum Tua SI was indirectly assisted by the central government's policy guidelines concerning the party. In accordance with the recommendation of its team investigating SI activities in the Outer Islands, the government decided in principle to award legal rights (*recht-persoon*) to each SI branch which sought such recognition.[16] Thus local Dutch authorities could only stop the party indirectly by preventing its initial development in their area. The Kaum Muda SI received recognition from neither the Central SI nor the government, but even so it made progress in several nagari already influenced by the Kaum Muda religious movement.

Alongside SI expansion in Minangkabau was the development of an "Indies" nationalist party, Insulinde. In 1916 under the influence of the Minangkabau educator and writer Marah Sutan, who was at that time chairman of the party branch in Batavia, several units of Insulinde were created in West Sumatra. Government school teachers, many of whom were former students of Marah Sutan, and urban penghulu formed the core of Insulinde support. After two years, they were granted autonomy by the Batavia branch. Several groups, such as Padang and Solok, had grown into full-fledged branches. As with the Kaum Tua SI, Insulinde's development depended to a large extent upon the personal influence of its promoters, and it drew upon the desire to participate in a new kind of "internal rantau." The Padang branch, led by Sulaiman Effendi, a radical coastal aristocrat, and Radja Ibrahim, a former civil servant, became the

---

15 *Oetoesan Melajoe*, January 27 and 29, 1917.
16 Frijling and Cligneet, "De Sarekat Islam in Zuid Sumatra (Lampung, Palembang, Bengkulen en Djambi)," in *Verbaal* November 27, 1915, No. 13. In its decision of September 9, 1915, the Council of the Indies recommended that the above-mentioned report be sent to all Governors and Residents in the Outer Possessions (see *Mailrapport* 2010/'15). Some of the report's suggestions were: legal recognition of local SI; granting facilities for local branches; establishing good relations with party leaders; and strengthening native officials. *Verbaal* November 27, 1915, No. 13.

first group to introduce the notion of political unity for the "Indies."

Many penghulu and "native" civil servants viewed the emergent political parties as a nuisance to the government and as basically detrimental to the adat-supported authority. Datuk Sutan Maharadja, the leader of the so-called "adat revolution of 1906," reacted by seeking an alliance with his former enemies, the adat-oriented Padang aristocrats. In September 1916, under his leadership, several penghulu from the interior joined coastal aristocrats in establishing the Sarekat Adat Alam Minangkab au (SAAM, Adat Association of the Minangkabau World). Shortly afterward, branches were organized in the interior.

Most SAAM members were adat functionaries or native officials. According to its statutes, the SAAM was designed to guard the alam Minangkabau, its adat and its religion against allegedly harmful activities by a number of intellectual and political movements. The party declared its desire to develop the Minangkabau people in accordance with the inherited values of their alam. Politically, the emergence of the SAAM and some of the later adat parties created a faction committed to the support of the government. The generally loyal stance taken by the adat parties created the popular belief that, despite their frequent criticism of government policies, they were no more than government parties whose ideology represented Minangkabau-centered cultural nationalism.[17]

The spread of the SI, the Insulinde (later called the Nationaal Indische Partij, NIP) and the SAAM, reflected the inability of adat institutions to deal with the contemporary situation. The parties offered institutions outside the adat through which individuals could advance their own ideas and even challenge the existing nagari council. In 1917, for example, a penghulu in Kamang, near Bukittinggi, was summoned by the nagari council of which he was a member. However, he preferred to discuss his case first with the president of his party, the Nationaal Indische Partij, rather than immediately obey the nagari council.[18] Apparently he no longer regarded the nagari council as the ultimate authority over a penghulu.

---

17 Abdullah, "Minangkabau 1900-1927," pp. 132-136. Hendrik Bouman, *Enige Beschouwingen over de Ontwikkeling van het Indonesisch Nationalisme op Sumatra's Westkust* (Groningen: J. B. Wolters, 1949), pp. 40-41.
18 Koloniaal Verslag, June 1917, *Mailrapport* 1712/'17.

In 1918, some shifts began to occur within the political parties. The moderate anti-government leaders of the Kaum Tua SI became close allies of the loyalist SAAM. Sjech Chatib Ali and Hadji Achmad had lost their influence among the numerous SI branches in the interior, and they now became advisors to the central board of the SAAM. The Kaum Muda SI, which had recently been recognized as an independent branch by the Central SI, developed into a moderate opposition party, forming an anti-government alliance with the vociferous NIP.

Several factors lay behind these shifts. The intensification of religious conflict between the Kaum Muda and the Kaum Tua ulama had caused a polarization in several communities. Through public preaching, especially at religious gatherings (*tabligh*), the Kaum Muda ulama attacked anything which they considered religiously unlawful. This served to cement cooperation between the Kaum Tua ulama and the adat-oriented leaders. In 1917 Abdul Muis stopped in Padang on his way to Europe.[19] He tried to reunite the two SI factions, but he failed and so aligned himself with the Kaum Muda side.[20] By so doing, he incurred the enmity of the Kaum Tua SI leaders, the early promot-ers of the SI in West Sumatra. His action also brought the Kaum Muda SI into the arena of political activism. In 1919 Resident LeFebvre, who had had friendly relations with the Kaum Muda group in Padang, was replaced by one of his Assistant Residents, Whitlaw. The new Resident had a reputation for distrusting anything connected with Islam. Whitlaw believed that the only way to rule Minangkabau was through its adat institutions and the penghulu.[21]

---

19 Abdul Muis was on his way to Holland as the SI delegate to a conference with metropolitan government representatives on the question of home defense for the Indies (*Indië Weerbaar*), On the early reaction to the defense question in West Sumatra, see K. A. James, "Indie Weerbaar, te Fort de Kock in 1914," *KT*, 2 (1916), pp. 1599-1603. Through 1916 and early 1917, the defense question formed the focus of political debates in Minangkabau newspapers. Datuk Sutan Maharadja, the editor of *Oetoesan Melajoe* and the leader of the adat party, strongly supported the idea that the Indies should defend themselves in cooperation with the Dutch government. He was challenged by Marah Sutan, a leader of the NIP, and by Noerdin Rassat, a leader of the Kaum Muda SI, who argued that the formation of a militia should be accompanied by greater participation of the people in the administration; this position was in accord with the position taken by the Java SI.
20 *Oetoesan Melajoe*, February 10, 1917.
21 In an article, Datuk Sutan Maharadja stated that Resident LeFebvre had been "a student of the hadji [Hadji Abdullah Ahmad] who is an enemy of the adat party." Resident Whit-law, on the other hand, "is a *tuan*, a gentleman who likes Minangkabau adat." *Oetoesan Melajoe*, May 4, 1920. Resident Whitlaw shared Ballot's opinion that the ideal administration for Minangkabau featured cooperation between adat institutions and the government's administrative machinery.

From 1918 until 1923, the major concern of the Kaum Muda political parties was to achieve political cooperation among themselves and to establish a means for dealing with popular grievances. Together with the loyalist adat parties, they demanded greater popular participation in the government apparatus through the establishment of a genuine Minangkabau council (Minangkabau Raad) entrusted with considerable power.

In June 1918, about thirty Kaum Muda political and educational organizations held a general meeting in Bukittinggi. They decided to form a Sumatran federation of organizations which could coordinate the activities of their numerous associations. Shortly after its establishment, the headquarters of the federation, which was called Budi Baik (Good Character), were transferred to Batavia. The transfer occurred at the instigation of several perantau intellectuals, in particular two Volksraad members, Abdul Rivai and Abdul Muis. They argued that such a Sumatran political party should have its headquarters in Batavia where it could function as a pressure group for "electing" suitable representatives from Sumatra to the Volksraad.[22] Now known as the Sarekat Sumatera or the Sumatranen Bond (Sumatran Union), this party served as the major link between political movements in Java and in Minangkabau, and as the spokesman for the local Sumatran parties in the capital. It had, however, lost its original character as a coordinating body for associations in Sumatra.

The scope of the Sarekat Sumatera was not limited to West Sumatra, and as a result, a need was felt for a body which could deal with purely Minangkabau problems. This feeling was intensified by the desire to formulate suggestions for a newly-constituted Herziening Commissie (Reform Commission) of the government.[23] In April 1919, Bagindo Djamaluddin Rassad, a graduate of the Agricultural College in Wageningen, Holland, took the initiative in organizing the Sarekat Combinatie

---

"A penghulu, however old and conservative he might be," according to Whitlaw, "is a man of distinction, whose influence should be used by the government." "Memorie van Overgave," 2488/'26, p. 14.

22 *Neratja*, September 21, 1918.

23 On this Reform Commission, see Van Niel, *The Emergence of the Modern Elite*, pp. 184 ff.; E. Moresco, "The New Consti-tution of the Netherlands Indies," *Asiatic Review*, 23 (1927), pp. 216-224.

Minangkabau (SCM, Federation of Minangkabau Associations). The members of the SCM were mostly Kaum Muda oriented organizations. Although at first it took a cooperative stance vis-a-vis the government, under the leadership of B. Djamaluddin Rassad and Sulaiman Effendi it soon developed as a spokesman for the radical factions of Minangkabau political and educational organizations.

Under the leadership of Sulaiman Effendi, the SCM was much influenced by Douwes Dekker's NIP in its political orientation. In June 1921, the SCM began to take part in political developments on Java; it participated in the autonomy movement designed to increase the participation of indigenous people in the administration. This movement was initiated by several Indonesian members in the Volksraad, but it failed because of central government hostility.[24] For the SCM, however, participation was a first step toward cooperation with political movements in Java. In June 1922, the SCM took part in the NIP-sponsored All-Indies Congress.

In July 1922, the SCM and its member organizations, particularly the local NIP and the Kaum Muda SI, hosted the first and only Congress of Sumatran Unity (Congres Persatuan Sumatra). Held in Padang, the congress was attended by several representatives from political parties in North and South Tapanuli, Atjeh, and the East and West Coasts of Sumatra.[25] It was presided over by Manullang, the chairman of a Batak Christian party. The congress proved a great success, for the notion of Sumatra as the island of the future and the call for unity among all the island's ethnic groups had a wide appeal. A stirring call was made for unity in the cause of independence and the development of Sumatra, a crusade which if possible should be carried to other parts of the Indies as well. The congress decided to form a central council for all Sumatra with its headquarters in one of the island's big cities, still to be selected.[26] The radical tone of the congress and the political activities of its leaders, however, directly caused the decline of the Persatuan Sumatra movement, for, shortly after the congress, several of its leaders were arrested. The cooperationist Sumatran leaders active in the Sarekat Sumatera,men

---

24 Van Niel, *The Emergence of the Modern Elite*, pp. 197 ff.
25 Abdullah, "Minangkabau 1900-1927," pp. 165-169.
26 Report of the Persatuan Sumatra Congress, Padang, July 1 and 2, *Mailrapport* 889/'22.

like Sutan Muhammad Zein and Sutan Pamuntjak, were alarmed by the radicalism of the congress. Moreover local problems soon distracted the Minangkabau from the Persatuan Sumatra program.

The Activities of Abdul Muis

Abdul Muis played a crucial role in the efforts by the political parties to become channels for popular grievances. This was particularly so after his extended visit to West Sumatra in 1918. A born orator, Abdul Muis not only put felt dissatisfactions into words, but, more important, he introduced the growing political public to a new way of viewing their problems. Instead of simply returning to an analysis based on the Plakaat Pandjang, a political myth that had never died out, Abdul Muis discussed the real meaning of colonialism and all its consequences.[27] As a member of the Volksraad and vice-president of the important SI, his speeches carried great weight in future decisions concerning the new politics of opposition. After he left, his activities were continued by SCM leaders, such as Djamaluddin Rassad, Sulaiman Effendi and Said Ali.

Opposition to government policies, as expressed in numerous public meetings and publications, took a more radical turn in 1920 as a direct reaction to a sharp increase in rice prices.[28] A minor economic slump began and lasted until 1924. Political activity intensified in 1922 in the wake of a government-announced plan to introduce a land tax. All parties, including the adat ones, voiced objections to the tax, to a government forest preservation policy, and to proposed taxes on communal adat houses (*rumah gadang*). The government's actions were taken as direct insults to Minangkabau concepts of property and to their sense of justice. The popular mood of 1908 seemed to be returning.

During this time of increasing political action, Abdul Muis, in his capacity as representative for the SI in the Outer Islands, came to Minangkabau.[29] He planned to stay permanently; he wanted to revive

---

[27] Official correspondence on Abdul Muis' visit is contained in *Verbaal* January 30, 1919, No. 45. Muis' own account is in *Neratja*, September 23-28, 1918.

[28] G. A. W. de Haze Winkelman, "Rijstcultuur en Overheids Bemoeinis ter Sumatra's Westkust," *De Locomotief*, 1925 (Sumatra issue).

[29] In 1923, after an internal power struggle, Muis had lost his position as vice-president and was replaced by Hadji Agus Salim. Deliar Noer, "The Rise and Development of the Modernist

the dying SI and also to guide local political activities. He soon moved to the fore in the campaign against the government, and, under his leadership, local political organizations organized a series of protest meetings, climaxing in a big meeting on November 4, 1923, in Padang Pandjang. The November meeting was attended by representatives from the political parties and other organizations and also by penghulu from many nagari in Minangkabau. They adopted a resolution rejecting the proposed land tax, the regulations concerning forest preservation and the adat house tax. The meeting also decided to form a Minangkabau Council (Kerapatan Minangkabau) to coordinate political activities. In general, however, the participants favored a cooperationist stance vis-a-vis the government, for most of them thought that cooperation was essential in order to solve the issues raised. Along these lines, the meeting urged the central government to establish the long-promised Minangkabau Raad as soon as possible.

The big November meeting proved the climax of Abdul Muis' political leadership in Minangkabau. When he had arrived in Padang in early 1923, Abdul Muis had been challenged by the newly-formed communist Sarekat Rakjat, whose leaders were followers of his political enemies, namely the communists who had been expelled from the SI.[30] Muis faced other opposition in his attempt to capture political leadership in West Sumatra, particularly from B. Djamaluddin Rassad, the chairman of the SCM. Using the support of the SI, Sulaiman Effendi's NIP, the Sumatran correspondents' association, and a newly organized adat party, the Bodi Tjaniago, Abdul Muis managed to out-maneuver the Sarekat Rakjat and at the same time to discredit B. Djamaluddin Rassad. The latter had rapidly declined in public esteem after his expulsion from the correspondents' association and removal as the director of the Bodi Tjaniago's Dutch-Native School, but the immediate cause of his fall was exposure of his mismanagement of the first big Minangkabau copra enterprise.

The success of Abdul Muis, however, proved a short-lived victory. Local officials regarded him as a stumbling-block hindering the

---

Movement in Indonesia During the Dutch Colonial Period (1900-1942)" (Ph.D. thesis, Cornell University, 1962), pp. 212-213.

30 Harry J. Benda and Ruth T. McVey (eds.), *The Communist Uprisings of 1926-1927 in Indonesia: Key Documents* (Ithaca: Cornell Modern Indonesia Project, 1960), pp. 99-100.

implementation of government policies. His influence was considered detrimental to the government's prestige. Early in 1924, Abdul Muis was expelled from Minangkabau and forbidden to live anywhere in the Outer Islands. His expulsion deprived Minangkabau of its most influential Western-educated leader. Sulaiman Effendi also soon left, going to Java permanently.[31]

Abdul Muis' exile also meant the removal of a strong opponent to the nascent communist movement; after his departure, the communists quickly radicalized the issues Muis had helped to formulate. The movement had already permeated the first "modern" madrasah, the Sumatra Thawalib of Padang Pandjang, which served as its intellectual center. Through the activities of the school graduates, the radical movement penetrated the Minangkabau nagari and laid the groundwork for "revolution."

The Growth of the Sumatra Thawalib

The Sumatra Thawalib of Padang Pandjang grew out of an ordinary traditional-style madrasah, which emphasized law and theology and was dominated by a single teacher.[32] In 1912 Hadji Rasul (Sjech H. A. Karim Amrullah), a pioneer of the Kaum Muda religious movement, became the teacher at the Padang Pandjang madrasah known as the Surau Djembatan Besi. He succeeded his friend, Hadji Abdullah Ahmad, the man who had made Padang a center of Islamic modernism. In 1918, Hadji Rasul introduced a graded class system into the school. He had been inspired by the experiments of one of his assistants, Zainuddin Labai el Junusi,[33] who had established the first modern elementary religious school. Slowly,

---

31 According to Rustam Effendi, a Minangkabau perantau intellectual and member of the Dutch parliament before World War II, his father left for Java in a great hurry and it was widely rumored that he had been expelled by the Dutch. Sulaiman died in 1966. Interview with Rustam Effendi, Djakarta, October 1968.

32 All religious schools were traditionally called *surau*. These can be subdivided into Quranic recitation schools and madrasah, where students also studied religious texts. Surau in this study refers to elementary religious schools and madrasah to advanced schools. This distinction is also used by Mahmud Junus in his study of religious schools in Indonesia, *Sedjarah Pendidikan Islam di Indonesia* (Djakarta: Pustaka Mahmudiah, 1960).

33 Zainuddin Labai el Junusi (1890-1924) was born in Padang Pandjang, the son of an influential local ulama. When he was young, he lived the life of an urang siak, traveling from one madrasah to another. For some years he studied and assisted Sjech Abbas of Padang Djapang. A self-educated man and a versatile writer, Zainuddin was one of the ablest Minangkabau religious scholars.

the methods of instruction, the curriculum, and the textbooks were "modernized" so that the madrasah became a model for other Kaum Muda schools. But, unlike most other Kaum Muda institutions, Hadji Rasul's school was very much under the control of its student organization and school board.

The origin of the madrasah student organization dated to a small reading club founded by Zainuddin Labai in 1913.[34] It had no direct connection with the Surau Djembatan Besi but many students joined the club. Zainuddin was not just a good religious teacher; he was also interested in secular subjects. His club therefore received newspapers and other publications from Java and from abroad, mainly Egypt. In 1916, when voluntary associations and political parties were generally on the upsurge, Hadji Habib, then a student at the Surau Djembatan Besi, initiated action to establish a student cooperative society.[35] Its main function was to supply the students' daily needs, such as soap and books. Its great success was a result of the lavish attention which Hadji Habib devoted to it.[36]

In 1918, inspired by the Jong Sumatranen Bond, which had branches in Bukittinggi and Padang, Zainuddin Labai and Djala-luddin Thaib changed the cooperative society into an organization with a wider scope of activities. The new organization was called Sumatra Thuwailib (Students of Sumatra). The school was reorganized under the same name and placed under the administrative control of a school board consisting mainly of graduates, junior teachers and local traders. The establishment of such a school board meant that the madrasah could no longer be considered the personal preserve of its master teacher. This represented a new era in the history of Minangkabau religious schools.

At about the same time, a student organization was established at the madrasah in Parabek (near Bukittinggi) of Sjech Ibrahim Musa, a moderate Kaum Muda ulama. On February 15, 1919, the students of Padang Pandjang and Parabek formed a federation known as the

---

34 M. D. Dt. Palimo Kajo, Speech at the Reopening of the Sumatra Thawalib of Padang Pandjang in 1968 (typescript).
35 Roesad, "Nota over de Godsdienstig-Politieke Beweging ter Sumatra's Westkust" (June 3, 1929), *Mailrapport* 1518x/'33.
36 *Tjaja Soematra*, August 22, 1922.

Sumatra Thawalib (General Organization of Students of Sumatra).[37] In 1921, Sjech Ibrahim Musa introduced the graded system and renamed his madrasah Sumatra Thawalib. Following the example of Padang Pandjang and Parabek, the Kaum Muda madrasah in Padang Djapang, Manindjau and Batu Sangkar were also renamed Sumatra Thawalib. A move was soon made to combine the students of these five schools into one organization.

On January 22, 1922, at the invitation of the students of the Padang Pandjang Thawalib, a general meeting of student representatives was held. The meeting decided to form a united Sumatra Thawalib student organization under a central board. One of its main goals would be the improvement of instruction and textbooks in the schools. Hadji Djalaluddin Thaib, who played an important role in the post-1927 period, was elected as the first chairman, and one of the advisers was Hadji Datuk Batuah, later the spiritual father of the communist movement in Minangkabau. All members of the board were senior students who also usually acted as junior teachers in their respective schools.[38]

The united Sumatra Thawalib student organization joined the SCM, which also had its headquarters in Padang Pandjang. The Sumatra Thawalib was the largest member organization of the SCM. B. Djamaluddin Rassad, in an effort to weaken the power the Sumatra Thawalib could wield, suggested changing its organizational structure to give more strength to the local branches, specifically by making them autonomous. He expected that such action would make the Thawalib branches dependent on ties to the SCM for unity, weakening their own central board. He argued that since the students belonged to the same school system, communication between branches could still be carried out. As part of the total effort to assert his influence, B. Djamaluddin Rassad suggested that the Thawalib organizations should not confine their activities merely to educational issues but should participate in economic and political movements.[39]

In a meeting on April 16, 1922, the Sumatra Thawalib accepted the proposal that its branches should have their own boards. The suggestion to expand activities beyond education issues gave rise to considerable

---

37 Tamar Djaja, "Pusaka Indonesia: Orang-Orang Besar Tanah Air," III (Manuscript).
38 Tjaja Soematra, January 26, 1922.
39 *Ibid.*, February 22, 1922.

debate. A representative from Padang Pandjang urged the participation of the Sumatra Thawalib in political activities, but he was strongly opposed by a junior teacher from Parabek. This reflected a fundamental difference which existed between the two institutions—Padang Pandjang had already become a center of anti-government political activities but Parabek remained a secluded religious school compound. The meeting at last decided that the organization should become directly involved in political activities but that the students should study the issues very carefully.[40]

The 1922 meeting was the first expression of an interest by the religious students in politics. After the April meeting, students of the Padang Pandjang Thawalib became more interested in political matters, a tendency which was encouraged by the nature of their religious training and by the increasingly radical trend among Minangkabau political parties. Hadji Datuk Batuah, one of the Thawalib's junior teachers and an adviser to the student organization, had already been influenced by communist doctrines, and, by early 1923, he began to introduce his students to this new ideology.

Hadji Datuk Batuah was born in 1895 in Kota Lawas, a nagari near Padang Pandjang. After graduation from a government second class school, he studied in Mecca, from 1909 until 1915. On his return to Padang Pandjang, he studied with and assisted Hadji Rasul, and, in 1922, he was elected an adviser of the Sumatra Thawalib student organization. In early 1923, he went to Sigli in Atjeh, where he met Natar Zainuddin, a Minangkabau streetcar conductor, who had received communist indoctrination in Java.[41] The meeting represented a turning point in Datuk Batuah's life, for his incipient anti-Dutch feeling could now be formulated in ideological terms. After his return to Padang Pandjang, he began propagandizing communism among his students.

---

40 *Ibid.*, May 4, 1922.
41 Office of the Attorney General, No. 1442 A.P., Weltevreden, May 3, 1924, *Mailrapport* 390x/'24. Natar Zainuddin was born in Padang and he graduated from a private second class school there. In 1903, he went to Atjeh where he worked as a streetcar conductor. In 1920 he attended the Congress of the Vereeniging van Spoor- en Tramwegpersonel (VSTP) in Semarang. He was the chairman of this leftwing union in Atjeh and, during the congress, he met with several Dutch communists such as Bergsma. In 1922, he joined the newly-established Communist Party. In 1923, as a member of the VSTP central board for the Outer Islands, he came again to Semarang for a congress. On his return to Atjeh he began to propagate communist ideology actively.

The climate in West Sumatra was right for the new doctrine, for political campaigns against the government were mounting and the Sumatra Thawalib students were already determined to study "politics." Datuk Batuah, understandably, became one of the most popular junior teachers, and soon exercised great influence over Thawalib students. Datuk Batuah was a penghulu and a religious teacher in his own nagari of Kota Lawas which allowed him to expand his influence there as well. He converted the younger members of the nagari council in Kota Lawas to his views by recalling to them how their nagari had risen against the Dutch in 1915 protesting the tax levies.[42]

The government meanwhile had expelled Natar Zainuddin from Atjeh for his political activities, and in mid-1923 he joined Datuk Batuah in Padang Pandjang, making it a center for "Islamic communism." The Sarekat Rakjat branch of Padang, which had been established in March shortly after the arrival of Abdul Muis, was now following the lead of Padang Pandjang. Hadji Datuk Batuah and Natar Zainuddin founded the International Debating Club and published *Pemandangan Islam*, a theoretical journal on Islamic-communism, and *Djago-Djago*, a fiery political organ. A large number of Thawalib students and junior teachers joined the debating club; they studied and discussed an ideology which could combine Islamic anti-kafir sentiment with Marxist doctrines on poverty. The extent of Datuk Batuah's influence among the students of the Sumatra Thawalib school was shown during a large protest meeting in November 1923, when some 200 students demonstrated outside the meeting hall, expressing their opposi-tion to Abdul Muis for his actions in isolating the communist leaders.[43] On that date, November 4, a Partai Komunis Indonesia (PKI, Indonesian Communist Party) section was officially established in Padang Pandjang.[44]

Datuk Batuah's influence in the Sumatra Thawalib directly challenged Hadji Rasul, the school's master teacher who not only opposed the

---

[42] Letter of the Resident of the West Coast of Sumatra to the Governor-General, No. 108, Padang, February 20, 1924, *Mailrapport* 390x/'24. On the rebellion, see C. P., "Eene Beschouwing over den in den Nacht van 21 op 22 December 1915 Plaats Gehad Hebbenden Overval van Padang Pandjang," KT, 5, No. 2 (1916), pp. 1209-1213.

[43] Datuk Tumenggung, "Geheim Nota voor de Adviseur voor In-landsche Zaken over het Communisme ter Westkust van Sumatra (July 30, 1925)," Kern Collection, #46.

[44] Benda and McVey, *Communist Uprisings*, p. 106.

participation of students in political activity but also condemned the new ideology as a deviation from Islamic orthodoxy. Hadji Rasul's attempts to influence Hadji Datuk Batuah and his colleagues only worsened relations between them. On August 2, 1923, a meeting was held between the two sides at the house of Datuk Batuah in Kota Lawas. Hadji Rasul was supported by several Kaum Muda ulama including Sjech Thaher Djalaluddin, a leader of Islamic modernism in Malaya who was currently visited his home nagari. The meeting ended in complete failure.[45] Subsequent meetings only widened the gulf between Hadji Rasul and Datuk Batuah.[46] Hadji Rasul realized that his traditional authority as a religious teacher to whom students owed respect and loyalty was being undermined, and he resigned from the Sumatra Thawalib. He was succeeded by one of his oldest and ablest students, Abdul Hamid Angku Mudo,[47] who managed to remain aloof from the controversy.

The resignation of Hadji Rasul resulted in open enmity between the Kaum Muda ulama and Datuk Batuah's group. When the government arrested Datuk Batuah and Natar Zainuddin on November 11, 1923, the younger generation of the religious Kaum Muda, who had been influenced by communism, accused Hadji Rasul of instigating the arrest. Datuk Batuah, despite his outspokenness, had still honored the traditional norms concerning the relationship between teacher and students in the madrasah. After his arrest, the Islamic communists no longer restrained their attacks on the Kaum Muda ulama.

The religious Kaum Muda movement had always stressed the need for religious and social reforms, but it now faced a major crisis. The Kaum Muda ulama feared that their movement was in danger of disintegrating. In Bukittinggi, Sjech Djambek, a persuasive ulama, expelled several

---

45 *Mailrapport* 581x/'24; *Verbaal* January 15, 1925, No. V.
46 In his biography of Hadji Rasul, Hamka recollects one such encounter. "One evening I saw Hadji Datuk Batuah, Djama-luddin Tamin and others come to his [Hadji Rasul's] house in Gatangan. They debated about communist doctrine. Their voices were equally high and loud; Hadji Datuk Batuah spoke with full enthusiasm." H. A. Malik Karim Amrullah, *Ajahku: Riwajat Hidup H. Abd. Karim Amrullah dan Perdjuangan Kaum Agama di Sumatra* (Djakarta: Djaj amurni, 1967), p. 132.
47 Abdul Hamid Angku Mudo (late 1880's-1959) came from a Sum-pur merchant family. His first teacher was Sjech Thaib Umar of Sungajang. In 1910, he began to study under Hadji Rasul. He wrote several books on religious questions, mostly in Arabic. Hamka, *Ajahku*, pp. 252-253.

students from his school upon discovering that they were attracted by Batuah's ideas. In Parabek, the moderate Sjech Ibrahim Musa did likewise and also forbade his students from involvement in politics. In early 1924, the organization of the Kaum Muda ulama, the PGAI, declared itself opposed to communism because communism could not be brought into accord with Islam. The communist followers, for their part, quickly denounced the ulama.[48]

The arrest of H. Datuk Batuah removed the spiritual leader of communism from the Padang Pandjang Thawalib. Even though its graduates continued to spread communist ideas in the rural areas, at the school itself the influence of the party declined. As a result of the conflict between Hadji Rasul and Datuk Batuah and the consequent resignation of Hadji Rasul, the school's enrollment began to decrease. Under the guidance of Hamid Angku Mudo the quality of education remained high, but the buildings had fallen into disrepair. The big earthquake of 1926 completely destroyed them. After this crisis, the school board recovered full control and began a rebuilding program. The communist leaders were gradually purged,[49] and the Sumatra Thawalib re-emerged as an intellectual center for anti-government political activities in Minangkabau.

The Communist Uprising

The arrests of the communist leaders did not halt the spread of the party's appeal, especially among petty traders suffering from the economic slump, and among the tarekat leaders. In Silungkang, where adat class consciousness was still strong,[50] communist leaders emphasized the

---

48 Schrieke, *Indonesian Sociological Studies*, I, pp. 153-154; Hamka, *Ajahku*, pp. 133-134.
49 In 1926 the Sumatra Thawalib school board circulated a list for contributions to its former graduates and donors. The Resident did not really believe that the sole intention of this action was to gain funds for a new building, but, according to him, "The political direction of the members of the Sumatra Thawalib board is not clear. They are not members of the communist party, although they might have been sympathetic to the extremist idea." Letter to the Governor-General, July 23, 1926, No. 448, *Mailrapport* 1044x/'22.
50 A. W. P. Verkerk Pistorius, "Iets over de Slaven en Afstam-melingen van Slaven in de Padangsche Bovenlanden," *TNI*, 2 (3rd S), No. 1 (1868), pp. 434-443. Most of the people that belonged to this lowest adat class were descendants of former prisoners from the Padri War. Though freed in the 1860's, they had remained in Silungkang.

notion of class struggle. They considered themselves the representatives of the "middle class," in opposition to traditional adat aristocracy.[51] In Kota Lawas, the nagari of Datuk Batuah, the party was led by penghulu who could influence the rest of the inhabitants. In 1925, the communist party members in Dangung-Dangung, a nagari in the Suliki district, proudly called their nagari "the second Moscow." In 1926 communist strength in the Batu Sangkar district was based in three nagari, referred to respectively as the "treasury," the "brain," and the "labor" centers.[52]

In Agam Tuo, however, Sjech Djambek was influential and the adat authorities were still powerful; here the communists could hardly expand their movement at all.

The graduates of the Sumatra Thawalib school successfully propagandized a philosophy popularly known as *ilmu kominih* (communist knowledge), which combined a religious argument with Marxist anti-capitalist and anti-imperialist ideas. Such communist promoters were described by the people as "the persons who have been to other places and who have visited big towns, where they had the opportunity to study communist knowledge and communist works."[53] Thawalib graduates were regarded as a new-style urang siak, people who had come from the rantau where they had studied a new *ilmu* (knowledge). Because of grievances accu-mulated from the various kinds of taxation and the government's forest policy, this new knowledge (*ilmu baru*) appeared to offer a promise for a better future. The social and economic ills allegedly caused by capitalist exploitation could only be cured through *kemevdekaan*, independence, which meant freedom both from the kafir government and from "adat feudalism."

In many ways, the spread of the communist movement reflected a growing awareness of the general rather than the particular character of popular grievances. Unlike the adat parties, which stressed the prime importance of Minangkabau, and unlike the previous Kaum Muda organizations, which took Sumatra as the symbol of their political struggle, the communist movement emphasized the notion of "The Indies." The

---

51 Benda and McVey, *The Communist Uprisings*, p. 102.
52 Politieke Politioneel Overzicht, 1927, *Mailrapport* 741x/'28.
53 L. Dt. Tumenggung, "Nota over de Toestanden ter Westkust van Sumatra, August 16, 1926," *Mailrapport* 934x/'26.

movement, therefore, cannot be separated from the early development of Indonesian anti-colonial nationalism.[54]

Throughout 1924, according to Dutch reports, the Communist Party was preoccupied with numerous public meetings. In 1925, it concentrated its activities on a lecture series about communism.[55] Under the leadership of Said Ali, a former leader of the SCM, the party established a close tie with its headquarters in Java and worked to consolidate itself in the face of mounting government pressure. By the end of 1925, however, adat authorities, with support from government and religious leaders, had successfully undermined the position of the party in many parts of Minangkabau. From the middle of 1925 until the middle of 1926, the Communist Party had to move its regional committee from Padang Pandjang to Padang and then back to Padang Pandjang again. In several places, it was forced to go underground.

During this period of uncertainty, when a reaction was setting in against the party in Java as well as in Minangkabau, the central committee convened a secret meeting at Prambanan, near Jogjakarta. At the meeting, held in December 1925, the party decided to prepare for a revolution in Sumatra and Java; though many party leaders disapproved, preparations were made.[56] Said Ali, who had represented the Minangkabau branches, instructed his followers to start collecting arms and to draw up a revolutionary strategy. In mid-1926, however, he was arrested and by the end of the year other party leaders had also been detained. Miscalculations in planning, disunity among the leaders and Dutch alertness reduced the intended revolution to no more than a series of desperate uprisings. In December 1926, scattered uprisings occurred in the outskirts of Batavia and in the residency of Banten, but in a very short time they were all crushed by government troops. In the Minangkabau region, whose revolt was supposed to signal the coming revolution, the rebellion did not break out until New Year's Eve. Though planned for Padang or the coal-mining town of Sawah Lunto, the rebellion in fact erupted in Silungkang, killing several people, including a Dutch official.[57] The rebellion was quickly put

---

54 Bouman, *Enige Beschouwingen*, pp. 94-95.
55 Benda and McVey, *The Communist Uprisings*, pp. 108-115.
56 McVey, *The Rise of Indonesian Communism*, p. 309.
57 Benda and McVey, *The Communist Uprisings*, pp. 158-177.

down and the government began an intensive campaign of repression throughout Minangkabau.

The rebellion had erupted in spite of, rather than because of, the communists' blueprint for revolt. It was a direct outcome of complex social phenomena. Schrieke, the chairman of the Investigation Commission on the Rebellion, pointed to the un-evenness of social development, the weakening of adat institutions, the divisive effects of government administrative policies in the nagari, the disruption caused by economic change, and the inherent conservatism of the Minangkabau social system when faced with the growing importance of individualism as some of the chief contributing factors to the rebellion.[58] Since the beginning of the century, Minangkabau had been the scene of social turmoil, including several rural uprisings, among others in 1904, 1908 and 1915. It had also experienced social and intellectual conflict, between the secular Kaum Muda and Kaum Kuno and between the religious Kaum Muda and Kaum Tua. Moreover, local administrators, from the residency to the district level, never properly learned the art of ruling the Minangkabau. Instead of pursuing a forward looking policy, the government preferred to maintain a status quo by supporting the adat authorities in their opposition to religious and secular movements.

Ironically, instead of keeping the nagari political structure intact, successive Dutch Governors and Residents had often undermined it. The government had failed to respect the Minang-kabau sense of justice and pride, sentiments which all social groups and factions shared and to which they appealed in times of crisis. Schrieke and his commission were perhaps correct in their contention that the rebellion was a reflection of "the crisis phenomenon," but its cause was rooted in the increasing hostility toward the government.

In several respects, the rebellion can be seen as a tragic result of Minangkabau's uneven social development. The earlier, rural uprising had demonstrated that desperate attempts at liberation from taxation and corvee only ended in death or exile. For more than ten years after the establishment of the SI, new interpretations of the colonial situation had penetrated to the nagari. The perantau and the urban intellectuals

---

58 Schrieke, *Indonesian Sociological Studies*, I, pp. 95-159.

who led Minang-kabau organizations had all participated in or observed political activities in Java and other regions. The increasing radicalism of the political parties and the persistence of Dutch conservative policies revived the militant spirit of 1908, but with important differences. The issues had been considerably enlarged; the inspiration came from outside; and the idea of returning to the traditional order (e.g., where taxes were unknown) had been replaced by the promise of a bright future. Now the government was labeled not just as "kafir" but also as "capitalist" and "imperialist," though often the driving force remained a belief in the ultimate "miracle" by which the strong and unjust ruler would be defeated.

The rebellion and its subsequent harsh suppression administered a profound psychological shock to the Minangkabau, for they saw that the accumulated resentment against the government had exploded in vain. The dream of kemerdekaan had turned into a nightmare. In this time of crisis, the people turned to adat and religion. Shortly after the rebellion was crushed, several nagari which had been influenced by the communist movement held traditional adat ceremonies to express remorse.[59] The nagari in the Solok district convened an adat conference to explore ways for strengthening adat institutions and adat bonds.[60] The leaders of the adat parties again voiced the need for a powerful Minangkabau Raad through which the people's representatives could directly participate in the administration. They demanded a change in the administrative system in order to improve the relationship between the penghulu and the people and between the government and the inhabitants (anak negeri). They wanted to restore what they regarded as the true adat political structure, that based on the nagari council.[61]

Outside the government sphere, the Kaum Muda and Kaum Tua ulama regained their leadership. The Kaum Muda ulama, whose authority had been gravely undermined by their former students, now regained the initiative from the Kaum Muda younger generation. The Muhammadijah,

---

[59] Datuk Tumenggung, "Dagboek," *Mailrapport* 718x/'27. After the anti-tax rebellions in 1908, several nagari also held such adat ceremonies. Ahmad Datuk Batuah, *Tambo Minangkabau* (Djakarta: Balai Pustaka, 1956), pp. 117-118.
[60] *Tjaja Soematra*, July 4, 1927.
[61] *Ibid.*, February 9 and 10, and July 2, 1927.

an organization which had its headquarters in Java, soon emerged as the only organization working to unite the splintered elements of the religious Kaum Muda. At the same time, it was the Muhammadijah that gave the younger Kaum Muda a chance to recapture the leadership from the Kaum Muda ulama.

CHAPTER THREE
THE GRADUATES OF THE KAUM MUDA RELIGIOUS SCHOOLS AND THEIR LEADERS

The emergence of Hadji Datuk Batuah and of the Sumatra Thawalib were significant events in Minangkabau. Both showed the extent of the influence exercised by the reform movement initiated by the religious Kaum Muda. They finally disproved the notion that religious reformation could continue without serious attention to political issues, such as the presence of an "infidel" government. Even though the Kaum Muda ulama had not hesitated to speak about the need to return to the true orthodoxy of Islam, they had consistently refused to relate the Islamic concept of political power to the political reality. The politicization of the Sumatra Thawalib, however, could also be interpreted as evidence that it was following the traditional role of religious schools as challengers of existing authority. These political factors have already been discussed, but the Thawalib's part in the religious movement has yet to be considered.

The main objectives of the movement were to promote orthodoxy, to change attitudes toward religious law and to create enthusiasm for modernity. These interrelated programs led the Kaum Muda ulama into open confrontation with heterodox tarekat leaders, traditionalist religious teachers, and adat functionaries. Religious developments since the Padri war included not only a deepening penetration of Islamic elements into the adat system but also a growing split between the tarekat leaders, experts on mysticism, and the religious teachers, experts on scriptural knowledge. According to Islamic doctrine, *fikh* (law), *tauhid* (doctrine on the oneness of God) and *tasauf* (mysticism) are all parts of religious knowledge, but divisions among experts had on occasion led to doctrinal conflict. The conflict in Minangkabau was intensified because the existing tarekat doctrines tended to emphasize traditionalism at the expense of the *sjariah* (religious regulations). At the beginning of the twentieth century, the tarekat were still very influential[1] but the number of other religious experts was increasing as more and more Minangkabau began studying religion in Mecca. When Sjech Achmad Chatib began his orthodox movement in the 1890's, he directed his appeals to this growing number of Mecca-trained religious scholars.

In 1906, some pioneers among the Kaum Muda ulama, including former students of Sjech Achmad Chatib, began to combine the drive for orthodoxy with a strong appeal for the use of akal (reason) and a consequent repudiation of taqlid attitudes, which meant blind obedience to established textual authorities. In emphasizing the need for a re-examination of the traditionally-accepted laws, the Kaum Muda ulama soon determined that they should no longer be bound by any one school of law (mazhab). Instead of simply following the precepts of the Shafiite school of law, to which the majority of Indonesian and Malayan Muslims belonged, the Kaum Muda ulama now formulated their religious judgments (*fatwa*) after examining the legal doctrines of other orthodox schools of law. The publications of this Kaum Muda group followed a similar practice, representing a departure from the type of religious arguments contained in the earlier Kaum Muda organ (*Al-Moenir*, 1911-1915).[2] The Kaum Muda ulama were thus abandoning the teachings of their own highly respected teacher, Sjech Achmad Chatib, an imam of the Shafiite school in Mecca. Sjech Achmad Chatib had in fact been highly critical of Islamic modernism as propagated at the turn of the century by the Pan-Islamist, Sjech Jamal ad-Din Al Afghani and his disciple, the Egyptian ulama, Sjech Muhammad Abduh. Though the Kaum Muda ulama continued to respect Sjech Achmad Chatib, they had more in common with his cousin, Sjech Thaher Djalaluddin, who had studied at

---

[1] Snouck Hurgronje believed the mystical brotherhoods would remain popular: "Because the tariqahs give to the individual inclination of the spirit of the true direction instead of simple teaching in general terms (like professors of Holy Science) what all should do and believe, it is obvious that these societies work much more powerfully towards the fur-therance and vivication of political ideas than study, not to mention the much wider circles which they influence.. .. In the tariqahs the practical consequences are drawn from such doctrines, and the glance of expectation is turned towards the sheikh of the Order. Among the ignorant masses however these consequences are expressed in all kinds of fanaticism." C. Snouck Hurgronje, *Mekka in the Latter Part of the Nineteenth Century*, translated by J. H. Monahan (London: Luzac, 1931), p. 281.

[2] Junus, *Sedjarah Pendidikan*, pp. 73-74; Hamka, *Ajahku*, pp. 106-108.

Al-Azhar University in Cairo and subsequently edited the first Islamic modernist journal in the Malay World—*Al Imam*, published in Singapore in 1906.

The appeals to abandon taqlid, to purify religion from syncretic practices, and to use akal in matters pertaining to religious law, divided orthodox religious teachers into two conflicting groups, the reformists and the traditionalists. The traditionalists, some of whom were also former students of Sjech Achmad Chatib, refused to acknowledge the right of an individual ulama to conduct idjtihad. They strongly restated their own loyalty to the Shafiite school of law. The conflict moreover caused the traditionalist, orthodox ulama to seek common ground with the mystical leaders in the face of the new enemy, the Kaum Muda ulama. Though Achmad Chatib had condemned the Naqsjabandijah order as a deviation from the correct path of Islamic orthodoxy, the traditionalist, orthodox ulama acknowledged it as a legitimate doctrine according to the mazhab of Shafei. The Kaum Tua ulama thus included the tarekat leaders and the traditionalist, orthodox religious teachers.

Adat authorities opposed any religious movement whatever because it would threaten their own role as the upholders of the *status quo* and social harmony.[3] Their commitment to the existing religious establishment was strengthened after the Kaum Muda ulama attacked particular religious rituals which had already been incorporated in adat ceremonies. Kaum Muda appeals for the abolition, revision, or simplification of various adat religious ceremonies, such as certain marriage and funeral rites or the traditional way of celebrating holy days, were interpreted by adat functionaries as direct attacks upon their own authority and hence threats to the stability of the adat. The adat authorities therefore allied themselves with the Kaum Tua ulama against the new religious threat.

Despite the apparent strength of the opposition, a number of factors combined to further the advance of the Islamic modernist movement. In the first place, of course, religious reformation was not a new phenomenon in Minangkabau. The Kaum Muda ulama, however, did not limit their activities to doctrinal matters; they also promoted broadly-based programs for the general improvement of society. They emphasized

---

3 Diradjo, *Mustiko Adat*, pp. 16-55.

activism, individual independence and frugality as means to overcome the disadvantages of contemporary economic changes. The deeper penetration of the money economy and the increasing importance of towns provided an appropriate background for the teachings of the Kaum Muda.

The status and function of religious teachers in the Minangkabau social system and the ambiguity of Dutch Islamic policies aided the Kaum Muda ulama. Two characteristics of the traditional Minangkabau nagari must be taken into account in order to understand the development of the religious reform movements. Each nagari was responsible for its own affairs. There was no functional adat organization above the nagari to enforce or hinder the introduction of any change in the nagari. There was no religious head or council which could give the final binding word on important religious issues. The main functions of the adat religious functionaries—such as the *imam, chatib* and *bilal*—were to perform religious ceremonies, to administer religious dues and to take care of the nagari mosque.[4] They were not necessarily religious experts, for their positions were inherited in accordance with the adat, through the uncle-and-nephew network. They presided over the Friday Council (Sidang Djumat), but this dealt only with minor religious matters. Non-adat religious experts gave the final judgment on important religious issues. Although outside the adat hierarchy, such experts did play an important role in the nagari, and, through their schools, they could expand their influence beyond nagari boundaries. Given the separation between religious expertise and ascriptive adat positions, nagari often recognized their most respected ulama as the nagari sjech. Although he remained outside the official hierarchy, the sjech's judgment on religious matters was considered binding on the nagari. Some pioneers of the Is-lamic modernist movement, such as Hadji Rasul of Sungai Batang and Sjech Thaib Umar of Sungajang, were recognized as sjech in their respective nagari.

Taking advantage of these aspects of society, the Kaum Muda ulama could claim religious superiority over adat religious functionaries in

---

4 A. W. P. Verkerk Pistorius, "De Priester en Zijn Invloed op de Samenleving in de Padangsche Bovenlanden," *TNI*, 3 (3rd S), No. 2 (1869), pp. 423-452.

their own nagari. In the supra-nagari sphere, they challenged the Kaum Tua ulama to face them in public debates. Laymen followed individual ulama who attracted them, thus intensifying the social polarization. Furthermore, no adat sanction existed which could force conformity with the religious views held by adat authorities. Until 1919, when the government decided to mediate the religious conflict,[5] the Kaum Muda ulama also had a favorable political climate. By their multiple programs and their insistence on the separation of religion from politics, the Kaum Muda ulama could take advantage of the loopholes in Dutch Islamic policy. Government officials were less suspicious of Kaum Muda activities also because they were centered in urban areas rather than villages.

Nineteenth-century Dutch administrative policy in Minangka-bau tended to be anti-Muslim. First, the government tried to exclude religious teachers, labeled the "independent spiritual leaders," and hadji from holding adat and administrative offices;[6] thus, it tried to prevent a hadji's election as a penghulu. Although Dutch administrative and economic actions had weakened adat institutions, particularly the balai and the office of the penghulu, the government defended these institutions in the face of threats by religious teachers. Officials had confused adat with a purely secular authority, separated from religion. In 1893, the government of the West Coast proposed that adat law should be codified in order to guard against the allegedly undermining influence of the religious movements. The proposal was rejected on the grounds that codification of adat law might imply a repudiation of the applicability of Western law. The Sumatra Regulation of 1899 was designed to strengthen the position of the penghulu by giving them more power to deal with religious teachers.

At the end of the nineteenth century, Snouck Hurgronje, Adviser for Arab and Native Affairs, suggested a more positive policy. He advised the central government to reject the proposal for the codification of adat laws; he argued that no single authority existed who could decide adat law for all areas of Minangkabau and the laws themselves did not derive

---

5 Schrieke presided over a debate between the Kaum Muda and the Kaum Tua in 1919. He took the case to Java and asked the opinion of the Javanese ulama; they unanimously condemned the Kaum Muda position. Schrieke, "Bijdrage tot de Biblio-grafie," pp. 249-325.
6 L. C. Westenenk, "De Inlandsche Bestuurshoofden ter Sumatra's Westkust," *KT*, 2 (1913), pp. 673-693.

from any one source. Rather than strengthen adat, Snouck thought that codification would lead to its petrification by destroying its flexibility and thus its ability to adapt to changing situations. Snouck declared it an illusion to believe that adat codification would protect adat from the encroachment of Islamic fanaticism: "The population of the West Coast of Sumatra and their chiefs are by heart Muslim believers, and there lies the future development of the 'Malay' family."[7] If the government tried to protect adat by combatting Islamic propaganda, he believed, it would merely provide religious teachers with an opportunity to accuse the government of being anti-Muslim, thus giving them an additional weapon. Snouck suggested an Islamic policy based on the assumption that Islam could be divided into a political and a dogmatic aspect. For dealing with political matters, Snouck recommended a strong-handed policy. In dealing with its purely religious concerns, in their social and individual forms, he urged the government to adopt a benevolent policy toward the former and a neutral one toward the latter.[8]

The first part of Snouck's recommendation was in fact a continuation of existing Dutch Islamic policy. Religious teachers had always posed a potential threat to the government. The religious schools and particularly the tarekat had often served as centers for rural rebellions. Snouck noted that religious and adat tracts written by these ulama always referred to the Dutch as *Ulando Setan* (Satanic Dutch).[9] An iron-handed policy had already been successfully employed to suppress various rural uprisings. Van Ronkel's report on the religious situation in Minangkabau in 1916 also recommended that the government should establish strict control over the rural religious schools, particularly those operated by tarekat leaders. He urged continuation of a repressive policy against the traditionalist and conservative religious teachers. In agreement with Snouck's recommendation, van Ronkel reaffirmed the wisdom of taking a neutral stand in dealing with the religious controversy between the Kaum Muda and the Kaum Tua groups. But he cautioned the government to observe carefully the activities of the Kaum Muda ulama.[10]

---

7 *Adatrechtbundels*, 1 (1913), pp. 31 and 21-44.
8 C. Snouck Hurgronje, *Nederland en de Islam* (Leiden: E. J. Brill, 1915), pp. 53-77.
9 *Adatrechtbundels*, 1 (1913), p. 34.
10 Ph. D. S. van Ronkel, "Rapport Betreffende de Godsdienstige Verschijnselen ter Sumatra's

Snouck insisted that religious neutrality should not mean official inactivity, for, in order to weaken Islam, he thought the government must pursue an "association policy" as part of an extensive educational program. A leading proponent of the "ethical policy," Snouck believed that educational programs, accompanied by a gradual process toward the "Indonesianization" of the administrative apparatus, would show the Indies people how Western civilization could benefit them. Such an "association policy" furthermore would create a class of progressive Western-oriented Indonesians loyal to the Netherlands.[11] Van Ronkel, although he did not share Snouck's optimism, supported the idea of expanding the Dutch school system. Although, according to van Ronkel, Western education could not be expected to alienate the youth from Islam, it might create liberal and less militant Muslims.[12]

Resident LeFebvre used these recommendations as policy guidelines during his tenure on the West Coast from 1916 till 1919. He severely crushed the uprisings which had begun in 1915, and he tried to curtail the spread of the Kaum Tua SI. LaFebvre shared van Ronkel's belief that the Kaum Muda ulama were neither anti-government nor interested in politics. The leader of the Kaum Muda ulama in Padang, Hadji Abdullah Ahmad, was apparently aiding the "association policy" idea with his successful HIS-Adabijah. The school received a financial subsidy from the government and also had a Dutch headmaster and two other Dutch-trained teachers.

Though LeFebvre's tenure was short, it was important. During his term, the adat authorities began to challenge the Kaum Muda ulama openly, and, by the time LeFebvre left, Kaum Tua ulama were allying themselves with the adat-party SAAM. In terms of conventional Dutch Islamic policy, the Kaum Muda group should be considered as the potential enemy. But LeFebvre was perhaps the only high Dutch official who did not believe in the policy of supporting the adat authorities. In his view, the penghulu

---

Westkust," *Verbaal* April 4, 1916, No. 54.

11 A Dutch observer of mid-nineteenth century West Sumatra also urged the government to introduce Western education because otherwise, "There is no middle power against the Mohammedans." A. Pruys van der Hoven (ed.), *Een Woord over Sumatra in Brieven Verzameld* (Rotterdam: H. Nijgh, 1864), II, pp. 36-37.

12 Van Ronkel, "Rapport," p. 33. His recommendation was approved by the Director of Administrative Affairs, Carpentier Alting, see *Mailrapport* 1351/'16.

were nothing but "stupid and backward" adat chiefs, and he believed the future of Minangkabau development rested with the secular and religious Kaum Muda.[13]

Ironically, Dutch policy toward religious conflict in Minangkabau actually resulted in a further spread of Islamic influence, for Snouck's policy guidelines had not included the eventuality of a conflict between traditionalist and modernist or reformist Islam. In the face of Kaum Muda religious and secular programs, the government had to make a number of temporary adjustments, especially in its conceptions about the division of Islam into a dogmatic and a political aspect.[14] Islamic doctrine does not recognize a clear distinction between temporal and spiritual powers, and Snouck's policy guidelines contributed to the spread of the Kaum Muda reform movement, because the ulama did not see Islam as separate aspects. But in their activities, the Kaum Muda ulama did draw a sharp distinction between "religion" for its own sake and "politics" which dealt with questions of secular power. Some leaders of the Islamic modernist movement, such as Hadji Abdullah Ahmad, regarded the Dutch government as an ally in their modernization program. Others maintained a good relation with Dutch officials; for example,Sjech Djambek's children were enrolled in prestigious government schools. Even Hadji Rasul, an outspoken and aggressive ulama whom van Ronkel had labeled "the fanatic," refused to question openly the existence of the Dutch political power. This attitude on the part of the Kaum Muda ulama helps explain why they were to some extent free from government suspicion, and why the government at first remained neutral in the religious conflict.

After 1919, however, government attitudes shifted and the Kaum Muda ulama came under increasing scrutiny. Beginning in 1923, according to Schrieke, local administrators began to use the adat apparatus against the Kaum Muda.[15] But by this time, the Kaum Muda religious movement had already entered a critical stage. Unlike their teachers, the students of the

---

13 J. D. L. LeFebvre, "Memorie van Overgave, July 22, 1919," *Mailrapport* 2904/'19, pp. 28-29.

14 Harry J. Benda, *The Crescent and the Rising Sun: Indonesian Islam under the Japanese Occupation, 1942-1945* (The Hague: van Hoeve, 1958), pp. 20-31. Benda calls Snouck's division "unrealistic" (p. 21).

15 Schrieke, *Indonesian Sociological Studies*, I, p. 159.

Kaum Muda ulama could not limit themselves to scholarly discussions about the Islamic teachings on temporal power. They began to cherish the idea of putting these teachings into practice.

No less important than these factors in the spread of the Islamic reform movement were the social and economic backgrounds of the pioneers and the methods they used to promote their ideas. Most of the prominent Kaum Muda ulama belonged to highly respected ulama and well-to-do families. Hadji Rasul was the son of Sjech Kisai, a greatly respected ulama and holy man from the Manindjau sub-district. On his mother's side, Hadji Rasul belonged to the adat upper class of Sungai Batang. Both the parents of Sjech Thaib Umar of Sungajang belonged to the *urang babangso*, the original settlers of the nagari. Sjech Djamil Djambek was a son of the Tuanku Laras of Kurai, Bukittinggi. Sjech Djambek is an extraordinary example of the transformation of a ruthless "independent young man" (*parewa*) into a persuasive and knowledgeable religious teacher. Hadji Abdullah Ahmad, the leader of the Kaum Muda in Padang, like Sjech Djambek, was not a "full-blooded" Minangkabau. His mother came from Bengkulen, on the southwest coast of Sumatra, but she had been acknowledged by adat as a Minangkabau.[16] On his father's side, he belonged to an ulama and trading family from Kota Lawas, near Padang Pandjang. His father was a rich merchant and an influential religious teacher. His uncle, Sjech Gapuk, served as the imam of the central mosque of Padang; this mosque was under the jurisdiction of Padang adat authorities. When Sjech Gapuk died in 1911, Hadji Abdullah Ahmad was appointed as his successor. Through this position, which he held for three years, Hadji Abdullah Ahmad began to gain influence in Padang. Almost all the less prominent Kaum Muda ulama also belonged to prestigious ulama families.

Some of the Kaum Muda ulama inherited religious schools operated by their fathers or uncles. Sjech Abbas and his brother, Sjech Mustafa, succeeded to the leadership of a school in Padang Djapang which their

---

16 An outsider who is accepted as a member of the adat community is termed "a nephew according to adat." Such newcomers are usually accorded second class status, and, in general, their descendants can not establish their own penghulu-ships. Rather, they remain under the "protection" of their host lineage. This regulation can be waived in some instances if all penghulu in the nagari approve. *Adatrecht-bundels*, 11 (1915), pp. 109-114.

grandfather had established during the Padri war. The Kaum Muda ulama usually began their careers as traditional religious teachers, reluctantly accepting the involved adat decorum which was accorded to a religious teacher. Only after they had established themselves as respected teachers in their own right could they begin to propagate their reform ideas.

The reformers used several methods in promoting their ideas. They issued numerous publications, established new schools, and held public debates with the Kaum Tua ulama, but their most effective medium was the tabligh, public religious lecture, which allowed more personal and intimate communications between the religious experts and the laymen. The Kaum Muda ulama would discuss religious problems in language which the people could understand; this represented a revolutionary change from traditional religious gatherings at which experts only read and explained religious texts. Instead of texts, the Kaum Muda ulama examined problems of daily life. No less important was their use of Malay or Minangkabau instead of Arabic in the Friday sermons. They adopted a slogan that "religion is only for those who can understand" and this proved important in the rapid spread of the reform movement.[17]

A close personal relationship which existed among the pioneers of the Kaum Muda reform also contributed to the movement's success. The prominent Kaum Muda ulama were able to complement each other's strengths or weaknesses. Hadji Rasul with his zest and aggressiveness sometimes enraged the nagari authorities and offended local administrators by denouncing anything which in his view constituted unlawful innovation. But Sjech Djambek with his well-known tact usually managed to ease the tension and turn the situation to the advantage of the Kaum Muda ulama. Hadji Abdullah Ahmad remained the most congenial ulama in the eyes of the Dutch officials. Commonly regarded as "the father of Islamic journalism in Sumatra," he worked actively among the educated and the trading groups in Padang. Sjech Djambek and Sjech Thaib Umar were able to win favor with the penghulu in their respective nagari.[18]

---

17 Junus, *Sedjarah Pendidikan*, pp. 76-79.
18 Hamka, *Ajahku*, pp. 231-245.

The progress of religious reform was clearly reflected by the increase in public debates, the proliferation of religious publications and the mushrooming of religious schools. During this period of economic change when the idea of kemadjuan spread out to the nagari, the presence of a religious school gradually came to be regarded as an additional source of prestige for the nagari and an indication of the religious devotion of its inhabitants. As a result, Minangkabau became the center of Muslim education in Sumatra and an important source for the Islamic modernist movement elsewhere in Indonesia. But Minangkabau also had to pay for these developments with a temporary but poignant polarization between the reformers and their opponents.

By the end of the first quarter of the twentieth century, religious controversies had reached the high water mark. The public debates had shown that the two groups of ulama could not find a common ground for their religious judgments. Having failed to convince the opposition, each side gradually abandoned discussion of the most divisive issues. They turned from debate on trivial doctrinal (*chilafijah*) matters and began to pay more attention to the spread of their school networks. The emphasis on education reflected the fact that many of the leading Kaum Muda and Kaum Tua ulama were former students of Sjech Achmad Chatib. In spite of their conflicts, these ulama still adhered to traditional ideas on the proper relationship among the disciples of the same *guru* (teacher). In the early 1920's, some Kaum Tua ulama began to copy Kaum Muda methods of disseminating religious instruction to the general populace through the tabligh. By the end of the 1920's, they had also begun to imitate the Kaum Muda educational system.

The New Madrasah and the Kaum Muda Educated Group

The madrasah, or religious school, has always been the focus of Muslim religious life. It was either under the guardianship of a *fukaha* (expert on religious law) or a mysticism teacher. Because Islam lacks social institutions for maintaining and elaborating legal and scriptural knowledge and for distributing these to the general populace, it has had to rely heavily on its religious schools. Not surprisingly, therefore, religious movements in Minangkabau usually identified the existing madrasah as their first target, and the first challenge was the founding of a new madrasah. In the long run, the most important aspect of the Islamic modernist movement was its school reform which formed the foundation for a rapid increase of its followers and for continuity in the movement. The reforms released students from complete obedience to their teachers and allowed them to elaborate their own knowledge.

The early Kaum Muda schools employed the traditional "circle" (*halaqah*) system; the teacher explained religious tracts to his students, who sat around him with their books and notes. The students included all ages and levels of knowledge; they were supposed to listen and to participate in the discussion. The best students were designated as the helpers. The halaqah method, according to Sjech Thaib, who was never able to change the system satisfactorily, could produce but one fine ulama out of a hundred students.[19]

The first substantial changes introduced by the Kaum Muda ulama in their schools were confined to the content of instruction. Although the Kaum Muda ulama had been fighting the heterodox tarekat schools and the taqlid attitude of the orthodox religious teachers since the beginning of the century, reform in the religious schools themselves only began in 1915. Zainuddin Labai, one of the ablest young ulama and a student of Hadji Rasul, began by taking the government schools as the model for his own elementary religious school. This school, the Dinijah, introduced the graded system in religious education, and, unlike the old schools, it also admitted girls as pupils. In 1918, the Surau Djembatan Besi in Padang Pandjang, where Hadji Rasul was the teacher and Zainuddin a junior teacher, also began to use the graded system. It proved relatively easy to modernize the Dinijah school. The children were divided into seven classes according to age and level of education. At the elementary levels, the pupils used books which were especially written by Zainuddin and by his colleagues. The upper classes used new textbooks from Egypt. From the early 1920's, the number of Dinijah schools continued to increase. Although the various schools were not administratively connected with each other, they were generally founded by former colleagues of Zainuddin, who took his Dinijah as their model. In 1923, a sister of Zainuddin, Rahmad el-Junusiah, founded the Dinijah Putri (Dinijah

---

19 Junus, *Sedjarah Pendidikan*, p. 50.

for Girls) in Padang Pandjang. The establishment of this school and its subsequent success not only made its founder one of the most important female pioneers in modern Indonesian history,[20] but also led to the formation of the energetic female Kaum Muda educated group, which played an important role in the wider Minangkabau social and political movement. Girls' schools were founded in many parts of Minangkabau and also in other areas of Sumatra and in Batavia.

The Sumatra Thawalib (the former Surau Djembatan Besi), following the example of the Dinijah, was divided into seven classes, but, unlike the Dinijah, the change proved very difficult to accomplish because the students varied greatly in age and training. Some of them were already well-trained in Arabic, while others could hardly read. Some of them were already adults, while others were still in their early teens.[21] For some years, the Sumatra Thawalib still had to use old textbooks.

The change in the school, however, resulted in a rapid increase in the number of "graduates," because religious studies were no longer considered as a process which ended only when the thirst for knowledge had been appeased or the teachers had been satisfied. The new madrasah unlike the traditional ones did not specialize in only one or two branches of religious knowledge. The Sumatra Thawalib offered instruction in all important religious subjects, and its students received a certificate (*idjazah*) allowing them to become teachers. The Sumatra Thawalib of Padang Pandjang was the model for other Kaum Muda schools, for example, those of Parabek, Padang Djapang, Manin-djau and Batu Sangkar. After the mid-1920's, the number of Kaum Muda schools rapidly increased, partly as a result of the spread of Kaum Muda influence and the improvement in the economic situation, but also because of the ambiguous educational policy of the government. Though promoting education, the government failed to meet the increasing demand for schools. Its policy was to encourage private schools, but, as far as possible, to avoid accepting any additional financial responsibility. In such a situation, religious schools, the dominant educational institutions of Minangkabau, presented the obvious solution to the people's needs.

---

20 Jeanne Cuisinier, "Les Madrasah Féminines de Minangkabau," *Revue des Études Islamiques*, 23 (1955), pp. 107-120.
21 Hamka, *Kenang-Kenangan Hidup* (Djakarta: Gapura, 1952), I, p. 41.

The educational policy of the Dutch government put more emphasis on the spread of elementary vernacular schools, the three-year volksschool. These schools, popularly called *sekolah desa* (village schools), were supported by the respective nagari communities but under the control of the Dutch government, from which they also received meager subsidies. The main function of these schools was to teach the basics of reading, penmanship and simple mathematics. After three years, the children were expected to return to ordinary village life. But after the 1910's, it became clear that such minimum schooling was far from sufficient. In order to accommodate children who wanted to continue their studies, two-year *vervolgschool*, or "continuation" schools, were established, but these also were few in number. In 1925, for example, there were 548 volksschool with an enrollment of about 33,440—about 40% girls—but there were only 55 vervolgschool plus eight schools for girls (*meisjesschool*).[22] As a result, the great majority of the children had to return to the village, although some enrolled in the new religious schools, particularly the Dinijah. After 1927, private secular schools also began to increase in numbers.

The graduates of the volksschool did not represent a problem because they could be easily absorbed into the community. Graduates of the vervolgschool and the vernacular five-year school program, the so-called second class school, did create difficulties because these schools had originally been established on the assumption that their graduates would become minor government officials.[23] Consequently, the graduates had been prepared to enter a new world, one somewhat detached from their own. The government, however, failed to furnish enough jobs, nor could it provide adequate higher education.[24] These shortcomings became more noticeable in the 1920's. In 1925, for example, the number of second class schools and vervolgschool reached 65, with an enrollment of about 13,850.[25] But there were only two *schakelschool* (connection schools) available to the graduates. The connection schools, introduced

---

22 A. I. Spits, "Memorie van Overgave, March 1937," *Mailrapport* 504/'37.
23 S. L. van der Wal (ed.), *Het Onderwijsbeleid in Nederlands-Indië 1900-1940* (Groningen: J. B. Wolters, 1963), pp. 142-151.
24 A 1915 second class school graduate who knew Dutch reported that many of his friends could not find jobs in positions which formerly had been open to them. *Soematera Tengah*, 15, 30, 33 (March and April 1915).
25 Whitlaw, "Memorie," p. 112.

in the early 1920's, gave graduates from the vernacular schools the chance to continue their education and earn diplomas equal to those from the seven-year Hollandsch-Inlandsche School (HIS). Dutch was used as the language of instruction, and a diploma from a HIS was required for admission to higher educational institutions and also for appointment to high status, high salary jobs.

The graduates of the second class schools and vervolgschool in West Sumatra pressed to enter the two teachers' training schools in Padang Pandjang. Though supplemented by three vocational schools, the available advanced education could not accommodate all who sought entry. Each second class school and vervolgschool could send only four or five of its best students to take the entrance examinations for the advanced schools, and only a handful of these would be admitted. As of 1916, the Bukittinggi Teachers' College, called locally the Sekolah Radja, only admitted graduates from a HIS or schakelschool. Only the children of a few select individuals, usually government officials, penghulu and rich persons, were admitted to the Dutch-language elementary schools. The number of both vervolgschool and second class schools did continue to increase prior to 1931, and quantitatively they were the most successful of the government schools.

In addition to the still limited number of private secular schools established by local educational organizations, the other important educational institutions available to the graduates of the second class schools were the new religious schools, particularly the Sumatra Thawalib. In 1928, the great majority of students at the Sumatra Thawalib had graduated from a second class school.[26] By the middle of the 1920's, the Sumatra Thawalib of Padang Pandjang and, to a lesser extent, the other Thawalib schools had succeeded in transforming themselves into "modern" religious schools. But, despite improvement in teaching methods and a continued emphasis on the need for *ilmu ashriah* (science suitable for the changing times), the Thawalib schools generally devoted most of their attention to theoretical religious studies.[27] This situation persisted

---

26 C. van der Plas, "Gegevens Betreffende de Godsdienstige Stroomingen in het Gewest Sumatra's Westkust," *Mailrapport* 527x/'29.
27 Hamka, *Kenang-Kenangan Hidup*, p. 43; Kadiman, "Peroebahan dalam Sekolah Agama," *Berita*, April 11 and 12, 1933; and *Pewarta*, May 4, 1933.

until 1931, when a new phase in religious school reformation began. By 1928, according to van der Plas, instruction in the Thawalib schools was "of very high quality, and, contrary to the old system of education, it is not based on learning by heart, but rather on thinking and comprehension."[28] Because Thawalib teachers insisted on a high quality of religious learning, many students in Padang Pandjang had to attend the Dinijah school in the afternoon to catch up on their religious studies.[29] Twelve years of study in the Al-Azhar school system were required, according to Mahmud Junus, a graduate of Al-Azhar, to finish what was completed in seven years in the Sumatra Thawalib.[30]

In the mid-1920's, the Thawalib schools began to use some important new textbooks. The students of the lower classes had, in addition to the old textbooks, new books written by their own teachers, Hadji Rasul and his associates. Students in the two highest grades studied from books written by great Islamic theologians and philosophers, such as Al-Ghazali, Ibn Rusjd, and Ibn Sina. In Quranic exegesis, the Thawalib schools used the work of the pioneer of the Islamic modernist movement in Egypt, Sjech Muhammad Abduh.[31] The teachings of the revolutionary Pan-Islamist ulama, Al-Afghani, were also available and known to Thawalib students. The literature used in the Thawalib schools belonged unquestionably to a "golden age" of Muslim theology and philosophy as well as a period of Islamic modernist thought.

In spite of the one-sided emphasis on theological problems, the Kaum Muda schools energetically cultivated the idea of individual rationality (idjtihad) and the spirit of reform. The gradual decrease in doctrinal conflict between the Kaum Muda and the Kaum Tua ulama saved the new generation from the kind of unproductive debates common in the 1910's.

The second generation of the Kaum Muda oriented students were influenced by numerous Islamic journals. Since the early 1920's, almost every important madrasah had its own journal. A few of them were colored by a particular political orientation, such as the "communist"

---

28 van der Plas, "Gegevens," pp. 8-9.
29 *Ibid.*, p. 9.
30 Junus, *Sedj arah Pendidikan*, p. 66.
31 *Ibid.*, p. 65.

Pemandangan Islam (Islamic View) published in 1923 and the radical *Doenia Achirat* (The World Hereafter) issued between 1922 and 1925. In general, however, the journals were purely educational and non-political; without exception, they emphasized the inherent greatness of Islam.

The concept of the inherent greatness of Islam gave graduates of the new religious schools a great psychological advantage, for it helped free them from the dilemma of the Western-educated intellectual, who must reconcile modernity with the desire to preserve his own culture. The modernist Islamic literature taught the new generation of the religious Kaum Muda that the West had risen to its position of power and technologi-cal development after receiving an initial stimulus from Islamic civilization. According to this position, the Western world began to develop independently after abandoning its own religion, Christianity, and accepting the new, materialist ethic. Islam, on the other hand, had fallen into obscurity because its adherents abandoned the true ethics of Islam and its rulers became increasingly interested in power for its own sake. The ulama, rather than nurturing the true spirit of rationality within the context of iman (belief), had entrapped their followers in blind obedience to a medieval obscurantism. The ulama had served as tools of the rulers instead of the guardians of the people.[32]

This dismissal of the "dark age of Islam" as a deviation from its legitimate history and the confidence in an eventual renaissance of Islam were clearly reflected in the speeches and writings of the Kaum Muda educated leaders. Typical of this genre was a booklet written in 1929 by Saalah Sutan Mangkuto, entitled *Soeloeh Moeballigh Islam Indonesia*. The author starts by explaining how a backward Arab nation was elevated to greatness in a relatively short time under the leadership of the Prophet, and how, under the banner of Islam, Arab civilization flourished for some centuries. But, in time, he writes, Islam's power and its élan declined.

> When the *ummat* Islam was at the peak of its greatness, it began to ignore [the true ethics of] Islam and began to move step by step

---

32 These ideas were clearly expressed in the first Islamic modernist journal, *Al Urwat al-Wuthqa*, edited by Al-Afghani and Muhammad Abduh and published in Paris in 1884. Charles Adams, *Islam dan Dunia Modern di Mesir*, translated by Ismail Djamil (Djakarta: Pustaka Rakjat, 1947), pp. 48-57.

toward decline. It eventually fell into the lowest possible state of humiliation and debasement.

The world fell to the mercy of the Western powers, who incessantly cultivated the sciences, but they also made many blunders and terrible wars. Thus men began to realize that the world could not be ruled by intelligence alone, and that divine regulations were also necessary.

> Now Islam and its ummat are climbing upward…; from day to day they are approaching their peak. The non-Muslims, Alhamdullillah [thanks be to God] have been continuously disclosing their falsehood;…every day they are approaching the deep valley of humiliation and debasement. Darkness will be replaced by light, the truth of Islam will become clearly visible.[33]

Despite this new trend, Saalah and the Islamic apologists stressed, the final outcome depended upon Muslims themselves. In order to attain glory now, and happiness in the world hereafter, believers had to cultivate seriously the true ethics of Islam as well as the modern sciences.

This conception of the nature of Islamic and Western civilizations permeated the political and educational movements among graduates of the Kaum Muda schools. They could find no place in the colonial system, for religious education was irrelevant to the government and their ideas abhorrent to the Dutch. The Western-educated persons because of their training could claim an appropriate status and function in the colonial system, but the younger generation of Islamic modernists could not aspire to participate even if they had wished to do so. Consequently, their relationship with the Dutch was not simply one of political confrontation but also of cultural estrangement. Dutch officials held the religious modernists in contempt, and they knew that the young Islamic intellectuals were inspired by genuinely anti-Western sentiments. Such anti-Western feelings became a source of weakness, however, because they prevented the young modernists from studying and applying modern political

---

33 Saalah Sutan Mangkuto, *Soeloeh Moeballigh Islam Indonesia* (Padang Pandjang: Boekhandel M. Thaib, 1929), pp. 30-44.

strategies and methods. On the other hand, such sentiments enabled the modernists to identify more completely with the population at large.

Until 1930, the most important educational institutions of the Kaum Muda were the Dinijah and the Thawalib schools. By 1928, there were 39 Thawalib schools with an enrollment of about 17,000 students. The biggest schools were the Thawalib of Padang Pandjang, Parabek, and Padang Djapang, which had about 750, 800, and 500 students, respectively. It was estimated that, from the mid-1920's until 1928, the Thawalib schools produced about 1,000 graduates.[34] This was important after 1927, when Minangkabau was recovering from its abortive rebellion, for it meant there already existed a large educated Kaum Muda group to provide leadership. The number is even larger if the graduates of the Dinijah schools are included.

Although such educated people represented only a very small percentage of the almost two million Minangkabau inhabitants of West Sumatra, the Kaum Muda enjoyed certain advantages. The intensity of religious conflict had subsided, and Kaum Muda religious ideas had spread throughout Minangkabau. Unlike the Kaum Muda ulama, whose legitimacy as religious teachers depended largely upon social recognition, the graduates of the Kaum Muda schools could claim recognition on the basis of their graduation certificates. In politics, the activities of Abdul Muis and the Islamic communist movement had paved the way for the activities of the Islamic modernists. Moreover, they did not have to face serious opposition from the Western-educated group, for in a religiously oriented society which admires rhetorical skill, the graduates of the religious schools were almost unbeatable opponents for the Western-educated persons. The latter were numerically weak but,more important,they had been trained to become government officials not religious preachers. Their skills were those of administration not of debate.

The Western-educated persons generally came from the higher strata of colonial Minangkabau society; their social status was based on position in the adat hierarchy and on relationship with the government. The older ulama generally came from ulama-fami-lies. But the graduates

---

34 van der Plas, "Gegevens," p. 9.

of the Kaum Muda schools came from many different social classes and occupational groups: some were from ulama families, others from trading backgrounds; some were the sons of school teachers, others were the offspring of civil servants. Within the community some were *urang datang* (new settlers) in their nagari, and others were from the urang usali (original settlers) and thus members of the adat aristocracy. In fact, some of the most important leaders of the Kaum Muda educated group were themselves penghulu.

The educated Kaum Muda group also benefited from the scattered geographical origins of its members. The Kaum Muda ulama had generally come from one of the religious centers in Minangkabau, such as Bukittinggi, Padang Pandjang, Batu Sangkar and Manindjau. The greater part of the Western-educated group came from the Bukittinggi region. The members of the Kaum Muda educated group, however, came from nearly all parts of Minangkabau. They also came from all class levels. In the coastal areas, for example, where the traditional class system remained stronger than in the interior, one finds that the graduates of the Kaum Muda schools cannot be identified with any particular social class.³⁵ At a time when adat authorities were struggling to maintain their status against outside competitors, the young Islamic modernists could operate within the nagari as internal forces for change. This role could also be played in the towns which were really conglomerations of satellite communities from the nagari. For example,the 1930 census showed that about 65% of the population of Pajakumbuh and 54% of Padang came from other nagari.[36]

The emergence of a group of Islamic modernists interested also in non-religious matters did not challenge the traditional Minangkabau concepts of leadership. There had always been an important role for *tjerdik -pandai*, or intelligentsia, alongside that of the penghulu and the ulama. Instead of becoming a counter-elite, the educated Islamic modernists could find their place within the traditional pattern. Their expertise in religious

---

35 The Kaum Muda educated group intensified the process whereby the importance of adat class declined within Minangkabau society. Schrieke, *Indonesian Sociological Studies*, I, pp. 114-130.
36 *Volkstelling 1930*, Vol. IV *Inheemsche Bevolking van Sumatra* (Batavia: Dep. Landbouw, Nijverheid & Handel, 1935), p. 38.

matters gave them the qualifications of an ulama, and, at the same time, their broad background in general affairs gained them recognition as part of the tjerdik pandai. Some prominent leaders of the Kaum Muda educated group, such as Hadji Djala-luddin Thaib, were able to combine their religious expertise with the ascriptive qualities of penghuluship.

Graduates from the Kaum Muda institutions could enter many different kinds of jobs. Some became writers, newspaper correspondents and editors for the numerous Islamic journals. A great number, however, made their living as traders in the towns or farmers in the villages, and they often served as religious teachers as well. A small percentage, usually those from well-to-do families, went to Mecca and particularly to Cairo to con-tinue their studies. When this group began returning in the 1930's, they initiated a new phase in religious school reform. Despite a common training as religious teachers, the Kaum Muda graduates found the community was unable to provide enough jobs for them as religious teachers or *muballigh* (religious preachers), and thus they needed to seek outside employment to sustain them.

An important difference between the older ulama and the younger generation of religious teachers was that the latter generally did not have the same independent personal status. Religious schools were no longer considered the personal property of the master teacher. Most of the new teachers had to seek employment in schools operated by others rather than establish their own institution. The withdrawal of Hadji Rasul from the Sumatra Thawalib in 1923 proved unprecedented in the history of religious schools in Minangkabau because the school continued despite loss of its founder-teacher. The traditional personal schools began to lose strength as they became more and more dependent on organizations of educational promoters. After the 1920's, a large number of religious schools were established and financed by local organizations rather than by individual teachers. Young religious teachers found that they could only join an existing school, or, if they wished to establish a new one, they needed the cooperation of others.

Many leaders of the Kaum Muda organizations were also teachers in the new schools. The organization for them did not represent simply a medium for propagating their ideas and ideologies; it was also an economic necessity.

Leaders of the Kaum Muda Educated Group

In 1918, shortly after its establishment, the Sumatra Thawalib sent one of its junior teachers to Tapak Tuan on the southwest coast of Atjeh. Many Minangkabau had lived in this area for generations and the Thawalib directors wished to introduce the new system of religious education there. The junior teacher was Hadji Djalaluddin Thaib, who was a penghulu in his home nagari, Balingka (near Bukittinggi),[37] His maternal family included many ulama, and his maternal uncles, Sjech Latif and Sjech Daud Rasjidi, were the most influential ulama in the nagari. Sjech Daud played a leading role in the spread of the Kaum Muda movement and was a junior partner of Hadji Rasul.

Djalaluddin was born in 1895. After graduating from a second class school, he went to Mecca in 1914, where he studied religion and Arabic until 1916. On his return, he continued his religious study first with Sjech Thaib Umar in Sungajang and later at the Surau Djembatan Besi with Hadji Rasul; he also served as a junior teacher in the latter school, remaining there until he was sent to Tapak Tuan. After a year, he was succeeded at Tapak Tuan by one of his colleagues from the Sumatra Thawa-lib. In 1920, Djalaluddin founded a Dinijah school in his nagari, but he remained active in matters connected with the Sumatra Thawalib. In 1922, he was elected chairman of the newly united Thawalib. Soon afterwards, this unity dissolved and the Thawalib of Padang Pandjang fell under the influence of Hadji Datuk Batuah's Islamic communist movement. Disappointed with this development, Djalaluddin abandoned the Thawalib,[38] and in 1925 he founded the Persatuan Guru Sekolah Agama (PGSA, Association of Teachers at Religious Schools), an organization of Dinijah school teachers. Until 1927, when he went to Kuala Lumpur as a religious teacher, Djalaluddin served as the chairman of the PGSA. On returning from Kuala Lumpur in 1928, Djalaluddin resumed the leadership.

He was one of the pioneers in the modernization of the school system, and he wrote several new textbooks for elementary religious schools.

---

37 Aziz Thaib, *Hadji Djalaluddin Thaib Dt. Penghulu Besar* (Fort de Kock: n.p., 1934); *Mailrapport* 861x/'34.
38 Hadji Djalaluddin Thaib's opposition to communism was based on Jamal ad-Din Al-Afghani's *Arradu 'ala Dahriyin*, which exposed the "fallacies of extreme materialism."

His Arabic textbook was used by all Dinijah schools and was thought to be the best of its time.³⁹ According to van der Plas, Djalaluddin was "a conciliatory figure," whose tactfulness was matched only by his organizational skill.⁴⁰ These qualifications later earned him wide respect as a "strong man" in Permi.

Another able and influential student of Hadji Rasul was Abdul Rasjid Sutan Mansjur, who played an important role although he rarely involved himself in politics. Born in 1895 in Manindjau, Sutan Mansjur came from an ulama family.⁴¹ After he graduated from the district second class school, the Dutch controleur nominated him as a candidate for the prestigious Sekolah Radja in Bukittinggi, but he turned it down because he preferred to attend the surau of Hadji Rasul.⁴² When Hadji Rasul moved to Padang Pandjang in 1912, Sutan Mansjur followed him and became one of his most trusted students. In 1917, Sutan Mansjur married Hadji Rasul's daughter.

In 1918, Sutan Mansjur was sent by the Sumatra Thawalib to Kuala Simpang, a small town in Atjeh, as a religious teacher. He was disappointed in his role because he felt that teaching was not a suitable job for him. During this time, Abdul Muis came to Kuala Simpang to promote the SI, and Sutan Mansjur began to ponder the possibility of joining this party as a remedy for his dissatisfaction. But membership in the SI required taking an oath to refrain from doing anything which was forbidden (*haram*) by Islam. Sutan Mansjur believed that by so doing the SI implied that God's sanction was insufficient and thus required supplementary sanctions. Such a dubious practice on the part of the SI was repugnant to Sutan Mansjur, an orthodox, reformist ulama.

He stayed two years in Kuala Simpang and then returned to become an assistant to his father-in-law in the Sumatra Thawalib at Padang Pandjang. In 1922, determined to give up teaching and become a trader instead, Sutan Mansjur took his family to Pekalongan in Central Java; many batik traders from Minangkabau and particularly from the Manindjau sub-district had businesses there. In late 1922, on one of his

---

39 Junus, *Sedjarah Pendidikan*, pp. 58-59.
40 van der Plas, "Gegevens," p. 15.
41 Hamka, *Ajahku*, pp. 257-260.
42 Interview, A. R. St. Mansjur, Djakarta, October 1968.

visits to Jogjakarta, he met Kiai Hadji Achmad Dahlan, the founder of the rapidly expanding Muhammadijah. Attracted by Dahlan's organization, Sutan Mansjur helped to form a branch in Pekalongan, and in 1923 he became its chairman. In the same year, he also founded a Minangkabau perantau organization, the Nurul Islam (Light of Islam), which became the backbone of the Muhammadijah in Pekalongan. In 1925, when Hadji Rasul visited the family of Sutan Mansjur, he was attracted by the organization and on his return home to Sungai Batang, Hadji Rasul founded a branch of the Muhammadijah there. The perantau traders of Pekalongan became the driving force behind this effort.

Shortly after the establishment of the Muhammadijah branch in Sungai Batang, Sutan Mansjur was appointed by the central board in Java as a propagandist-at-large. He took his family back to Sungai Batang and began to travel throughout Sumatra and Sulawesi. In 1927, he and Hadji Fachruddin, the most popular Javanese leader of Muhammadijah, managed to organize several branches, including some in Atjeh. Sutan Mansjur took over the leadership of the Muhammadijah in Minangkabau in 1930, and he built it into a strong organization despite the increasing popularity of radical political parties. Under his leadership, the Muhammadijah emerged as the organization doing the most to promote education.

Before Sutan Mansjur assumed leadership, the most influential Muhammadijah leader in Minangkabau was Saalah Jusuf Sutan Mangkuto. Unlike most leaders of the Kaum Muda educated group, Saalah had never studied formally with any Kaum Muda ulama. A self-made man, he was more of a politician than a teacher. Born in 1901, Saalah was a son of a respected Naqsjabandijah leader. On his maternal side, he was descended from an original settler of his nagari, Pitalah, near Padang Pandjang. After finishing his education in the second class school in 1917, he became a parewa, the traditional Minangkabau "freedom loving-youth,"[43] but he still continued his religious education. In 1918, a nephew of his father took him to Padang, for, as he put it, it was not proper for a young man to remain living "under the roof of his mother's house." In Padang he

---

43 A somewhat idealized picture of the parewa life is given in Hamka's novel, *Tenggelamnja Kapal van der Wijck* (Medan: Pedoman Masjarakat" 1938).

worked as an apprentice in several jobs, but he was usually fired. As a former parewa and skilled in the Minangkabau art of self-defense (*silat*), Saalah saw no need to restrain his quarrelsome nature. In 1921, under the guardianship of a neighbor who was a retired public prosecutor (*djaksa*), he studied law and six months later he became a *pokrol bambu* (unlicensed attorney).[44] He left this job in 1923 because very strong and harsh criticism had been voiced against this occupation in the Volksraad. His legal experience, however, influenced his style of leadership in Muhammadijah.

When Abdul Muis began publishing a newspaper in Padang in 1923, Saalah went to work for him, and the SI leader served as his first mentor in politics. After the expulsion of Abdul Muis from Minangkabau in 1924, Saalah returned to Pitalah, where he established an adat organization, Berlian Minangkabau (The Jewel of Minangkabau). This organization was intended to unite all the penghulu and adat functionaries in Pitalah and serve as a first step toward a greater adat organization which would include other nagari. But he was a non-penghulu and his attempt to organize the penghulu aroused enmity among the adat authori-ties of Pitalah. Rejected by the penghulu, he went first to Padang Pandjang, and, in early 1925, along with his friend, a rich penghulu called Datuk Sati, Saalah went to Java to study the *pergerakan* (political movement). In Batavia, they met Agus Salim, the only Minangkabau perantau leader in that city whom they knew. He explained aspects of political life in Java. In August 1925, with a letter of introduction from Hadji Agus Salim, Saalah and Datuk Sati traveled to Jogjakarta to attend the Al-Islam Congress. There they met the most famous political leader of that time, Tjokroaminoto, the president of the SI.[45] The organization of the congress and his meetings with the Muslim leaders in Java left a deep impression on Saalah. A turning point in his life occurred when he was introduced to Hadji Fachruddin, from whom he learned about the Muhammadijah and its goals. Saalah and his friend remained about a month in Jogjakarta, the

---

44 Interview, Saalah Sutan Mangkuto, Djakarta, November 1968.
45 The Al-Islam Congress in Jogjakarta, August 21-27, 1925, was the third. Its main objectives, as initiated by the SI and the Muhammadijah, were to achieve Muslim unity in Indonesia and closer ties with Muslims abroad. It was strongly influenced by political Pan-Islam. J. Th. Petrus Blumberger, *De Nationalistische Beweging in Nederlandsch-Indië* (Haarlem: Tjeenk Willink, 1931), pp. 77, 84-90.

center of Muhammadijah activities, before returning to Padang Pandjang in early 1926.

Here, they were snubbed as part of the *kaum hidjau* (green group) from Batavia. Their former friends had already joined the communist *kaum merah* (red group). Soon afterwards Saalah went to Djambi, but it was not easy for a Minangkabau to cross the Residency boundary. Since he did not have a pass, he was arrested and imprisoned for two months after which he was expelled from Djambi. On his return to Pitalah, he established a Muhammadijah group.

The different styles of leadership shown by Sutan Mansjur and Saalah can to some extent be explained in terms of their individual backgrounds. Sutan Mansjur was an ulama who looked to Muhammadijah as a means for reforming the ummat. Saalah, although he shared Sutan Mansjur's ideal, was more a politician than an ulama. Sutan Mansjur represented the urang siak at its best; Saalah was by temperament a parewa who loved action.

Hadji Uddin Rahmany, like Hadji Djalaluddin, was a religious teacher who later turned to politics. Born in 1901 in Lubuk Basung, he failed to finish his secular education in the second class school because of illness, but he did continue his religious training. From 1914 till 1920, he studied in the madrasah which later became the Sumatra Thawalib of Manindjau. When the teacher of the school, one of his maternal uncles, died, Uddin's older brother took over. After Uddin finished his education in 1920, he became a junior teacher in the school and when his brother went to Mecca in 1926, Uddin succeeded him. In late 1927, after returning from a pilgrimage, Uddin founded a Dinijah school in Manindjau. He gave up teaching and busied himself with the direction of the Manindjau Thawalib and Dinijah schools .

While still a junior teacher, Uddin had already begun to educate himself in secular knowledge. Like many of his friends, he was initially attracted to the communist movement, and he joined the party. In 1925, during the fasting month vacation, he went to Padang Pandjang to study the party and its ideology, but he found himself in heated disagreements with the party leaders. He wanted to know how communism could be in accord with Islam, if, as maintained by some party leaders, "religion is a poison to the people"? On his return to Manindjau, Uddin was expelled from the party, and he soon joined the adat authorities and the older ulama in combating local communist influence.⁴⁶ In spite of his preoccupation with his two schools and his unhappy experience with the communist party, Uddin retained an interest in politics. He put this interest to work after Hadji Abdul Madjid and Datuk Singo Mangkuto established a branch of the Partai Sarekat Islam (PSI) in Manindjau in 1928. Until his arrest in 1933, Uddin was one of the most influential leaders of the PSI in Minangkabau.

Hadji Abdul Madjid and Datuk *Singo Mangkuto* perhaps should not be included among the Kaum Muda educated group, but they played an important role in the activities of this group. Hadji Abdul Madjid was a moderate leader of the Kaum Tua ulama in the Manindjau sub-district, and, in 1921, he was the vice-president of the Ittihadul Ulama, the first organization of Kaum Tua ulama and one which challenged the Kaum Muda ulama's PGAI. His participation in the movement of the Kaum Muda ulama and their students began when he, as leader of the Kaum Tua group, took an active part in opposing the proposed Guru Ordinance. Thereafter, he always joined the political activities of the Kaum Muda educated group, although he disagreed with them in religious matters. When the PSI branch was established in 1928, Hadji Abdul Madjid became its adviser. In 1930, when the Sumatra Thawalib was transformed into the Persatuan Muslimin Indonesia (commonly known as Permi, though until 1932 abbreviated as PMI), he was its first chairman.

Hasanuddin Datuk Singo Mangkuto was born in the 1890's. He was a penghulu of Sungai Batang, in the sub-district of Manindjau. For some time he was a perantau trader in Atjeh, and during the early 1920's he was active in the SI movement there. In 1925, he was sentenced to two years' imprisonment for his political activities.⁴⁷ Upon his release from prison, he returned to Sungai Batang and was soon active in nagari politics. Like Hadji Abdul Madjid, he first became important in the political movement of the Kaum Muda educated group when his newly established party, the Persatuan Adat (Adat Association), took an active part in the opposition to the Guru Ordinance. He served as the first chairman of the PSII branch in Minangkabau.

---

46 Statement of Hadji Uddin Rahmany, *Mailrapport* 861x/'34.
47 "Report of the Assistant Resident of Agam, Fort de Kock, September 3, 1928, no. 98," *Mailrapport* 966x/'28.

These six persons were important leaders in the period between 1927 and 1933. But, after 1930, they were forced to share their leadership with new returnees from the Middle East, particularly Cairo. In spite of the rapid ascendancy of the better educated and more cosmopolitan newcomers, the above six persons and their colleagues were important, for they laid the foundation for the later predominance of the political and educational organizations of the young Islamic modernist intellectuals.

The post-1927 leaders shared a common experience in the rantau—Mecca, Java and elsewhere. Although the particular rantau did not necessarily determine the course of action they took later, their rantau experiences influenced their activities on return to Minangkabau. An example of this is seen in the difference between Sutan Mansjur and Datuk Singo Mangkuto, both of whom came from Manindjau and both of whom went to the same rantau, Atjeh. Aggressiveness in public debate, skills in organization, expertise in religious knowledge and a broad knowledge of general affairs contributed to the prominent positions which these men assumed vis-a-vis their colleagues. Wealth helped in the careers of some, such as Hadji Djalaluddin Thaib, but this was not the case with Saalah and Sutan Mansjur. While striving to reform society, these leaders could not avoid dissension. Moreover different personal inclinations, family backgrounds and experiences led to the establishment of competing organizations. The first organization to develop rapidly after the 1927 rebellion was the Muhammadijah, but it was soon followed by others.

CHAPTER FOUR
MUHAMMADIJAH AND LOCAL POLITICS

In April 1927, a Minangkabau journalist warned his readers not to be influenced too readily by the new organization from Java, the Muhammadijah. He claimed that the Minangkabau people were always very susceptible to any organization whose ideology or propaganda was based on Islam. In 1916, for example, many Minangkabau joined the SI although they knew little about it. Later many were influenced by the communist party, which claimed an Islamic basis. The Muhammadijah maintained that it was a religious organization, but the journalist reminded his audience, "The communists also used religion,...the consequence was disaster." He warned that the spread of Muhammadijah might reawaken religious controversy between the Kaum Muda and the Kaum Tua groups, because the Muhammadijah was clearly a Kaum Muda organization.[1]

His reaction was typical of those who were concerned about the maintenance of social order in the wake of the rebellion of three months earlier. But, seem from another perspective, the Muhammadijah might in fact be an effective means for attaining social harmony and development. If so, the possibility of re-surgent religious conflict was a risk worth taking. The promoter of Muhammadijah in Minangkabau, Hadji Rasul, said in May 1927, that a religiously based organization was important in terms of the three basic spiritual needs of human beings. Man, he believed, was destined to depend on "three friends." The first was God the Merciful without Whom there was no life. Man's second friend was *nafsu*, or natural desire, without which he could not live. Nafsu was like fire, because if man did not control it, it could destroy life itself. The third

---

1 *Tjaja Soematra*, April 16, 1927.

friend was man's fellow human being, for man could not live by himself. Those who failed to live with these friends would regret it "in this world and the world hereafter."[2] Hadji Rasul asserted that Muhammadijah's goal was to guide its members in their relationships with these three friends. A religiously based organization would remind one of his obligation to God and to society and would direct his natural desires toward good ends. Hadji Rasul saw Muhammadijah as a community of believers, one which emphasized social activity in order to create a religiously perfect society.

Hadji Rasul introduced the Muhammadijah to his nagari, Sungai Batang, and to Minangkabau, in June 1925, after returning from a visit to Java. He had been greatly attracted by the activities of the organization on Java. It had been founded, in 1912, by Kiai Hadji Achmad Dahlan, a Javanese reformist ulama. Not only did Muhammadijah embody Hadji Rasul's own ideals, but also he believed it could serve as a tool for combating the activities of his former students, now active in the communist party. And, in fact, Muhammadijah soon provided an alternative for the non-communist graduates of the Kaum Muda schools. It was also an organization in which Kaum Muda ulama and their students could find a common ground. The PGAI, founded in 1919, was an organization of teachers only; the Sumatra Tha-walib was specifically a student organization. But Muhammadijah included both, and, moreover, it was neither a professionally nor a geographically limited organization. Like the SI, it directed its appeals at the ummat as a whole, rather than any particular segment of it. After the rebellion, Muhammadijah became the major organization for graduates of the Kaum Muda schools, one in which they could pursue their different objectives. Muhammadijah acted not only as an educational organization working to establish religious and secular schools, but also it served as a political party questioning the political situation and the legitimacy of current holders of political power.

The history of Muhammadijah at this time reflects both the nature of political activities among the Kaum Muda educated group and also the operation of Dutch Islamic policies. The growth of the organization demonstrates certain aspects of Minangkabau political behavior at

---

2 Politieke Politioneel Overzicht, 1927, *Mailrapport* 849x/'27.

the village level. Muhammadijah first spread in the nagari rather than in the towns, and its success depended on its ability to influence adat authori-ties as well as perantau traders and religious teachers. One could view the development of Muhammadijah in terms of the confrontation between adat-based authority and pecuniary prestige. The expansion of Muhammadijah also reveals the growing influence of the idea of kemadjuan and the declining role of the religious element in nagari conflict. Early in the twentieth century, when the Naqsjabandijah was in conflict with the other tarekat and the religious Kaum Muda was first developing, competition centered on control of the mosque, one of the pillars of the nagari according to adat. The victory of one party over its rival was symbolized by its ability to control the nagari mosque. If a stalemate occurred, one side might build a new mosque or the old mosque might be divided into two "congregations." For Muhammadijah, however, the control of the school rather than the mosque was considered the symbol of a group's influence in the nagari.

Sungai Batang: The First Stronghold of Muhammadijah

In 1907, Hadji Rasul's father, Sjech Kisai, died. Since he was the most revered ulama in the nagari, the people of Sungai Batang wanted to hold an elaborate adat funeral ceremony. But Hadji Rasul, who had just returned from Mecca, thought that such a ceremony, with its extravagant feasts, was haram (forbidden) according to Islamic law. Because of this opposition, Hadji Rasul was accused of having sinned against his father and of obstructing adat. The tuanku laras, the nagari chief, and the majority of the penghulu supported the traditionalist religious teachers in the view that Sjech Kisai deserved the highest adat honors. As a result, Hadji Rasul was rejected as a religious teacher, but nonetheless, a few months later a group of penghulu from Kubu, part of Sungai Batang, invited him to teach in their surau.[3] It was at the Kubu surau that Hadji Rasul really began his career as a religious reformer.

In 1923, after his religious views had already been widely accepted, Hadji Rasul withdrew from the Sumatra Thawalib in Padang Pandjang

---

3 Hamka, *Ajahku*, pp. 80-83.

because his stands on communism and on student participation in politics had cost him the loyalty of his students and assistants. Hadji Rasul therefore returned to Sungai Batang, and, in October 1924, he encouraged his brother Hadji Jusuf Amrullah, the highest adat religious functionary in Sungai Batang, and Datuk Penghulu Besar, a retired government official, to establish an educational organization, the Sandi Aman (Foundation of Peace). In spite of its leaders' prestige, the Sandi Aman failed to attract people, and by 1925, it had only fifteen members.[4] One major reason for its weakness was the use of Hadji Rasul's *Sandi Aman Tiang Selamat* (Foundation of Peace, Pillar of Happiness) as an ideological guide. This work, published in 1922, was considered an anti-adat and anti-penghulu treatise.

The book was written at a time when Hadji Rasul was engaged in a legal dispute with an adat expert[5] and it was intended as a document on religious ethics. But it not only showed how to lead an ethical social and individual life but also attacked some aspects of adat. These attacks openly revealed Hadji Rasul's orthodox Islamic concept of secular power. He also renewed the attack, begun by his teacher Sjech Achmad Chatib, on adat inheritance law. He sharply criticized what he regarded as the penghulu's arbitrariness in dealing with their people. Hadji Rasul also questioned the government's right to impose taxation. Because the legitimate holder of power was God the Creator, all laws and regulations made by man should be based on His laws. Thus, he said, the secular administration should always consult the ulama, the experts on religious law, otherwise God's law and man's law would conflict. If this occurred, Hadji Rasul warned, "it is better to die than to live." One who obeyed laws which were not in accord with God's law was in effect no less than a kafir.[6]

Given this background, the name Sandi Aman alone was sufficient to arouse suspicion that the organization was anti-adat, even though

---

4 Report of van Dam, the controleur of Manindjau, November 14, 1925, no. 1747, *Mailrapport* 1453x/'27.
5 Hamka, *Ajahku*, pp. 119-122.
6 Quoted by van Dam in his report of November 14, 1925, *Mailrapport* 1453x/'27. Ibn Chaldun, a fourteenth-century North African social philosopher, explained this as a conflict between law made by men and that made by God. Hadji Rasul thought that the ideal state was one in which religious law was dominant. But he recognized the political reality and sought at least to create a situation in which religious opinion would have a place in the execution of temporal political power.

its chairman was a penghulu. Hadji Rasul's failure to influence people in 1907 and again in 1925 is significant. On the first occasion, he was snubbed by his community despite his position as an heir of Sjech Kisai. In 1925, although his religious views were widely accepted, his Sandi Aman project was not. Personal status, apparently, could not guarantee the success of a venture which attacked existing values and practices. After Hadji Rasul reorganized the Sandi Aman into Muhammadijah, in June 1925, it quickly developed into a major force in Sungai Batang, and the nagari became Muhammadijah's first base in Sumatra. The Muhammadijah differed from earlier projects because it was built on the existing social system and economic situation of the nagari.

The inhabitants of Sungai Batang believed it was the oldest nagari in the Manindjau sub-district. According to local traditions, Sungai Batang and nine other nagari in the area had been settled by the same group of early explorers. The people of the ten nagari considered themselves bound to each other by adat ties (*setali adat*), and almost every suku in each nagari could identify a *belahan* (presumed blood relationship) in other nagari in the sub-district. The consciousness of belahan was particularly strong between nagari which were thought to have split in the recent past, as for example Sungai Batang and Tandjung Sani, which in adat matters functioned as a double nagari. Notions of belahan helped preserve peace between the nagari, but, more important, they made an excellent channel for inter-nagari communication. A new development in one nagari could easily be initiated in another by clever manipulation of the belahan system. A member of the suku Tjaniago in Sungai Batang, for example, could theoretically exploit his belahan in the same suku in other nagari.[7]

In terms of the traditional political system, the Manindjau sub-district belonged to the Bodi Tjaniago tradition, which recognized the equality

---

[7] Noer Sutan Iskandar, a novelist who came from the Manindjau region, tells in his autobiography that, after he completed his education in the elementary teachers' school, he established a volksschool in the nagari. His father was an influential former nagari head, so many people from the area sent their children. Many came from nagari across the lake; while at school, "They had to live with their relatives, their fellow suku or belahan in my village. The fellow suku took care of the children gladly...I realized at that time what a good thing the custom of my nagari was. ...I did not have to concern myself with building dormitories for the children from other nagari because the 'adat dormitory' would take care of them." Noer Sutan Iskandar, *Pengalaman Masa Ketjil* (Djakarta: J. B. Wolters, 1949), pp. 238-239.

of all penghulu. But unlike most other nagari which belonged to this tradition, Manindjau nagari had rather liberal provisions concerning the selection of penghulu. A new penghulu could be elected or appointed if the old penghulu had died or was too old to function properly. A new penghulu-ship might be instituted if the original matrilineal family had become too large, and new families from other regions could establish their own penghuluships. Such newcomers were thus not only recognized as belonging to the adat community of the nagari but were also given an opportunity for upward mobility in the local adat hierarchy.[8] Such provisions resulted in a rapid increase of the number of penghulu in Manindjau in contrast to other parts of Minangkabau.

At the end of the nineteenth century, the appointment of new penghulu became part of wider village politics. In order to strengthen his own position, a tuanku laras would work to appoint new penghulu.[9] In 1914, the office of tuanku laras was abolished, but the social consequences of the increased number of the penghulu persisted. The Nagari Ordinance of 1914 was intended to reactivate the traditional nagari council (balai), and it therefore established guidelines which limited council membership to the supposedly original penghulu. But the law was strongly opposed by the penghulu, whose positions were equal according to adat.[10] The ordinance was based on the logical assumption that too many members would decrease council efficiency, but it created divisions among the penghulu. Although all had equal prestige according to adat, those whom the government recognized as original penghulu now had greater authority. This awkward mixture of government-recognized authority and adat-created prestige resulted in rivalry between the two groups of penghulu when those who were not balai members became aware of the consequences of their loss of power. Deprived of their seats in the nagari council, the penghulu now sought to increase their status in other ways, for example by participating in the new voluntary associations. But they rejected the Sandi Aman because it did not offer an appropriate channel

---

8 "Nota van de Controleur der Danau-district en Matoer van 15 November 1888 omtrent Penghulu Andiko Verheffingen in de Onderdistrict," *Adatrechtbundels*, 11 (1915), pp. 109-114.
9 Hamka, *Ajahku*, pp. 68-71. Noer Sutan Iskandar, himself the grandnephew of a tuanku laras, confirms Hamka's story. *Pengalaman*, pp. 194-222.
10 Report of the Controleur of Manindjau, Spits, April 6, 1917, no. 379/13, *Verbaal* March 4, 1919, No. 23.

for penghulu; it was considered too inimical towards adat and adat's assumptions.

The sub-district of Manindjau was geographically isolated from the main roads. It was one of the most sparsely populated regions, having only 71.1 persons per square kilometer; it was also the least prosperous in natural resources. Sungai Batang, the largest and most densely populated nagari in the sub-district, had less arable land than its much smaller neighbors.[11] Rice cultivation provided only 6.46% of the income for the population of the sub-district; other agricultural products, such as cinnamon and coffee, provided only another 10.30%. The biggest sources of income were non-agricultural, from fishing, cottage industries and, especially, commerce. More than many other parts of Minangkabau, this area was heavily dependent on the perantau traders. The number of perantau fluctuated greatly, increasing when business in the rantau was good. Every year, however, new adults always went to the rantau to become apprentices of relatives who had preceded them. According to the census of 1930, about one-fifth of the persons born in the area lived outside it. In the district of Manindjau, about 23.5% of the heads of families were women.[12]

This dependence on the perantau combined with the insignificant role of agricultural production meant that despite its geographical isolation the region was sensitive to economic fluctuations and political developments which occurred far beyond its boundaries. In the absence of strong leadership from their penghulu, the inhabitants were more receptive to outside influences introduced by the perantau. It was to these prestigious perantau traders that Hadji Rasul finally turned after the failure of the Sandi Aman.

When he went to the batik center of Pekalongan in Central Java, Hadji Rasul found the Minangkabau perantau active not only in their own organization, the Nurul Islam, but also, under the leadership of his son-in-law Sutan Mansjur, they were important in the local Muhammadijah. Hadji Rasul was supported by this perantau community in his efforts to establish a religious school in Sungai Batang and to introduce the

---

11 Sutan Maaruf, *Riwajat X Koto Manindjau* (Bukittinggi: Pem-bela Negeri, 1931); *Volkstelling 1930*, IV, pp. 11, 132.
12 *Volkstelling* 1930, IV, p. 65.

Muhammadijah there. On his return to Sungai Batang, he proposed the dissolution of the Sandi Aman and the formation of a Muhammadijah group. With financial support from the perantau traders, Hadji Rasul was able to build a Muhammadijah elementary religious school. The school employed graduates from the Thawalib schools of Padang Pandjang and Manindjau, and it soon attracted many pupils—having 250 by the end of 1925. The early success of the school contributed to a further expansion of Muhammadijah.[13]

The financial support of the perantau traders was a major factor in the early success of Muhammadijah, for it did not need to be dependent on popular contributions. Muhammadijah made its appearance on the scene through the establishment of the first "modern" religious school in Sungai Batang. Rather than launching an ideological attack, it began by making a positive contribution to the community. The fact that the organization was founded under the auspices of the perantau gave it a great advantage in a nagari so dependent on its perantau. This was further strengthened by the return of three influential traders from the community in Pekalongan. They were, respectively, Djafar Datuk Madjo Lelo (a younger half-brother of Hadji Rasul), Datuk Nan Bareno and Sutan Maradjo. Joining with former leaders of the Sandi Aman, they endowed the Muhammadijah leadership with high adat status as well as assurance of continued financial support from the rantau. Datuk Madjo Lelo was a penghulu of the suku Tandjung, the suku of the current nagari chief. Datuk Nan Bareno was a penghulu of the suku Melaju, and Datuk Penghulu Besar was the most respected penghulu of the suku Piliang. Tandjung and Melaju were two of the four biggest suku in Sungai Batang.[14] Inter-suku marriage proved an important channel facilitating the spread of Muhammadijah. All Hadji Rasul's brothers and half-brothers were promoters of the organization. Under the leadership of Datuk Penghulu Besar, the chairman, and Hadji Jusuf Amrullah, the secretary, the organization expanded to Tandjung Sani.

Unlike previous organizations in Sungai Batang, Muhammadijah did not directly challenge existing adat authority. It provided instead a new means for gaining position in the community, and its penghulu

---

13 van Dam's report, *Mailrapport* 1453x/'27.
14 Hamka, *Ajahku*, p. 42.

promoters used the adat system to spread their movement. As a member of the nagari council of Sungai Batang, Datuk Madjo Lelo sought its agreement for the establishment of a second class school offering a religious education. The initial financing would come from the rantau. There was only one government second class school in the sub-district, at Manindjau, and so the proposal was accepted. In September 1925, the Muhammadij ah second class school was opened under the auspices of the nagari council. The school proved so popular in Sungai Batang and the neighboring nagari that, by late 1926, it was competing for students with the government school in Manindjau. In spite of its allegedly unqualified teaching staff, many parents preferred to send their children to the Muhammadijah school. As a result, enrollment at the government school dropped to 68, while the Muhammadijah school had no less than 165 students.[15] The next year enrollment in the government school regained its former maximum of 165 pupils, but the Muhammadijah school was already successfully established. Through wise manipulation of the existing system, the Muhammadij ah in Sungai Batang was able to mobilize not only the educated segment of the population, the former students of the Kaum Muda schools, but also the numerous penghulu.

The Muhammadijah had two subsidiary organizations which also played an important part in its development, the boy scouts, called Hizbul Wathan (The Party of the Fatherland), and the women's association, the Aisjiah. The Aisjiah was established in Sungai Batang in early 1926, and its first members were wives and female relatives of the Muhammadijah promoters. Originally the Aisjiah was under the direct guidance of the Muhammadijah leaders; members of the Muhammadijah local board presided over its meetings. With the return of Hadji Rasul's daughter (the wife of Sutan Mansjur) from Pekalongan in mid-1927, the Aisjiah began to stand by itself. The contribution of the women's section to the success of the movement as a whole can hardly be exaggerated. The women also provided important financial support for several Muhammadijah ventures. The Hizbul Wathan was established in Sungai Batang in early 1927. It was intended:

---

15 This infuriated Wilminck, the new inspector of education. See his letter of January 4, 1927 in *Mailrapport* 214x/'27; also Politieke Politioneel Overzicht, April 1927, *Mailrapport* 711x/'28.

To promote the education of children and youths outside the school walls and at home, and also to teach and to educate them so that they will become honorable persons, respectable and useful to society, and healthy and strong. These [qualities] must be based on Islam.[16]

The Hizbul Wathan acted as an effective propaganda instrument for Muhammadijah. According to its statutes, members should be under eighteen, but, until the end of 1928, the majority of Hizbul Wathan members in Sungai Batang were adults.

In April 1927, it was estimated that about 600 men and 512 women were registered as members of Muhammadijah in Sungai Batang-Tandjung Sani.[17] By November, the number had more than doubled, totaling about 2,440 persons, of whom half were women.[18]18 This amounted to almost one-fifth of the whole population of Sungai Batang-Tandjung Sani. One cause of this rapid development was the visit of Hadji Fachruddin, the Javanese vice-president of the Muhammadijah Central Board. His stay in Sungai Batang though short enhanced the prestige of the Muhammadijah and his speeches rekindled Minangkabau pride. He explained the ideas and activities of Muhammadijah but, more than that, he asserted that Islam in Java was now more progressive than in Minangkabau. In several Aisjiah meetings, Hadji Fachruddin explained the reformist concept of equality between men and women and the importance of organization for women. His speeches were enthusiastically received by audiences in Sungai Batang and elsewhere. During his visit, the Sungai Batang branch founded the Penolong Kesengsaraan Umum (PKU—Helpers of Public Suffering) to organize social work and public health programs. A plan for establishing a Muhammadijah HIS was also drawn up. By the end of 1927, the Muhammadijah in the Manindjau area already had two religious schools and two second class schools.

Muhammadijah had developed into the most powerful organization in Sungai Batang. Already in April 1927, the Dutch Assistant Resident of Agam complained that Sungai Batang was controlled by religious

---

16 *Aqidah Moehammadijah Bahagian Hizboel Wathan* (Jogjakarta: n.p., 1927), p. 2.
17 Politieke Politioneel Overzicht, April 1927, *Mailrapport* 711x/'27.
18 *Ibid.*, *Mailrapport* 741x/'28.

teachers and that they had effectively undermined the nagari council, the official intermediary between the government and the population. The religious teachers could now say, according to this Dutch official, "*L 'etat, c 'est moi*."[19] The regency administration now began to see a potential countervailing force against Muhammadijah in Datuk Singo Mangkuto, who had recently returned to Sungai Batang after a long absence in Atjeh.[20]

Because Muhammadijah was already the major force in Sungai Batang, Datuk Singo Mangkuto had first joined that organization, becoming one of its second echelon leaders. But he continued to look for ways to enlarge the scope of his own activities. A penghulu of his suku, he organized a consumer cooperative under the leadership of the other penghulu. The others tentatively agreed, on April 24, 1927, to found a cooperative "for the benefit of the people in the nagari." It was announced at a public meeting on May 12, 1927, and a board of thirteen executives headed by Datuk Singo Mangkuto was elected. Seven of the board members were penghulu of Sungai Batang. Two of these were also leaders of Muhammadijah, and Hadji Jusuf Amrullah, the secretary of Muhammadijah, was appointed as adviser. The cooperative represented the first attempt by the adat functionaries to improve the people's welfare by means other than the official nagari council.

In addition to this penghulu enterprise, on May 14, Datuk Singo Mangkuto founded an adat-based organization, the Sarekat Adat (Adat Association) of Djorong Labuh, a section of Sungai Batang. The purpose of the association was "to seek consensus (mufakat) for the sake of nagari welfare." In order to achieve this goal, the association intended to regain popular confidence by activities in agriculture, education, adat and religion.[21] The association later changed its name to the Persatuan Adat (Adat Union) as it expanded to other sections of Sungai Batang and Tandjung Sani. By the end of 1928, there were six units of the Persatuan Adat in the double nagari, having a total membership of about 300 persons. Like the Muhammadijah, it also had a women's subsidiary. Although membership in the association was open to anyone, the board of

---

19 Report of the Assistant Resident of Agam in April 1927, *Mailrapport* 847x/'27.
20 *Ibid.*
21 Report of the Demang of Manindjau, *Mailrapport* 847x/'27.

executives had to consist of adat functionaries. The association represented an attempt by Datuk Singo Mangkuto to mobilize adat functionaries on the basis of their adat positions and responsibilities. Some leaders of the Persatuan Adat were also members of Muhammadijah. Until August 1927, Datuk Singo Mangkuto himself was still one of Muhammadijah's propagandists,[22] but then a split began to develop between him and the Muhammadijah leadership. The plan to establish the consumer cooperative proved stillborn, for the Muhammadijah leaders, who were also members of the proposed cooperative, were not really enthusiastic about it. In addi-tion, Datuk Singo Mangkuto was involved in a political struggle for the position of nagari head of Sungai Batang; this created a major crisis.

The crisis had originated after a rigged election for nagari head in 1926. It was always difficult to find a man who was respected by the people, particularly by his penghulu colleagues, and also trusted by the government. In 1926, the government was concerned about the communist movement and took an immediate interest in all local affairs. Thus the demang (district head) exerted direct "gentle pressure" to gain election of a particular candidate though the man was unpopular.[23] The constantly growing influence of Muhammadijah, combined with an improvement in the political climate after the suppression of the 1927 rebellion, led to an accelerating movement to oust the nagari head. By exerting its influence among the members of the nagari council, the Muhammadijah was able to isolate the nagari head and finally force him to retire at the end of July. Competition soon began among the penghulu over his successor. In early August, on behalf of the Persatuan Adat, Datuk Singo Mangkuto saw the Assistant Resident, seeking support for his own candidacy.[24] But by this time the government had decided that Datuk Singo Mangkuto himself was politically unreliable because he was a former SI leader in Atjeh and had been imprisoned there for political activities. In the meantime, the Muhammadijah had decided to support the candidacy of its vice-president, Datuk Siri Bandaro. After the failure of Datuk Singo

---

22 On July 2, 1927, for example, Datuk Singo Mangkuto presided over an important Muhammadijah meeting. See Politieke Politioneel Overzicht, 1927, *Mailrapport* 741x/'28.
23 Hamka, *Ajahku*, pp. 178-179.
24 van der Plas, "Gegevens," p. 24.

Mangkuto's bid for government support, the Muhammadijah candidate won the election in September. The competition over the post of nagari head, however, had weakened the cooperation between the leaders of the Muhammadijah and the Persatuan Adat. This gave rise to a new type of political bickering in the villages. The Persatuan Adat, the party of the penghulu, emerged as the self-styled opposition party against the nagari council, which was dominated by the Muhammadijah.

The first half of 1928 was not a good time for either Muhammadijah or the Persatuan Adat in Sungai Batang. The economic boom which had been developing since 1925 reached a peak in 1928.[25] Economic activities in the rantau became more important, and, ironically, the economic boom tended to deflect interest from Muhammadijah. At the same time Hadji Rasul criti-cized the leaders of Muhammadijah for their lack of religious knowledge, and he sharply rebuked the young leaders who blindly followed directions from Java. He said Muhammadijah leaders had become taqlid to the Central Board on matters of religion instead of attempting to find solutions through their own rational efforts (idjtihad). He denounced the religious performance of the Muhammadijah on such matters as the collection and distribution of alms. He also criticized Aisjiah activities as deviations from the correct religious path.[26] Hadji Rasul was, of course, the most fundamentalist of the Kaum Muda ulama.

At the same time, a conflict was brewing between Datuk Singo Mangkuto and the nagari head. In accordance with its own program, the Persatuan Adat wanted to establish a new school and set up a communal farm. But the new school would need money. The Muhammadijah was building a permanent HIS, so the nagari head was opposed to the idea of another locally-financed school. The communal farm would have been beneficial economically but would create serious adat problems. In Minangkabau, family land is inalienable and to use the communal nagari land (tanah ulajat) requires the approval of all penghulu, including those on the rantau. The resulting controversy became so intense that the nagari head refused to hold further discussions and furthermore he arbitrarily forbade the Persatuan Adat to open an office near the market of

---

25 A. I. Spits, "Memorie van Overgave, March 1937," *Mailrapport* 504/' 37. The peak years in Minangkabau economic development were 1928 and 1929.
26 Hamka, *Ajahku*, pp. 64-65.

Sungai Batang. On February 23, 1928, the Persatuan Adat invited several leaders of Muhammadijah from Sungai Batang and Padang Pandjang to a protest meeting. Datuk Singo Mangkuto wanted the approval of the Muhammadijah for his plan to oust the nagari head. When the move failed, the Persatuan Adat elected one of its members to act as a "shadow nagari head." Datuk Singo Mangkuto said that his organization would submit protests against the nagari head to the Resident, the Governor-General, the Volksraad, and, if necessary, the Dutch parliament.[27]

The protest was ineffective but it demonstrated the overtly political character of the Persatuan Adat. Meanwhile, beginning in early 1928, Datuk Singo Mangkuto had worked actively to expand the Persatuan Adat to other nagari. He wanted to mold the association into a forum for all the penghulu throughout Minang-kabau, but he was hampered because he was still unknown outside the Danau region. At association meetings, he gradually introduced the notion of a national struggle against the colonial regime. The adat party no longer confined itself to the problem of reviving the bond between the penghulu and their people; it began to promote ideas of Sumatran unity and nationalism as the first step toward a larger unity, Indonesia. In his attempt to make the Persatuan Adat a more effective organization, Datuk Singo Mangkuto realized he could not compete with Muhammadijah, and thus he introduced a secular ideology and appealed to an extended sense of loyalty.[28]

In the second half of 1928, Datuk Singo Mangkuto and the Muhammadijah leaders made a common cause from their opposition to the Guru Ordonnantie (Teachers' Ordinance). Under the leadership of Hadji Rasul, Sungai Batang and other nagari in the Danau sub-district led the fight against the ordinance. The campaign gave Datuk Singo Mangkuto

---

27 Politieke Politioneel Overzicht, lste Kwartaal, 1928, *Mailrapport* 881x/'28.
28 The Dutch police suspected that the Persatuan Adat was influenced by Sukarno, who had just established his Nationalist Party. *Ibid.*

Among other things, Datuk Singo Mangkuto tried to popularize a Sumatran anthem written by Muhammad Sjafei (founder of the INS) and based on a popular song from the *komedi bangsawan*. One stanza from the song read:
"We sincerely love you
Every day; every night
Sumatra is always in our minds
Your soil is fertile
From North to South
Sumatra, we will never forget you."

an opportunity to extend his leadership outside the nagari boundaries of Sungai Batang. Muhammadijah was able to use the campaign to strengthen its own position in the Danau region and to expand rapidly in other parts of Minangkabau.

The Growth of Muhammadijah

The success of Muhammadijah in Sungai Batang and Tandjung Sani proved that an organization which had been imported from outside could become a part of the nagari. In other places in West Sumatra, however, Muhammadijah sometimes encountered prejudice and indifference. The first Muhammadijah group outside the Danau region was established in Padang Pandjang.

On June 20, 1925, several students at the Sumatra Thawalib who came from the Danau region founded a debating club called the Tabligh Muhammadijah. The students studied and practiced the techniques of preaching, tabligh. The speeches were later collected and published in the first journal of Muhammadijah, the *Chatibul Ummah*.[29] Though at first membership in the Tabligh Muhammadijah was exclusively Danau area students, gradually it became seen as an alternative for Thawalib students who did not want to join the Communist Party. As a result, the club soon became the target of attack for Thawalib students in the Communist Party; they opposed it because it was under the guardianship of Hadji Rasul and also was affiliated with a Javanese Muslim organization which received a Dutch subsidy.[30] But in fact the Tabligh Muhammadijah was even more distrusted by the government, which was concerned about Hadji Rasul's obvious importance in the organization.[31] The aggressive frankness of Hadji Rasul in attacking everything he considered contrary to religious

---

29 Report of the Assistant Resident for Batipuh/Pariaman, no. 322, December 30, 1925, *Mailrapport* 1453x/'27. Hamka describes the early days of this club in *Kenang-Kenangan Hidup*, I, pp. 77-78.
30 "Hate and suspicion toward Muhammadijah as a tool of 'imperialism and capitalism' which received a subsidy from the Dutch, had deeply influenced the attitude of the Sumatra Thawalib students who were under the communist spell. After they failed to block the establishment of the first Muhammadijah, several Thawalib students, who were members of the Sarekat Rakjat, were instructed to join the new organization. [Their intentions were] to investigate and to influence [the Muhammadijah]." Hamka, *Ajahku*, p. 136.
31 Letter of the Resident of the West Coast of Sumatra, Whitlaw, to the Office for Native Affairs, January 1, 1926, no. 9, *Mailrapport* 1453x/'27.

law made him one of the most distrusted ulama in the eyes of Dutch officials, notwithstanding his strong anti-communist stand.[32] Given the unfavorable climate, the Tabligh Muhammadijah remained a debating club unable to expand. A student from Sitjintjin tried unsuccessfully to form a similar organization there. Nagari authorities were then under strong attack from the Communist Party, and they would not tolerate the activities of yet another outside organization.

A more formidable Muhammadijah unit was assembled by Saalah Sutan Mangkuto in Pitalah, near Padang Pandjang, in August 1925. Unlike the Tabligh Muhammadijah, it was composed of adults and had a subsidiary, the Perkumpulan Tani (Farmers' Association). Pitalah, however, was also one of the strongest bases of the Communist Party, and the authorities identified the Muhammadijah as another threat to the nagari.[33] Furthermore, Saalah himself was not popular among the penghulu.

Reacting to the unfavorable situation in Pitalah and the stagnation of the Tabligh Muhammadijah, Hadji Jusuf Amrullah, Muhammadijah secretary in Sungai Batang, took the initiative in December 1926. He dissolved the debating club and established a branch of Muhammadijah in Padang Pandjang, making the Pitalah unit a subordinate. Shortly afterward, Sjech Muhammad Djamil of Djaho, the most influential Kaum Tua ulama in Padang Pandjang and head of one of the biggest madrasah in Minangkabau, joined with Saalah's group. His participation was motivated, among other things, by his belief that Muhammadijah could become a bulwark against communist influence.[34] He was elected the first chairman of the new branch, and, under his guidance, Muhammadijah made an important break-through in Padang Pandjang. Another Kaum Tua ulama, Sjech Muhammad Zain, a Simabur tarekat leader, also joined

---

32 Resident Whitlaw's contempt for Hadji Rasul pervaded his final report upon leaving the residency. "I think he [Hadji Rasul] has two faces; that is why he belongs to neither party. Neither the communists nor the government trust him." Whitlaw further quotes from an anonymous letter which he received: "In appearance he [Hadji Rasul] sides with the government, but in his heart he belongs to the communists. You can see by yourself, Your Excellency, that almost all of his students are leftists." W. A. C. Whitlaw, "Memorie van Overgave, April 1926," *Mailrapport* 2488/'26, pp. 51-52.
33 Letter of the Controleur of Fort van der Capellen to the Assistant Resident of Tanah Datar, March 29, 1927, no. 172, secret, *Mailrapport* 523x/'27.
34 Schrieke, *Indonesian Sociological Studies*, I, p. 154.

the Muhammadijah and influenced many penghulu of the nagari to join as well. In a relatively short time the group expanded to more than 400 registered members.[35]

Nagari authorities forced the Pitalah Muhammadijah to act within or through existing adat institutions. They ruled that because Muhammadijah claimed to be a religious organization, it should hold its meetings in the nagari mosque rather than in private houses, but to do this, the Muhammadijah first needed the approval of the nagari penghulu and religious teachers. In November 1926, the nagari authorities' resolution was accepted by the district head (demang) of Padang Pandjang.[36] The Muhammadijah leadership saw this statement as an indication that the adat authorities were determined to obstruct its activities, because the statement was designed to put the organization under the direct control of the nagari head and the nagari council. Ignoring the nagari head's statement, the Muhammadijah continued its activities and even joined the newly established branch in Padang Pandjang. The nagari council of Pitalah reacted on December 2, 1926, with a *kebulatan* (resolution) stating:

> The Perkumpulan Tani and Muhammadijah are [now] dissolved. Religious tabligh can be held at any time in the mosque, provided consent is given by the sidang Djumat and the ulama.

But the kebulatan was only made public on January 28, 1927, while the government was still engaged in suppressing the remnants of the Silungkang rebellion.[37]

In the meantime, Saalah, always an energetic Muhammadijah promoter, had been involved in a confrontation with a Dutch controleur. Shortly after the January rebellion, Saalah went to Labuh, a nagari near Batu Sangkar and a place where he had many friends, to promote the Muhammadijah. The local controleur, however, was conducting a vigorous campaign against "communist rebels." He forbade Saalah from carrying out his propaganda campaign on the grounds that he had not

---

35 Politieke Politioneel Overzicht, 1927, *Mailrapport* 741x/'28.
36 Statement of the Demang, November 15, 1926, no. 2428/8, *Mailrapport* 524x/'27.
37 Resolution of January 28, 1927, no. 20, *Mailrapport* 524x/'27.

gotten a license from the nagari council. The controleur was doubly concerned because Saalah came from Pitalah, a most infamous nagari in official eyes. This implied identification of the Muhammadijah with the Communist Party provided Saalah with a sufficient reason to protest to the Office for Native Affairs in Batavia. The controleur, however, wisely washed his hands of the affair and turned it over to the nagari council of Labuh.[38]

Dutch officials objected to the political character of Muhammadijah. Muhammadijah leaders had not refuted the anti-government statements of communist leaders but rather had used to their own advantage the anti-government sentiments aroused by the communists. Moreover, the fact that the spread of the communist movement had benefited from the participation of former students of the Kaum Muda schools, such as Sumatra Thawalib, made the local administration suspicious of anything in which this group was involved. Because Resident Arndt had failed to foresee the earlier rebellion, he was now overly cautious to the point of intolerance in dealing with Muhammadijah. His attitude was widely shared among the assistant residents and controleur, who believed that the government should refuse to recognize Muhammadijah as a legal corporate body in the Residency. Assistant Resident Winkelman of Batipuh/Pariaman, for example, warned against the possible danger of a "Muhammadijah terror" since this organization was holding secret meetings. In his view: "Who can guarantee to me that extremist elements in the nagari do not hide themselves behind the banner of Muhammadijah?" Assistant Resident Karsen of Tanah Datar agreed that Muhammadijah members "should not be treated differently" from other extremists.[39]

The events in Pitalah and Labuh caused considerable concern in the Office for Native Affairs in Batavia. Saalah took his case to the Batavia authorities. He also requested assistance from the Central Board of Muhammadijah in Jogjakarta, and its strong support of his case made a great impression on the Office, which did not wish to alienate the Muslim

---

38 Report of Controleur Veen to the Assistant Resident of Tanah Datar, March 29, 1927, no. 172,secret, and Saalah's complaint to the Office for Native Affairs, March 2, 1927, both in *Mailrapport* 524x/'27.
39 Letter of Resident Arndt, April 11, 1927, no. 1103, secret, in *ibid.*

organization. In Java, the rapidly growing Muhammadijah had retained a social and educational character and as far as possible had remained aloof from politics. Consequently, it was on good terms with the government and received a small subsidy for its schools. At this time, the Muhammadijah was estranged from its onetime partner, the Partai Sarekat Islam (the former SI), which now followed a non-cooperative policy.[40] It was feared that the hostile attitude of local administrators in West Sumatra might adversely influence the Central Board of Muhammadijah, which was "a very loyal organization." Within the circle of the Office for Native Affairs, generally, the idea of combating radical movements by counter-propaganda rather than repressive action had great currency.[41] The Office believed the government would have a formidable means of combating the remnants of the communist movement if Muhammadijah in Minangkabau were under the direct control of the Central Board.

The Office initiated action shortly after being informed by the Central Board of Muhammadijah that Hadji Fachruddin, the vice-president, was about to make a propaganda trip to Minangkabau. On April 15, 1927, van der Plas, an adviser to the Office, appealed to the Governor-General to instruct the Resident of the West Coast to end his hostile attitude toward Muhammadijah, for in Java, the Muhammadijah was not only loyal but also could be considered "the representative of Islam."[42] On behalf of the Office, van der Plas also sent an urgent letter to the Resident urging him

---

[40] Among the various causes of conflict between the two Muslim organizations were: friction between their leaders; SI "envy" of Muhammadijah's rapid development while it itself was in decline; and difference in political attitude. Muhammadijah's view of the conflict is discussed in *Bintang Islam*, 7, 8, 9 (June-July 1927), contained in Kantoor voor de Volkslectuur, *Overzicht van de Inlandsche en Maleisch-Chineesche Pers*, 29, 33, 34 (1927). For more detail on the conflict itself, see Alfian, "Islamic Modernism in Indonesian Politics: The Muhammadijah during the Colonial Period, 1912-1940" (Ph.D. thesis, University of Wisconsin, 1969), pp. 385-387.

[41] In 1924, the Resident of West Sumatra, supported by the Attorney-General, proposed that H. Datuk Batuah and Natar Zainuddin be exiled. R. Kern, Adviser in the Office for Native Affairs, objected on the grounds it would only make the two communist pioneers "martyrs"; he reminded the government that "the blood of martyrs is the seed of the church." Instead, he thought, communism should be countered "by arousing anti-communist trends among the people themselves." *Mailrapport* 581x/'24. Van der Plas shared this outlook for dealing with radical political movements. "Neutraliseering en Bestrijding van Revolutionnaire Propaganda onder de Inheemsche Bevolking, in het Bijzonder van Java en Madoera," *Verbaal* May 1, 1929, C 9.

[42] Letter of van der Plas to the Governor-General, April 15, 1927, no. 264, *Mailrapport* 524x/'27; Letter of van der Plas to the Governor-General, April 20, 1927, no. 135, secret, *Mailrapport* 527x/'27.

"to demonstrate a more sympathetic attitude toward the organization" during the visit of Hadji Fachruddin.[43] The Governor-General proved receptive to the argument and instructed the Resident to change the attitude of the local administration because the central government did not want Hadji Fachruddin to gain a bad impression during his visit.[44]

Hadji Fachruddin was indeed one of the best leaders ever to serve on the Central Board of Muhammadijah.[45] When he visited Minangkabau, he immediately made a good impression on the local authorities. If Hadji Fachruddin was disturbed about the local administration's treatment of Muhammadijah he did not express it in his reports. He ignored the Pitalah incident, even though his host was Saalah, the man behind the incident.[46] His visit cemented the understanding between the Office for Native Affairs and the Central Board of Muhammadijah concerning the latter's activities in Minangkabau and initiated a period of paternal guardianship by the Central Board over the Minangkabau branches. The Office approved this step, and the understanding continued to govern Muhammadijah to some extent until 1930.

Hadji Fachruddin's visit was a major propaganda triumph for Muhammadijah in Sungai Batang and Padang Pandjang. At every religious gathering attended by the Javanese visitor, numerous contributions were collected which enabled the establishment of several Muhammadijah religious schools. During the visit, a plan was worked out to open a Muhammadijah HIS in Padang Pandjang.

Despite this success, however, the Muhammadijah suffered a setback shortly after Hadji Fachruddin's visit. Sjech Djamil Djaho and Sjech Muhammad Zain, who had contributed much to the early development of the organization, gradually lost their interest in Muhammadijah. In

---

43 Letter of van der Plas to the Resident of the West Coast of Sumatra, April 14, 1927, *Mailrapport* 524x/'27.
44 Secret Telegram no. 84x, Buitenzorg, April 21, 1927, *Mailrapport* 524x/'27.
45 In a 1934 lecture, van der Plas said: "Since the death of Hadji Fachruddin in February 19 29, the Muhammadijah no longer has a religious leader with such great authority." Ch. O. van der Plas, "Mededeelingen over de Stroomingen in de Moslimsche Gemeenschap in Nederlandsch-Indië in der Nederlandsche Islam-Politiek," *Verslagen der Vergadering van het Indisch Genootschap* (February 16, 1934), p. 260.
46 *Bintang Islam*, 7-14 in *Overzicht van de Inlandsche Pers*, 29, 33, 34, 40 (1927). On the basis of the articles, G. F. Pijper, an assistant adviser in the Office for Native Affairs, reported favorably to the Governor-General on December 7, 1927. *Mailrapport* 1453x/'27.

early 1927, they attended its Sixteenth Congress in Pekalongan, at which it was decided to create a "Council of Opinions" (Madjelis Tardjih) to pass judg-ment on religious issues.[47] By so doing, the Muhammadijah clearly announced that it would not follow blindly the established textual authorities. This issue had been at the heart of the controversy which had caused the split in Minangkabau between the Kaum Muda and the Kaum Tua ulama two decades earlier. Sjech Djaho and Sjech Zain, both prominent Kaum Tua ulama, realized that they had joined the wrong organization. The gradual withdrawal of Sjech Djaho was a serious loss for the Padang Pandjang branch, for it left the organization under the leadership of younger men.[48]

Except for the opening of the HIS in July 1928, the Padang Pandjang branch failed to expand any further. In other places, however, local leaders founded branches independently, without the promotion of Padang Pandjang leaders. Bukittinggi is a case in point. After the outbreak of rebellion, little activity occurred in Bukittinggi, much to the annoyance of local graduates from the Sumatra Thawalib who wanted to establish a boy scout organization for religious school pupils. None of them had experience in boy scouting, but when they asked the Assistant Resident to suggest someone in the administration who could help them, he replied that the Thawalib graduates should help themselves. They therefore decided to affiliate with another organization which already had a boy scout program. On September 11, 1927, a meeting was held at Sjech Djambek's surau. Hitam Sutan Mudo, later an important Muhammadijah leader, led the meeting, which decided to organize a Muhammadijah branch in Bukittinggi with a women's section (Aisjiah) and a boy scout group (Hizbul Wathan).[49] As finally organized, the total membership was 138 persons, including women. In the first year and a half, the number of members increased more than five times. Sjech Djambek was to

---

47 The Madjelis Tardjih was also envisioned as a counterpart of the SI Madjelis Ulama. Noer, "The Rise and Development," pp. 127-129.
48 "After he returned from Pekalongan, he gradually withdrew from the organization. As a great ulama he did not say anything, he neither criticized nor slandered [the Muhammadijah]. He no longer fulfilled his obligation as the chairman of Muhammadijah, thereby I, the writer of this book, as the vice-chairman, had to take his position. But before he withdrew, I had the opportunity to work closely with him." Hamka, *Ajahku*, p. 249.
49 van der Plas, "Gegevens," pp. 25-26.

the expanding Muhammadijah in Bukittinggi what Hadji Rasul had been to the Sungai Batang branch. Sjech Djambek's surau served as the headquarters for the organization, and his sons and daughters joined its leadership. His sons, Abdul Gafar and Muhammad Zen, became two of the most energetic Muhammadijah leaders, and Muhammad Saleh led the Hizbul Wathan. Like Hadji Rasul, Sjech Djambek also was not a registered member of Muhammadijah. Both remained loyal members of the PGAI, the first organization established among the Kaum Muda ulama.

No further Muhammadijah branches were established until the campaign against the Guru Ordinance in the second part of 1928 gave Muhammadijah and other organizations a rallying issue. The Muhammadijah was then still engaged in the difficult process of developing its own schools, so far including only four religious and four vernacular schools.

During and after the campaign against the Guru Ordinance, Muhammadijah branches were established by local traders and religious teachers in Padang (September 12), Batu Sangkar (December 13) and Pajakumbuh (December 21). Although all were directly under the Central Board in Jogjakarta, their composition and activities reflected very much the views of the local leaders. The financial basis of the branches also varied according to place. Regular financial contributions from the members played a lesser role than occasional gifts marked for definite purposes, such as the establishment of schools or the conduct of religious celebrations. Religious gatherings, or tabligh, were one of the most important means of collecting such gifts. Not unlike traditional adat gatherings, tabligh were used to stimulate and exploit the sense of Minangkabau pride. Articulate speakers (muballigh) played on traditional Minangkabau sentiments by reminding audiences not only of their obligations to God and society but also their pride as devout Muslims and worthy Minangkabau.[50] The visit of Hadji Fachruddin had demonstrated how religious gatherings could be manipulated. Moreover, it was shown that the size of contributions reflected the fame of the speaker. The Muhammadijah branches therefore frequently cooperated to gain speakers who attracted large audiences; among the most popular were Hadji Rasul and Sjech Djambek. Because

---

50 Hamka, *Ajahku*, pp. 155-156.

the method of collecting contributions through tabligh proved successful, the Muhammadijah never developed a more permanent fund-raising mechanism, and this proved to be an important handicap.

A major step towards unification of the Muhammadijah branches was taken at the Fourth Regional Conference, held in Simabur on May 18-21, 1929. The conference decided that all branches and groups on the West Coast of Sumatra should join a Persatuan Muhammadijah Minangkabau (PMM, Union of Muhammadijah in Minangkabau) under a regional executive board. This could act as the intermediary between branches in Minangkabau and the Central Board in Jogjakarta as well as between the organization as a whole and the local authorities. Saalah Sutan Mangkuto was elected chairman of the regional executive board,[51] and Padang Pandjang became its unofficial headquarters. The first active step taken by the PMM was to send promoters to various parts of Minangkabau, Atjeh and Benkulen.

The PMM provided the Central Board in Java with a more direct channel for exercising its control over the activities of the Minangkabau branches. Government officials believed that such control would facilitate efforts by the Central Board to "cleanse" Minangkabau branches of their politically-oriented leaders. Resident Gonggrijp warned that the Muhammadijah in Minangkabau was run by organizationally experienced leaders who had come of age during the communist movement.[52] The Central Board was already under pressure from the Governor of Jogjakarta to sever its relationship with these "suspect" branches in Minangkabau. At a conference of Residents from the Outer Islands, held in Bogor on January 28, 1929, Resident Gonggrijp broached the subject, but van der Plas disclosed that the Central Board had already begun consolidating and purifying the branches.[53]

After the Bogor conference, van der Plas made an official visit to Minangkabau in order to study the Muhammadijah.[54] In his report

---

51 Members of the Regional Board were: Chairman, Saalah Sutan Mangkuto; Secretary, Hadji A. Kamil; Treasurer, Sutan Mah-mud; Members, A. Malik Karim Amrullah Dt. Indomo (Hamka) and Hitam Sutan Mudo. Politieke Politioneel Overzicht, lste Halfjaar, 1929, *Mailrapport* 793x/'29.
52 G. F. E. Gonggrijp, "Memorie van Overgave, January 2, 1932," *Mailrapport* 360/'32, p. 2.
53 Extracts from a Report of the Conference with Heads of Regional Administrations, Buitenzorg, January 28-29, 1929, *Mailrapport* 538x/'30.
54 Van der Plas left for Padang two weeks after the Governor-General approved his proposal.

delivered in May, van der Plas criticized the local authorities for painting a bleaker picture than the situation warranted, and he accused them of arbitrariness in their dealings with the Muhammadijah. He said that the Resident did not conceal his animosity toward the organization, and, as a result, junior officials did not hesitate to obstruct its activities. One assistant resident had rebuked the penghulu of a particular nagari because they had been unable to block a Muhammadijah campaign. Another assistant resident boasted of his success in undermining the position of Muhammadijah in his region. Muhammad Saleh, a son of Sjech Djambek, had been dismissed from his job in the telephone office because of his leading position in the Hizbul Wathan.[55] Van der Plas argued that Muhammadijah should not be considered a dangerous organization and the Governor-General agreed with him.[56] Consequently, in the middle of June, Resident Gonggrijp sent a secret circular to all Dutch officials instructing them to assume a neutral position in dealing with Muhammadijah affairs. This new policy was aided by local developments. The numerous schools of Sumatra Thawalib and their graduates were seeking a new unity, and many young Muhammadijah leaders who were Thawalib graduates found this new organization more attractive. Local authorities were encouraged; they thought it would be easier to handle such a separate radical organization as it was not affiliated with any "large, very loyal organization on Java."[57]

The progress of Muhammadijah, the establishment of the PMM, and the change of attitude on the part of the local administration influenced the decision of the Central Board to hold the Nineteenth Congress in Minangkabau. This was the first congress ever held outside Java. Shortly after the decision was made, a special regional conference was held in

---

Mailrapport 321x/'29.
55 van der Plas, "Gegevens," pp. 41-42.
56 Governor-General de Graeff was widely known for his paternalistic, liberal policies. It was ironic that the communist rebellions broke out during his tenure. The Dutch socialist historian Koch described de Graeff as "an aristocrat of blood and of mind...He would be willing to give in to the demands of the Indonesian nationalists provided these did not threaten the position of the Netherlands...." Koch said that de Graeff, however, could not avoid the tragedy of a man of good intentions who had to guard the colonial position; he could not find a way which would satisfy both sides. D. M. G. Koch, *Menudju Kemerde-kaan: Sedjarah Pergerakan Kebangsaan Indonesia Sampai 1942*, translated by Abdul Muis (Djakarta: Jajasan Pembangunan, 1951), pp. 116-117.
57 Politieke Politioneel Overzicht, 3de Kwartaal, 1929, *Mailrapport* 1099x/'29.

Bukittinggi, from August 14 to 17, 1929, at which Saalah Sutan Mangkuto was elected chairman of the preparatory committee. A new local board was also elected for Bukittinggi. Beginning in mid-August, an extensive campaign on behalf of the forthcoming congress was conducted throughout Minangkabau, for the local Muhammadijah was determined to make the congress a magnificent success. Every nagari in the regencies of Agam and Batipuh/Pariaman was propagandized by Muhammadijah leaders. Bukittinggi, site of the upcoming meeting, was dominated by a congress mood.[58]

The congress was held on March 14 to 21, 1930 and was a great success. President Hadji Ibrahim led the Central Board delegation. Two hundred and forty representatives, from 99 chapters in Java, one in Kalimantan, and one in Sulawesi, attended. The fifteen branches and groups of Muhammadijah in Minangkabau sent delegates. And 158 delegates from 30 sections of Aisjiah also came. Almost all local organizations in Minangkabau sent observers.[59] The many meetings of the Aisjiah, Muhammadijah and Hizbul Wathan were well attended. On March 15, a big rally was held. It was attended by 15,000 to 20,000 persons, even though admission was charged.[60] The congress differed from previous ones held on Java more in style than magnitude, though it was in fact much bigger. Speakers from Java concentrated upon the role of Muhammadijah in social welfare and educational development under the banner of Islam, but Minangkabau speakers used the congress as a forum for criticizing the government. Saalah Sutan Mangkuto spoke about the use of power which made the people suffer, and Hadji Rasul, with his usual forthrightness, lectured on the past glory of Islam.[61] One illustration of the different character of the delegates was a debate between the famous Muhammadijah ulama from Java, Kiai Hadji Mansjur, and Hadji Rasul on the subject of female speakers in a mixed audience. Hadji

---

58 *Peringatan Congres Moehammadijah Minangkabau ke-XIX di Boekittinggi, 14-21 Maart 1930* (Jogjakarta: n.p., 1931).
59 Petrus Blumberger, *Nationalistische Beweging*, pp. 344-345.
60 Report of de Vries, April 2, 1930, no. 57/M, *Mailrapport* 431x/'30. The largest Muhammadijah rally on Java was held at the time of the XVI Congress in Pekalongan, but it was attended by only about 2,000 persons. *Bintang Islam* (April 1927), *Overzicht van de Inlandsche Pers*, 26/1, 1927, pp. 408-409.
61 Concerning the speeches given, see Petrus Blumberger, *Nationalistische Beweging*, pp. 345-347 and Alfian, "Islamic Modernism," pp. 451-454.

Rasul, who had also criticized the activities of the Aisjiah in one of his books, believed that it was forbidden (haram) for a woman to speak to a mixed audience. Kiai Hadji Mansjur, who was supported by younger Muhammadijah leaders, questioned the validity of this judgment. Finally, the ulama agreed that a better judgment should be that it was *mubah*, not recommended. Since it was judged inappropriate for women to address a mixed audience at this particular congress, a leader of Aisjiah from Padang Pandjang lost the chance to speak at the biggest rally ever held in Minangkabau.[62]

Nevertheless, the most important event at the congress was the struggle behind the scenes between the young Minangkabau leaders and the Central Board. The leaders from Java were attacked by Saalah and Zain Djambek, who opposed the acceptance of government subsidies.[63] The young leaders also demanded that the Muhammadijah in Minangkabau should be allowed to establish a closer relationship with the Sumatra Thawalib. Saalah, in speeches prior to the congress, had stressed the importance of cooperation between these two organizations of Kaum Muda educated people. He himself was also a member of the executive board of the Sumatra Thawalib. At the congress, however, Saalah and his colleagues were severely rebuked by Sjech Djambek and other Kaum Muda ulama who feared that closer ties with the Sumatra Thawalib would adversely affect Muhammadijah's relations with the local authorities. For its part, the Central Board insisted that its branches maintain a good relationship with adat and local authorities.[64] The congress, at the insistence of the Central Board, agreed to restrict the activities of the politically oriented leaders; this would show that Muhammadijah in Minangkabau was intended solely as an educational and religious organization.

In order to guarantee the success of this directive, the congress decided to establish in each residency a "Consulate" which could act as the representative of the Central Board. The "Consul" (*Konsol*) would be appointed by the Central Board itself and be directly responsible to it. As

---

62 "Kaoem Moeda di Minangkabau," *Pandji Islam*, 9 (March 3, 1941), p. 8875; Hamka, *Ajahku*, pp. 165-168.
63 de Vries Report, *Mailrapport* 431x/'30.
64 Gonggrijp, "Memorie," pp. 6-7.

a result of this decision, the newly-organized PMM was replaced by the Muhammadijah "Consulate" in Minangkabau.

The congress decisions represented a victory for the Central Board and the moderate elements in Muhammadijah. The Minangkabau young leaders had used the forum of the congress to deliver their political speeches, but now they were given the alternative of divorcing themselves from politics or withdrawing from active membership in Muhammadijah. Although Saalah and Zain Djambek, the two most outspoken leaders, remained active leaders of Muhammadijah, many of their friends left and joined the Sumatra Thawalib. The institution of consulates provided a good solution for coping with the problems that arose as Muhammadijah spread to regions outside Java. But before the decision could be implemented in Minangkabau, Muhammadijah had to fight the local authorities.

Dutch officials thought that the congress was influenced by the Sumatra Thawalib. They were angered by the anti-government speeches and by the way in which the local congress committee had treated government representatives. Assistant Resident Groeneveldt of Agam felt that the local administration had contributed much to the success of the congress He had provided the congress with many facilities out of respect for Sjech Djambek, who had been awarded a silver star for his assistance in combating the communist movement.[65]

A few days after the congress, Groeneveldt summoned Sjech Djambek to his office and berated the old ulama, blaming him for not restraining the political speakers. The Assistant Resident was especially annoyed because Sjech Djambek's sons, Gafar and Zain, had been two of the most outspoken members of the Congress Committee. He told the ulama that, from that date, the close relationship between the regency administration and the Muhammadijah was ended, and, in a drastic move, he prohibited the Muhammadijah from holding its regular religious meeting in Parit Rantang, a nagari in the vicinity of Bukittinggi. The nagari council tried to avoid this issue by declaring the tabligh a nagari affair. But the Assistant Resident suspected that the nagari council had been infiltrated

---

65 Letter of the Assistant Resident to the Resident, March 29, 1930, no. 168, secret, *Mailrapport* 431x/'30. An appropriate place at public meetings for government representatives was required by law.

by Muhammadijah and reim-posed his decision. The nagari mosque was guarded by the police, and the district chief was instructed to dissuade the people from attending. In other nagari, such as Sarik, similar incidents occurred. The Assistant Resident proudly announced that "from now on the holding of tabligh will be decided by the Assistant Resident not by Muhammadijah."[66]

Resident Gonggrijp actively supported the actions taken by his subordinate. In his report to the Governor-General on April 16, the Resident described the Muhammadijah as "a disloyal and anti-Western organization" which was "not a purely religious but rather a political organization which used religion as an overcoat." For this reason, he said, "The Muhammadijah on the West Coast of Sumatra can no longer be considered merely a branch of the same organization on Java." Resident Gonggrijp reiterated his proposal that the Central Board should cut its ties with the Muhammadijah in his residency.[67] From the time he took office in late 1927, Resident Gonggrijp said, he had believed that the Muhammadijah was an organization of "so-called modernists, who formed a small revolutionary minority."[68] They deliberately "used the sometimes outward religious fanaticism of the Minangkabau."[69]

This highly unfavorable assessment of Muhammadijah was disputed by Gobee, an adviser in the Office for Native Affairs. He criticized Gonggrijp's "unbalanced judgment" and pointed out that labeling the modernists as "revolutionaries" was unjustified. They could be called revolutionaries only in the sense that they "strive toward the rejuvenation of religion." In Minangkabau, there were several modernist ulama, such as Dr. Hadji Abdullah Ahmad, who were loyal to the government. Furthermore, Gobée pointed out that there were no statistical data to prove Gonggrijp's contention that the modernists formed only a minority; in any event, he said, they "are more than a small minority, and, in the foreseeable future, there is no doubt that they will become the majority."[70]

---

66 The correspondence and reports relating to this issue are contained in *Mailrapport* 431x/'30 and 712x/'30.
67 *Ibid.*
68 Letter of the Resident to the Governor-General, April 16, 1930, no. 354, secret, *Mailrapport* 431x/'31.
69 Gonggrijp, "Memorie," p. 2.
70 Gobée, letter to the Governor-General, July 15, 1930, no. K 67, secret, *Mailrapport* 712x/'30.

In the course of the government debate, the Fifth Annual Regional Conference of Muhammadijah was held in Pajakumbuh at the end of May. The executive board of the Union of Muhammadijah in Minangkabau (PMM) announced that the Central Board would gradually assume control over the local branches and groups. Sutan Mansjur was nominated as the first "Consul" in Minangkabau. This was subsequently approved by the Central Board.[71] Shortly after the conference, representatives of the Central Board went to Batavia to protest the harassment of the Muhammadijah in Bukittinggi and elsewhere. They also reassured the central government that the Central Board was taking over the Minangkabau branches.[72] Gobée's sharp rebuttal of the West Coast administration, combined with developments in Muhammadijah, influenced the Governor-General, and he instructed Resident Gonggrijp to study Gobée's criticism carefully.[73] Finally, on August 14, 1930, the Attorney-General informed the Governor-General that no action would be taken against Muhammadijah. By that time, the Central Board has already taken over the local branches, and the newly established Perhimpunan Muslimin Indonesia (PMI, Association of the Indonesian Muslims) was providing an alternative forum for the politically oriented elements from Muhammadijah.[74]

Under Sutan Mansjur, the Muhammadijah carried out a plan for consolidation and "purification." At this time, however, a new force in Minangkabau political life was beginning to develop and, by the beginning of 1931, it had forced the Muhammadijah into the background. A new dynamic force swept the nagari and challenged the nagari authorities; it took the shape of two new radical parties, Permi and the PSII.

The Muhammadijah and the Adat Authorities

From its early development until the end of the Dutch colonial period, Muhammadijah constantly had to overcome opposition from adat authorities. A close look at this conflict explains the characteristics of

---

71 Politieke Politioneel Overzicht, 2de Kwartaal, 1930, *Mailrapport* 812x/'30.
72 *Soeara Moehammadijah*, June 29, 1930 in *Overzicht van de Inlandsche Pers*, 27/1930, p. 2.
73 Letter from the First Government Secretary, W. G. Stroband, to Resident Gonggrijp, July 27, 1930, no. 193x, *Mailrapport* 712x/'30.
74 Attorney-General's Office, August 14, 1930, no. 1707/A.P., secret, *Mailrapport* 841x/'30.

Muhammadijah as well as the nature of Minangkabau political and social movements at the nagari level.

The Muhammadijah campaign to improve and reform social conditions by definition implied that the existing situation was far from satisfactory. On this basis alone, conflict between Muhammadijah, an organization outside the adat system, and the adat authorities, the traditional protectors and leaders of the people, was inevitable. According to adat, the penghulu were responsible for the welfare and the development of their people. Social criticism, inherent in Muhammadijah's program, would necessarily be seen as a direct challenge to the penghulu's leadership. The identification of certain social conditions as unsatisfactory suggested that the penghulu had by and large failed in their adat functions. Resentment against this criticism was intensified by a tendency among Muhammadijah promoters to view their organization as the only channel for social improvement. Moreover, Muhammadijah reinforced its position by asserting that the reforms it sought comprised a religious obligation. In a bitter article, one penghulu wrote:

> If [Muhammadijah] wants to develop Islam, it should do so tactfully. Particularly, since it wants to spread its Muslim organization in a region which had been Islamized for hundreds of years.[75]

Ideology, however, was not the main point of contention with the adat authorities. By their very existence, the Muhammadij ah and similar associations challenged the nagari authorities. They not only provided new channels for people who were dissatisfied with the existing adat institution, but they also decreased the influence of the adat authorities. Balai Selasa provides a case in point. In August 1928, a leader of Muhammadij ah from Padang Pandjang founded a branch in Balai Selasa, a small coastal town in the south. For two years, the organiza-tion developed and expanded without friction with the adat authorities. In 1930, however, it began to grow rapidly and friction soon developed, necessitating the intervention of the district administration. At the time of its founding, only seven of the 55 branch members came from Balai Selasa. The rest were perantau

---

75 *Warta Hindia*, January 5, 1929.

traders from the Danau region.⁷⁶ Local adat authorities regarded the organization as their "guests" (urang datang), but the moment it began attracting the local population, it was considered to be encroaching upon the jurisdiction of the adat authorities.

The early success of Muhammadijah in rural areas had depended largely on its ability to infiltrate the nagari council, the most obvious examples being Sungai Batang and Tandjung Sani. But in Sulit Air, in 1929, a penghulu was dismissed from the nagari council for promoting Muhammadijah over the opposition of other council members. According to the council, the penghulu had committed serious mistakes. He had considered Muhammadijah as the representative of religion, and he had ignored the traditional function of the penghulu to maintain harmony between adat and religion.

In general, there was a tendency among the penghulu to use adat machinery to obstruct the spread of Muhammadijah in their nagari. A typical case was Pasar Ambatjang, a nagari in the vicinity of Padang. In December 1928, a local notable, one Mat Dahlan, who was a trader and religious teacher, decided to introduce the organization in his nagari. For this purpose, he planned to hold a big religious gathering in the nagari mosque, and he invited Hadji Rasul and Sjech Djambek to be the principal speakers. He asked the permission of the nagari council to use the mosque, but the request was rejected on the grounds that the nagari mosque could not be used for promoting an outside organization. Mat Dahlan later asked the nagari council's approval for holding the tabligh in his own surau. At the council meeting, a debate developed concerning the jurisdiction of the penghulu over a privately owned surau. The penghulu contended that, even though the surau belonged to Mat Dahlan's family, it should be treated as public property because it existed to serve the community. Therefore, the penghulu could legitimately determine its use. Mat Dahlan argued that the surau served the community not because it belonged to the community but because of the surau owner's generosity. A privately funded surau reflected one's duty to God and to the community at large, both local people and travelers who needed accommodation.

---

76 Politieke Politioneel Overzicht, 3de Kwartaal, 1928, *Mailrapport* 1173x/'28.

Though failing to get approval, Mat Dahlan decided to carry out his plan anyway. Pretending illness, Hadji Rasul and Sjech Djambek sent their apologies and said they would be unable to attend. Several young Muhammadijah leaders from Padang Pandjang did come, as did many people from surrounding nagari. Before the meeting began some penghulu stood up and challenged Mat Dahlan and his colleagues. A heated debate took place until the representatives from Padang Pandjang finally had to calm down their supporters in Pasar Ambatjang. The debate ended only because both factions realized that they had reached the point at which social harmony was endangered. Muhammadijah thus had to wait another year before it succeeded in expanding to neighboring nagari.[77]

The preventive action against Muhammadijah proved the best policy for nagari authorities, especially as it was encouraged by the local administration, and it could prevent the conflict between adat and government laws. According to government regulations (*Staatsblad* 1919, no. 27), a voluntary association whether a political party or a social and educational organization, could be established without the authorization of the government. So long as the organization did not transgress government laws, the local administration had to allow it to carry out its activities. In other words, it was the administration not the adat authorities which had final authority over the voluntary associations. A conflict between an organization and the adat authorities might expose differences in criteria used by the administration and adat authorities. This legal dualism explains the problems which the local administration faced in dealing with the Muhammadijah. The so-called "Kubang affair," which embarrassed even the central government, illustrates these problems and also how Muhammadijah attempted to infiltrate nagari institutions.

The Kubang Affair

On April 30, 1930, the Governor-General cabled Resident Gonggrijp asking him to report on an "incident" which had allegedly occurred in

---

[77] Somewhat pro-Muhammadijah accounts of the incident are contained in *Tjaja Soematra*, December 27 and 28, 1928; pro-penghulu accounts in *Warta Hindia*, January 5, 1929. A *Tjaja Soematra* correspondent accused district authorities of siding with adat leaders (January 14, 1929).

Kubang. On May 3, the Resident replied that the problem concerned an order by the nagari head of Kubang, with the full agreement of the nagari council, that the Muhamma-dijah close its adult courses and orphan school.[78] The incident had started, in the words of a Dutch controleur, as "a storm in a glass of water,"[79] but it soon became a public issue about which the government had to report to the Volksraad.[80] What really happened in Kubang? In order to understand the incident a discussion of some aspects of the Kubang community is necessary.

Kubang is a nagari in the sub-district of Guguk, district of Suliki, about twenty kilometers from the regency capital, Pajakumbuh. Kubang is one of the most prosperous nagari in the regency of Lima Puluh Kota. In addition to rice, an important source of income comes from a cottage textile industry. The nearest market for manufactured products is Pajakumbuh, to which Kubang is connected by a very good communication system. Although in earlier times the producer and the seller were usually the same person, by the early 1920's the textile producers began to sell to intermediaries, also usually Kubang people. The more successful businessmen began to live in Pajakumbuh, dealing in textiles woven by their relatives back home, but both middlemen and producer-dealers frequently visited Kubang. As a consequence of the new situation matriarchal authority over individuals began to slacken. This process was accelerated by the growing trend toward individually-owned houses, as many well-to-do traders and their families moved out of their matrilineal communal houses.[81]

Kubang belonged to the Koto Piliang political tradition with its recognized difference of rank among the penghulu and its vertical distribution of power. But the authority of the upper level political units rested on the support of the lower ones. The nagari was divided into several *koto*, each koto consisted of four suku and each suku was a conglomerate of several lineages. The lowest level of political organization was the

---

78 *Mailrapport* 451x/'30.
79 J. B. F. Sartorius (controleur of Suliki), Partijstrijd te Koebang (onderafdeeling Soeliki), May 7, 1930, *Mailrapport* 538x/'30.
80 Question of Volksraad member T. Njak Arief about the attitude of the West Coast administration towards Muhammadijah, *Mailrapport* 1233x/'30.
81 Only 49.93% of the dwellings were communal, matrilineal houses (rumah gadang) while 34.46% were individually-owned. *Volkstelling 1930*, IV, pp. 64-67.

extended kinship group. Each level of political organization was led by a penghulu.[82] All penghulu, regardless of rank, were members of the nagari council. But the Nagari Ordonnantie of 1914 allowed only the so-called core-penghulu, those who headed the two highest political levels, to serve as members of the council; lower penghulu were stripped of power over nagari affairs. This artificially sharpened the distinction between the core and the lower penghulu and had an important psychological effect. Now that the lower penghulu were detached from responsibility for village affairs, they had little to lose in any attack against the nagari council.[83] The lower penghulu thus became the promoters of Muhammadijah in Kubang and intentionally used it to challenge the nagari council.[84]

The Muhammadijah issue arose from competition between the core and lower penghulu (supported by traders and religious teachers) over the control of an orphan school founded in the last quarter of 1928.[85] The school was begun by several lower penghulu aided by non-penghulu traders in Pajakumbuh and religious teachers. The nagari council had approved establishment of the school and the building itself belonged to the nagari. The struggle between the school's promoters and the nagari council began when Muhammadijah was intensifying its activities after its successful anti-Guru Ordinance campaign. A Muhammadijah branch was formed in Pajakumbuh and most of the Kubang leaders joined. Fearing a possible expansion of the organization to Kubang, the nagari council issued a resolution, on January 9, 1929, which forbade holding religious gatherings having outside speakers or activities by outside organizations without the prior approval of the nagari authorities. From the point of view of other nagari authorities and the local administration in the regency, the resolution appeared to be a good preventive measure, and other nagari in the regency later followed suit. The issue of the orphan school remained unsettled, although the school continued to expand. It

---

82 More detailed information on the penghulu ranks is contained in a report by the controleur of Suliki, H. J. D. Veen of March 1918, *Verbaal* March 4, 1919, no. 23.
83 Schrieke, *Indonesian Sociological Studies*, I, pp. 132-133.
84 Communist sympathizers had boasted earlier that the sub-district of Guguk was a "second Moscow." On the participation of lower penghulu in the movement, see Sartorius' report in *Mailrapport* 538x/'30.
85 Except as otherwise noted, the sources for the Kubang Affair are the reports and official correspondence contained in: *Mailrapport* 451x/'30, 538x/'30, 558x/'30, 841x/'30 and 1232x/'30.

followed the system of the Dinijah schools and had twenty pupils under a well-trained teacher.

A one-sided solution for the uneasy relationship between the school promoters and the nagari council was apparently reached by chance. In March, several Kubang families whose sons were studying at the Thawalib school in Parabek decided to build a surau for students in the Parabek compound. Others joined these families in the project. In June, the three highest grades of the Thawalib school were moved to Bukittinggi and this included the majority of the Kubang students. Thus a new surau was no longer necessary. Some school promoters suggested that the materials which had already been collected should be used for a permanent building for the orphan school. The suggestion was warmly approved and penghulu Datuk Manggung Padang donated a piece of his family's land as a religious gift (*wakaf*) for the proposed building. Most members of the nagari council, however, strongly opposed this plan. According to adat, only the council had the right to initiate such action. The school promoters viewed the matter as a koto level issue instead of a nagari one. Since the school was to be built in Koto Baru, however, the issue had to be settled first by the penghulu there. Datuk Manggung Padang and his penghulu colleagues in that koto were quite influential.

In January 1930, the school building was completed, and the promoters decided to hold an opening ceremony with village festivities on January 13 and 16. The heads of families throughout Kubang and from some neighboring nagari were invited. Not one core-penghulu was honored as host. The ceremony demonstrated the school promoters' victory and it publicly snubbed the core-penghulu. Reacting to the humiliation, nineteen core-penghulu saw the controleur of Suliki on January 19 and complained that the promoters of the orphan school had been collecting contributions of rice, coconuts and money from the people without the consultation, let alone approval, of the nagari council. This represented a grave offense against the traditional rights of the core-penghulu, and they urged the Dutch official to close down the school. The controleur, no matter what his personal opinion of the affair, thought this request was an overreaction. As an official, he had to maintain the Resident's secret instruction that the Dutch administration should take, as far as possible, a neutral stand. The school was not closed but its promoters wisely discontinued collecting contributions. Furthermore it was now the fasting month. To celebrate the end of the holy month (idulfitri), the school promoters held a communal festivity in Dangung-Dangung, a neighboring nagari and the capital of the sub-district. On this occasion, they received many contributions. In the meantime, the Muhammadijah branch in Pajakumbuh also held a donation-evening on behalf of the Kubang orphan school. Thus, though not directly encroaching on the nagari council's authority, the school promoters could still collect contributions.

On March 28, 1930, a week after the successful Nineteenth Congress of Muhammadijah in Bukittinggi, the school promoters decided to dissolve their own organization and form a Muhammadij ah group. They planned to use the new school building for adult and Aisjiah courses. The establishment of Muhammadijah was a direct repudiation of the resolution of the nagari council, and the nagari head reacted quickly by informing the newly elected executive board of the Muhammadijah group that he was strongly opposed. But he did not force the executive board to dissolve the new group, and this precipitated a confrontation with the nagari council. In the meantime, various political intrigues were going on within the council itself. A certain Datuk Perisai, half-brother of the nagari head and known for his strong ambition to become a nagari head himself, exploited the Muhammadijah case as a means for exercising his own influence. He persuaded the council to hold a special meeting which resulted in a resolution on April 10, 1930 that reinforced the resolution of January 9 and forbade outsiders from holding religious gatherings. It restated the vital importance of gaining prior agreement from the penghulu. An infringement against this resolution could result in exclusion from the adat community. Since the Muhammadijah and its subsidiaries had been founded without approval from the nagari council, the promoters had in fact committed a serious adat offense.

Shortly after the meeting, the nagari head requested that the Muhammadijah submit a complete list of its members. The next day he tried to force the two religious officials who were members of the Muhammadijah executive board to resign from the organization. When they refused, he dismissed them from their nagari positions. Since Muhammadijah refused to dissolve itself voluntarily, the nagari head issued a statement which declared that the Muhammadijah should be dissolved and its schools closed down because the organization had not yet been "recognized by the penghulu or members of the nagari council of Kubang."[86] Unknown to the nagari head, however, four days before he issued the statement, on April 12, the Muhammadijah branch in Pajakumbuh had officially recognized the Kubang group. Dissolution of the group was therefore no longer simply an internal nagari affair. On April 18, branch representatives visited the sub-district chief and protested the nagari head's actions. This posed a dilemma for the official. On the one hand, the nagari council was right according to adat; it had not been consulted by the Muhammadijah promoters. On the other hand, the transfer of the orphan school to Muhammadijah was only reasonable; almost all of its promoters were members of that organization in Pajakumbuh. Moreover, Muhammadijah was also a legally recognized body. According to law, the organization had not committed any offense. The assistent demang, being a minor native official, transferred the problem to the Dutch controleur, who subsequently ordered the nagari head to reopen the orphan school. But the controleur used the opportunity to "lecture" the representatives of the Muhammadij ah branch, when they saw him on April 24, on the important role of the penghulu in maintaining law and order in the nagari.

The "lecture" of the controleur on Minangkabau adat and other matters convinced the Muhammadijah leaders that the official in fact favored the nagari council. He had treated them as though they did not understand their own adat. The reopening of the orphan school was ordered only for the sake of the children. The Muhammadijah's adult courses were still closed, and no decision was made concerning the legality of the Muhammadijah itself in Kubang. Dissatisfied with this temporary solution, the secretary of the Kubang group went to Padang Pandjang to solicit aid from Saalah Sutan Mangkuto, a former unlicensed lawyer and an astute local politician. He took advantage of this last opportunity before he was succeeded by a Consul of Muhammadij ah to embarrass the provincial administration which had always been at odds with him. In a meeting in Pajakumbuh on April 27, he told the audience that, according to law, the nagari council had no right to dissolve Muhammadijah because it was a legally recognized organization. He said the Kubang group should leave

---

86 Resolution of the Kubang nagari council, no. 19, April 10, 1930, *Mailrapport* 538x/'30.

the school closed but replace its signboards which the nagari authorities had removed. In this way, Saalah hoped to show that the Muhammadijah itself was still in operation but that its schools were forced to close down by the nagari authorities. He also sent an urgent cable to the Central Board in Jogjakarta, informing it of the incident and asking the Central Board to discuss it with the Office for Native Affairs.

The next day, the orphan school was closed again. On April 29, the nagari head and the members of the nagari council, realizing that they played an ill-advised game, summoned the secretary of Muhammadijah and informed him that he could reopen the orphan school. But when the secretary also inquired about the adult and Aisjiah courses, the nagari council did not reply. The Muhammadijah leader knew that he had the upper hand and refused to accept a temporary solution; the meeting ended in failure. The nagari council statement had indeed been ill-considered and the sanction of exclusion from adat had been unwarranted. But, on the other hand, for the sake of its own prestige, it could not accede easily the Muhammadijah leader's demand.

In the meantime, the cable sent to the Central Board had begun to have far-reaching effects. The Central Board had protested immediately to the Office for Native Affairs. Gobée like van der Plas had been very critical of the local administration's handling of Muhammadijah matters, and he brought the case directly to the Governor-General. In December, after some debate among the high officials, the Governor-General instructed Gonggrijp to change his policy and commanded that the Kubang Affair be satisfactorily resolved.[87] The Muhammadijah and its schools were reopened; the organization in Kubang had won a victory.

The "Kubang Affair" stimulated public debate throughout Minangkabau. Why did the penghulu obstruct the development of Muhammadijah, an organization which worked for the sake of education and religion? What were the limits of the penghulu's authority? Could they exclude people arbitrarily from adat? The penghulu's supporters argued that there was nothing inherently wrong in Muhammadijah, but that it should not ignore the traditional responsibilities of the penghulu.

---

87 Government Secretary Kiveron to the Governor of Sumatra's West Coast, December 4, 1930, 388x, *Mailrapport* 1232x/'30.

It was the duty of the penghulu to guard the nagari against any undesirable influence. The experience during the communist movement had shown that, if the penghulu were not on guard, disaster was sure to come.[88] There was nothing new in these arguments, but they were to be repeated again and again. The debates only demonstrated once more the uneven social situation. The changing attitudes toward traditional power had to confront a strengthened nagari council supported by the government.

The opposition of the adat authorities to the Muhammadijah was in some cases prompted by provocative attitudes taken by Muhammadijah followers. In some parts of Agam, for example, the penghulu and village elders were annoyed by the activities of the Hizbul Wathan. In August 1929, the Agam adat party SAAM officially protested the Hizbul Wathan's activities in its district.[89] Quasi-military pretensions were a common phenomenon in the early growth of the boy scouts, and the Hizbul Wathan proudly called itself "the soldiers of Muhammadijah." The military tendency in the Hizbul Wathan was perhaps typical of the early boy scout movement in a colonial society. Uniforms and quasi-military drill annoyed the penghulu, but they had a positive psychological effect on the youth.[90]

Conclusion

The main objectives of Kiai Hadji Achmad Dahlan when he established Muhammadijah were religious purification, betterment of social life and modernization of religious schools. He shared the ideals of the Minangkabau Kaum Muda ulama, and he was thought to be a loyal subscriber to the first Kaum Muda journal, *Al-Moenir*. Both Dahlan and the Minangkabau Kaum Muda ulama were influenced by the Egyptian religious reformer, Muhammad Abduh. But while the Kaum Muda ulama were still pre-occupied with their conflict with the Kaum Tua, Kiai Dahlan and his Muhammadijah were slowly mobilizing the *santri* Muslim community in the heartland of Javanese court culture. Dahlan and his colleagues had to advance their programs among the prevailing

---

88 *Tjaja Soematra*, May 22, 30 and August 20, 1930.
89 Politieke Politioneel Overzicht, August 1930, *Mailrapport* 316x/'29.
90 *Ibid.*, 1928, *Mailrapport* 1173x/'28.

traditionalist attitudes of a santri community surrounded by the *abangan* element of Javanese society. They also had to compete with increasingly active Protestant and Catholic missionaries receiving financial support from the government. The Kaum Muda ulama in Minangkabau, on the other hand, worked in the midst of a basically homogeneous religious society and did not face a major challenge from outside. In comparison with the early struggle of Muhammadijah in Java, the Kaum Muda ulama in Minangkabau had a much more favorable social situation. They did not need a strong organization for their followers. They were satisfied with an organization of their own peers, the PGAI. They did not have adverse local circumstances which necessitated an organization such as Muhammadijah with a strong ideological foundation. But the emergence of the communist Sarekat Rakjat, which to a large extent recruited its cadres from among the Kaum Muda students and followers, destroyed the latter's early and somewhat unorganized, attempts to reform society.

After its initial establishment in Sungai Batang and Padang Pandjang in 1925, the Muhammadijah benefited from three important developments. In Padang Pandjang, the organization benefited from the general frustration following the communist rebellion, because it could provide a forum for people who had been disappointed with both the communist movement and the government. Its initial character was best defined by Resident van Heuven, who called it "a combined organization for very heterogeneous political or religio-political elements and aspirations."[91] The campaign against the Guru Ordinance, which gained momentum in August 1928, and the Nineteenth Congress of Muhammadijah in March 1930, were the two events that promoted the expansion of Muhammadijah and the spread of its school network. Opposition against the Guru Ordinance provided an opportunity for the Muhammadijah to propagandize and for the Congress to show its strength. Although by the beginning of 1931 the Muhammadijah was forced into the background in Minangkabau, it continued as the biggest organization backed by a rapidly expanding school network.

---

91 B. H. F. van Heuven, "Memorie van Overgave, December 31, 1934," *Mailrapport* 254/'35, p. 2. Interview with Saalah Sutan Mangkuto, Djakarta, November 1968.

From the government's point of view the most obvious difference between the Muhammadijah in Java and in Minangkabau was the latter's involvement in politics. These political tendencies resulted from the nature of the Minangkabau political tradition on the nagari level, the timing of the Muhammadijah activities, which began to accelerate significantly after the communist rebellion, and the personal inclinations of the leaders, who had been exposed to nationalist political activities in Java. No less important was the hostile attitude displayed by the local administration. Since 1923, when some Kaum Muda oriented organizations began to participate in the opposition against certain government policies, particularly the land tax and forest preservation programs, the Kaum Muda educated group had become the object of government suspicion. The rebellion of 1927 increased the government's hostility. The attitude of the Dutch officials on the West Coast of Sumatra became a source of friction between themselves and the advisers of the Office for Native Affairs. The function of the Office was more "academic" in nature and it tended to seek solutions through understanding the local situation rather than through repressive policies. In dealing with Muhammadijah, the Office subscribed to the idea that radical tendencies in society could be combated by supporting counter-elements. Given direct guidance from the Central Board, the Muhammadijah could be expected to combat the still existing radical elements in Minangkabau.

In the final analysis, however, the determining factor that caused friction between the Office and local officials was their differing view of what was politically expedient. The local officials were particularly concerned with political questions in their regions; whereas the main interest of the Office for Native Affairs, as a part of the central government, was the political and social stability of the Netherlands Indies as a whole. Given this scope of interest, the position of Java was crucial, for it was the focal point from which the real challenge to colonial government might arise. This concept explains the policies of the Office, which were supported by the Governor-General, concerning the Muhammadijah. A hostile stand against Muhammadijah in Minangkabau could alienate the

Table 1

The Development of Muhammadijah from
August 1928 till the end of 1930

	August 1928*	December 1930
I. Branches/Groups		
1. Branches	4	26
2. Groups	?	75
II. Schools		
A. "Secular" schools		
1. HIS	3	3
2. Schakelschool	-	2
3. Second class/ standard	1	2
4. Volksschool	-	1
B. Religious schools		
1. Elementary	3	7
2. Secondary	1	1
3. Tabligh	-	1
C. Special schools		
1. Orphan	-	2

* Politieke Politioneel Overzicht, 1925-1928; van der Plas, "Gegevens," *Islam*, September 20, 1930, in *Overzicht van de Inlandsche Pers*, 43/1930.

"loyal organization" in Java, thereby strengthening greatly the non-cooperative political parties. The adamant attitude taken by the Central Board in defending its branches in Minangkabau forced the central government to restrain the local administration.

In retrospect, the Muhammadijah episode in West Sumatra represents one of the last important chances for the Office for Native Affairs to influence the decision-making process with regard to Indonesian political movements. Under the liberal Governor-General de Graeff, the Office still acted as the "conscience" of the government. But, thereafter, the Office's influence rapidly declined. It became no more than a "bureau for complaints" (*Klachtenbureau*), and its officials lacked adequate power to redress the complaints.[92] The time soon came when a Dutch controleur, a former student of Snouck Hurgronje lamented: "What a long time since Snouck Hurgronje left us."[93]

---

92 Benda, *The Crescent and the Rising Sun*, pp. 68-82.
93 D. van der Meulen, *Ik Stond er Bij: Het Einde van ons Koloniale Rijk* (Baarn: Bosch & Keuning, [196?]), p. 106.

CHAPTER FIVE
SCHOOLS AND THE FORMATION OF POLITICAL PARTIES

The Kaum Muda considered the central government plan to introduce the Guru Ordinance throughout the Netherlands Indies as a direct challenge to their school network and reformist zeal. The Kaum Muda educators were in the process of expanding their schools and modernizing the curriculum and method of instruction. The ordinance would in effect put religious teachers and religious propagandists under government control. The Kaum Muda believed it was a government attempt to hinder their efforts to recover from the internal crisis stemming from communist actions. The formulation of the ordinance was somewhat vague, and it appeared that it might also affect the numerous surau mengadji. These Quranic recital schools were the most important part of the Minangkabau educational system, because all Minangkabau children were expected to spend some time studying there. The Kaum Muda feared the ordinance might result in the subjection of Islam itself to government control. Opposition to the plan was based not only on the fact that it affected the major occupation of the Kaum Muda leaders but, more importantly, that religious schools had always occupied a key position in Islamic life. Hostility to the plan soon led to concerted action among the numerous religious and educational organizations. It provided an opportunity for the intensification of the Muhammadijah's expansion drive. Political parties re-emerged as active elements in the ferment occasioned by the proposed ordinance. Organizing for the anti-Guru Ordinance campaign, the scattered Sumatra Thawalib schools were gradually unified under one leadership. By the end of 1930, this education organization had been transformed into a strong, politically-oriented, socio-economic organization, Permi. Shortly after the campaign, a branch of the Java-based radical Islamic party, the Partai Sarekat Islam (PSI), was established in Minangkabau.

From early 1927 until the middle of 1928, the Muhammadijah and other minor Islamic organizations were engaged in consolidating their position. During this process, the older ulama occupied prominent positions and their participation and support were essential for the success of the numerous activities undertaken by the Kaum Muda educated group. These organizations directed their attention toward their own districts or Minangkabau as a whole. After the campaign against the Guru Ordinance, new trends began to develop. Muhammadijah was no longer the only alternative for the Kaum Muda educated group, and their main concern was no longer restricted to the expansion of school networks. Their scope of interest had continually enlarged in step with the growing popularity of the still vague notion of Islamic nationalism. Non-cooperative political views were becoming more influential, and the increasing activities of the Kaum Muda educated group threatened to renew religious controversy. In the middle of 1928, several important Kaum Tua ulama began to organize themselves and their schools into one common association.

The period from the middle of 1928 until the end of 1930 represented a transitional phase in the educational and political movement of the Kaum Muda educated group. Their activities and programs were to some degree influenced by developments in Java, such as the increasing popularity of political parties, the intensification of conflict between the Muhammadijah and the PSII, and the deepening division between the Islamic reformists and traditionalist organizations. By the end of 1930, the Kaum Muda educated group was also being affected by the return of students from the Middle East and of several perantau who had been active in politics in Java. These people radicalized Minangkabau political parties, engaged in a search for a suitable ideology and laid the groundwork for the reformation of religious schools.

Opposition to the Guru Ordinance

The Guru Ordinance was a new version of a similar regulation first issued in 1905 and applied in Java and Madura. According to the 1905 statute, "any native non-Christian priest" must have a teaching license from the "native chiefs" before he could give religious instruction. Religious teachers must keep lists of their pupils and the regent, or other chief, could control the religious schools.[1] The government hoped thereby to supervise the activities of the independent religious teachers (kiai), who in the past had been the major challengers of secular authority. This infringement upon the activities of religious schools faced a crucial test when the Muhammadijah and the SI began to expand in the mid-1910's. Both organizations continuously demanded that the government repeal the 1905 Guru Ordinance. Nevertheless, the government felt that the ordinance had proved effective in Java, and, therefore, in 1920, it prepared to extend the regulation to the Outer Islands.

After the 1915 uprisings in Minangkabau, local authorities pressed for extension of the Guru Ordinance to West Sumatra. Without such control, they believed, the fanatic religious teachers could continue to manipulate people's grievances.[2] Van Ronkel, who arrived several months after the uprising, also recommended the implementation of a teachers' ordinance in Minangkabau.[3]

The new ordinance was finally passed in 1925. It stipulated that: "Anyone wishing to give instruction on the Mohammedan religion to persons other than his immediate family should inform the regent, or patih, in Java or the district chief in the Outer Regions." The notice should be submitted on a special form supplied by the district office. Although official permission was no longer required, the prospective teacher should have a letter of registration from the district office.[4]

From the outset, the Islamic organizations viewed the new ordinance as one more infringement upon Islamic prerogatives. There was in fact no real difference between "a license" and "a letter of registration." Both were issued by the district office or the regent's office. The new Guru Ordinance, more importantly, did not differentiate between "education" and "preaching." The expression "anyone wishing to give instruction on Mohammedan religion" could include the Quranic recitation teacher

---

[1] *Staatsblad* 1915, no. 550.
[2] Note from the Assistant Resident of Batipuh/Pariaman included in Resident LeFebvre's letter to the Governor-General, Padang, January 27, 1916, no. 1186, *Verbaal* June 15, 1916, no. 41.
[3] van Ronkel, "Rapport," *Verbaal* April 4, 1916, no. 4.
[4] *Staatsblad* 1925, no. 219.

(guru mengadji) as well as the religious preacher (muballigh). In effect, the ordinance could encompass the whole process of disseminating religious knowledge and religious propaganda, making it subject to government control. The ordinance further stipulated that a religious teacher should keep complete data on his pupils and the curriculum of his school; this imposed a large burden on him. In December 1926, the Bogor Al-Islam Con-gress called by the PSI rejected the new Guru Ordinance. At Muhammadijah's Seventeenth Congress in February 1928, members re-emphasized their opposition to the ordinance. Rejecting the government's argument that Muslims would also benefit from the measure because it would improve the quality of religious teaching, the Muhammadijah Congress argued that the regulation obstructed the spread of Islamic knowledge and, moreover, it impeded the development of Islam itself. According to a congress resolution, Muslims in the Indies should be granted "a considerable measure of freedom in spreading Islamic teachings."[5]

According to the central government plan, the timing and method of implementation of the ordinance in the Outer Islands should be determined by particular local conditions. In January 1927, for example, the Guru Ordinance was implemented in Atjeh, East Sumatra, Riau, Palembang, Tapanuli, Minahasa and Lombok. In Minangkabau, local opposition to the ordinance had begun after 1926, when the central government first announced its intentions. Opposition had intensified after the Muhammadijah Congress of 1928. When Sutan Mansjur visited Minangkabau after attending the conference, he told his father-in-law Hadji Rasul about the expected consequences of any attempt to introduce the Guru Ordinance in West Sumatra. He said it would deprive religious teachers of their freedom to propagate their faith.[6] The need for urgency in mounting a concerted opposition increased after the representative of the Office for Native Affairs in Sumatra, Dr. de Vries, began a campaign to persuade religious teachers to accept the ordinance.

On June 14, 1928, Hadji Rasul invited some twenty Kaum Muda ulama and their former students to a closed meeting in the surau of Sjech

---

5 Resolution of the Muhammadijah Congress, Jogjakarta, February 1928, *Mailrapport* 1003x/'28.
6 Hamka, *Ajahku*, pp. 150-151.

Djambek in Bukittinggi. After examining the possible implications of the ordinance, they decided to organize opposition to it.[7] The younger participants would visit all parts of Minangkabau in order to contact religious teachers and invite them to a general meeting planned for August.

From mid-June, the Kaum Muda ulama and their assistants contested with de Vries for the support of local religious teachers. In his report, de Vries stated that in June he had initially gained the support of religious teachers in Lubuk Sikaping, Sawah Lunto, Muara Labuh, Balai Selasa and Kerintji. But in the Padang area and in heartland regions, such as Pajakumbuh, Padang Pandjang and Batu Sangkar, the Kaum Muda ulama had great influence. In these areas, neither religious teachers nor nagari heads would give a definite answer. They asked de Vries for three months in which to think it over. In early July, several important religious teachers in Bukittinggi seemed to have accepted the proposed Guru Ordinance, but, by the end of the month, they had begun to waver again.[8]

At the end of July, the opposition gained new momentum after the visit of a Javanese Muhammadijah leader. He spoke widely about the ill effects of the 1905 ordinance and the even more serious consequences that might result from the new Guru Ordinance.[9] On July 19, the Committee for a Conference of Ulama in Minangkabau (Comite Permusjawaratan Ulama Minangkabau) was formed under the chairmanship of Hadji Abdul Madjid. He also established a local religious council consisting of the Kaum Muda and Kaum Tua ulama in Manindjau.[10]

The Conference of Ulama in Minangkabau was held on August 19, 1928, in the surau of Sjech Djambek. About 800 Kaum Muda and

---

7 *Peringatan (Verslag) dari "Madjelis Permoes j awaratan Oelama Minangkabau" Membitjarakan "Goeroe Ordonnantie" pada Tanggal 19 Agoestoes 1928 dan "Madjelis Permoesjawaratan Oelama" pada Tanggal 4 Nopember 1928 Menerima Verslag Perdjalanan Oetoesan Menghadap Toean Gouverneur Generaal* [A. Emran Djamil & H. A. Karim Amrullah, eds.] (Fort de Kock: n.p., 1928), pp. 1-2. On the preparations see Hamka, *Ajahku*, pp. 151-152.
8 Dr. de Vries' report to the Resident and to the Office for Native Affairs, Fort de Kock, September 5, 1928, no. 41/ secret, *Mailrapport* 966x/'28.
9 Politieke Politioneel Overzicht, 2de kwartaal, 1928, *Mailrapport* 1173x/'28.
10 In August 1927, Hadji Abdul Madjid and Hadji Muhammad Siddik (a Muhammadijah leader from Bukittinggi) formed a provisional committee to work for the establishment of a Minangkabau religious council (*raad agama*) in Bukittinggi. *Tjaja Soematra*, August 23, 1927.
    The chairman of the Manindjau council was Hadji Hasan Basri, with Hadji Abdul Madjid as vice-chairman. Tjaja Soematra, August 10, 1928.

Kaum Tua religious teachers from all parts of Minangkabau attended, representing some 115 religious and local organizations.[11] Dr. de Vries, several high Dutch officials and other government representatives also attended the conference. The big attendance at the conference enabled Hadji Rasul and its other promoters to overcome the initial setback they had received when Hadji Abdullah Ahmad, the chairman of the PGAI, and other influential ulama had announced their support for the Guru Ordinance.

The speeches delivered at the conference were highly emotional and attacked several ulama who were still wavering about their stand on the ordinance. Some influential Kaum Tua ulama, such as Sjech Djamil of Djaho and Sjech Arrasuli of Tjandung, who reportedly leaned towards approval of the ordinance, left the conference in dismay. A certain Chatib Maharadja, one of the earliest opponents of the religious Kaum Muda in Padang in the early 1910's, was shouted down when he suggested that the ordinance should be accepted temporarily. Hadji Rasul made a strong emotional speech which discussed the dangers of disunity among the ulama and warned of the threat against Islam, As a result, the Conference finally accepted a resolution which rejected the ordinance.[12]

The resolution (kebulatan) stated that it was obligatory for all Muslims to offer religious instruction and that there was no way of avoiding this obligation. It warned that the Guru Ordinance might undermine the relationship between the government and the Muslim community. "The kind of Islam of the ummat Islam in the West Coast of Sumatra does not disturb public order," and even if a disturbance occurred, many measures already existed in the penal code which could be applied. The statement concluded: "It is obvious and clear that the Guru Ordinance will eventually weaken the freedom of the Islamic religion."[13]

Since the ordinance was seen not merely as a question of the freedom of religious schools but also as a threat to Islam as a whole, the conference decided that a delegation of religious and adat leaders should be sent to Batavia. Hadji Abdul Madjid, the chairman of the conference, and Datuk

---

11 *Peringatan "Madjelis Permoesjawaratan,"* p. 4.
12 The meeting is described fully in Alfian, "Islamic Modernism," pp. 429-441.
13 The text of the resolution is contained in an appendix to *Peringatan "Madjelis Permoesjawaratan."*

Singo Mangkuto, the chairman of the small adat party in the Danau subdistrict, were elected as delegates. On the day he was selected, Datuk Singo Mangkuto wrote to the Governor-General requesting an audience. Writing as a penghulu rather than a religious scholar, he explained that the Minangkabau people were by nature easily upset whenever the central government introduced new decrees, particularly if they sensed these might be to their disadvantage. He reminded the Governor-General of the scattered anti-tax rebellions in 1908 and of the cruel "pacification campaign which wounded the hearts of the people" after the 1927 rebellion.

> For a hundred years the ummat Islam in Minangkabau has had no freedom in its home country. It has had to endure different kinds of suffering because of the numerous burdens put upon its shoulders by the central government.

Protesting against the very presence of a colonial government, Datuk Singo Mangkuto asserted:
The Islamic religion is the religion of Allah. For this reason, no single temporal power can dominate it. He repudiated government policy which he said tried to divide the penghulu from the ulama, a policy based on the fallacy that adat and religion were separable.

> The Islamic religion is the soul of adat; adat is only the body. So it must be clear to Your Excellency that body and soul cannot be separated.[14]

Datuk Singo Mangkuto had in effect expanded the scope of the opposition by representing it as a protest against the presence of the colonial regime itself. The opposition to the Guru Ordinance had become, as a commentator put it with a little exaggeration, a kind of "small-scale holy

---

14 Letter of Datuk Singo Mangkuto to the Governor-General, Fort de Kock, August 19, 1928, *Mailrapport* 1001x/'28. The Assistant Resident sent a letter suggesting that theoretically Datuk Singo Mangkuto could not represent the "adat group" as he had not been elected by either representatives of the adat councils or the adat parties. Letter of September 3, 1928, no. 98/secret, *Mailrapport* 966x/'28.

war (*perang sabil*) for the Minangkabau."¹⁵ This was the prevailing mood as the delegation left for Batavia in September 1928.

An intense suspicion about the government's true intentions was a major contributing factor to the opposition against the Guru Ordinance. "The only desire of a kafir government," a young Muhammadijah leader bluntly told de Vries, "is the repression of Islam."¹⁶ This suspicion spread, fired by the personal influence of Hadji Rasul and channeled through the network of Kaum Muda schools. From the day he had learned about the Guru Ordinance, Hadji Rasul was determined to oppose it at any cost. He was, indeed, the "spiritual father" of the opposition movement, and through him, the Danau sub-district became the hard core of the movement.¹⁷ The conference was clearly dominated by ulama from this region, and, significantly, both Hadji Abdul Madjid and Datuk Singo Mangkuto came from there. The numerous Thawalib and Dinijah schools along with the expanding Muhammadijah school system provided the instrument for spreading the opposition movement. On the other hand, in the district of Bukittinggi, where the penghulu were very powerful, religious schools schools had been under the direction of the adat councils since the early 1920's. Here the Guru Ordinance provision that religious teachers must register at the district office was seen by the penghulu as an encroachment upon their own newly-acquired power.

The appointment of de Vries and the manner in which he conducted his "investigation" also damaged the government cause. Before his arrival, a local newspaper reported that he was an investigator "whose work is to spy on religious and political trends on the West Coast of Sumatra."¹⁸ De Vries was never able to overcome this initial image or establish good communications with Minangkabau ulama. Any serious effort to win the cooperation of the ulama also backfired, because then he was accused of ignoring the penghulu.¹⁹ Though a good Arabist and an honest administrator, de Vries was handicapped by his ambiguous position; despite his position in Djakarta at the liberal Office for Native Affairs, in

---

15 *Fadjar Asia*, September 27, 1928 in *Overzicht van de InlandschePers*, 39/1928, pp. 14-15.
16 Report of de Vries, *Mailrapport* 966x/'28.
17 *Ibid.*; Politieke Politioneel Overzicht, 3de kwartaal, 1928, *Mailrapport* 1173x/'28.
18 Quoted by van der Plas, "Gegevens," p. 49.
19 *Peringatan "Madjelis Permoesjawaratan,"* pp. 23-24.

West Sumatra he was attached to the office of the Resident, a man who had always been suspicious of the Kaum Muda group.

The Conference of the Ulama demonstrated that de Vries had lost the contest with Hadji Rasul for influence over the religious teachers. Realizing that under the circumstances the Guru Ordinance could not be imposed, Resident Gonggrijp acted immediately, because he did not want the Kaum Muda religious teachers, the initiators of the conference, to benefit from any delay. Three days after the conference, he sent a circular letter to all assistant residents, controleur and district chiefs, in which he instructed them to inform the people that the postponement of the ordinance had nothing to do with the protest meeting of the Kaum Muda ulama. "According to my mind," Resident Gonggrijp wrote, "it is better to explain [to the people] through the nagari heads that the government has no intention of withdrawing from [eventual] introduction of the Guru Ordinance."[20]

The Resident's circular was unexpected, because implementation of the Guru Ordinance depended entirely on the Governor-General. How could the Resident anticipate postponement while emphatically stressing its eventual introduction? In an article in December 1925, Schrieke warned the government that it should consider carefully the difficulties that might arise from the application of the Guru Ordinance to Minangkabau.[21] Later, while chairman of the investigation commission examining the rebellion of 1927, Schrieke criticized the fact that in several places—apparently in the Bukittingi district—it was decreed that a prospective teacher should ask the permission of the penghulu before opening his school. Schrieke again cautioned that tactless introduction of the Guru Ordinance might lead to disaffection among the religious teachers.[22] To inquire into the possibilities of promulgating the regulation in Minangkabau, Gobée of the Office for Native Affairs visited there in February 1928. His visit convinced him that the ordinance could create serious problems. In his report to the Governor-General, he stated that there were twelve regions in which the Guru Ordinance was still not in force: the West Coast of

---

20 Circular of the Resident, Fort de Kock, August 22, 1928, no. 6244/17, *Mailrapport* 64x/T28.
21 B. Schrieke, "De Islam op Sumatra," *Koloniaal Weekblad*, 25, No. 53 (December 31, 1925), pp. 4-6.
22 Schrieke, *Indonesian Sociological Studies*, I, pp. 158-159.

Sumatra, Bangka, Billiton, Djambi, Bengkulen, Lampung, Southeast and Southwest Borneo, Bali, Celebes, Maluku and Timor. Information from these areas was not complete. Gobée proposed, however, that Djambi, Bengkulen and West Sumatra should be temporarily exempted. In Djambi, the authority of the chief religious functionaries still needed to be assessed, as did the extent of the influence exercized by religious teachers. The religious situation in Bengkulen was unstudied. Echoing the warnings of Schrieke, Gobée suggested that West Sumatra needed further investigation and deliberation.[23] The suggestion was approved by the Director of Education, and the Governor-General also seemed to agree with it. On June 11, through the First Government Secretary, the Governor-General instructed the Resident of the West Coast of Sumatra to inquire about the "possibilities and advantages" of implementing the ordinance in his region. The Secretary warned that no mention should be made that the ordinance might be introduced on the West Coast.[24] The resulting de Vries investigation, as we have noted earlier, intensified the opposition movement.

The opposition movement started before the central government had arrived at a decision. The Office for Native Affairs was itself divided on the issue. Gobée, in spite of his warning against hasty introduction of the ordinance, in principle, favored it. Another adviser, van der Plas, strongly argued against the ordinance.[25] Because of this indecisiveness on the part of the central government, the opposition movement won the battle. The movement lived up to the predictions that the Guru Ordinance would encounter strong objection. In October 1928, when Hadji Abdul Madjid and Datuk Singo Mangkuto had their audience with Governor-General de Graeff, they were told their trip had not been necessary.

---

23 "Letter of Gobée, Weltevreden, May 19, 1928, no. J/162 secret" and "Approval of the Director of Education, May 31, 1928, no. Ax 21/1/8 secret," *Mailrapport* 1001x/'28.

24 "First Government Secretary H. A. Helb, Weltevreden, June 11, 1928, no. 237 secret," *Mailrapport* 608x/'28.

25 In a report to the Governor-General, van der Plas stated that the Guru Ordinance was practically "worthless" (*waardeloos*). *Mailrapport* 205x/'31. In a later lecture to the Indisch Genootschap, he said that: "The overburdened civil servants know that the ordinance is worthless, that no inflammatory nor dangerous propaganda can be detected by using the ordinance." van der Plas, "Mededeelingen," p. 268.

The government has not made a decision and it is also in no hurry to decide whether or not the Guru Ordinance should be introduced on the West Coast of Sumatra.

The Governor-General explained that de Vries' task was only to discover the opinions of the Minangkabau people.[26]

From the point of view of the central government, the Governor-General was telling the delegates the truth. But the way in which de Vries handled his task, combined with the circular sent by Resident Gonggrijp, convinced the opposition leaders that the government was indeed preparing the way for introduction of the ordinance. The Governor-General's remarks were interpreted as signs that the opposition had achieved a complete victory. Overnight, the issue of the Guru Ordinance developed as a new "political myth" in Minangkabau history, a myth in which, under the guidance of the Kaum Muda ulama, the Minangkabau people had scored a great victory.[27] This "myth" influenced the later course of the Minangkabau political movement. The psychological effect of the opposition movement was intensified by other government actions which were considered direct affronts to Islam. During this period, the local administration arrested Sjech Thaher Djalaluddin, one of the earliest pioneers of Islamic modernism in the Malay World, and confiscated several books written by Sjech Thantawi Jauhari, a reformist Egyptian ulama.

In March 1928, Sjech Thaher, a Minangkabau ulama who had been living in Malaya, returned home to visit his family and to take his wife back with him. On arrival in Bukittinggi, however, he was immediately arrested and charged with having once been a communist conspirator.[28] Resident

---

26 First Government Secretary H. A. Helb's letter to the Resident of the West Coast of Sumatra, October 15, 1928, no. 407 secret, *Mailrapport* 1001x/'28; *Peringatan "Madjelis Permoesjawaratan,"* pp. 24-25.
27 Two examples of this interpretation are: Hamka, *Ajahku*, p. 153 and Thaib, *Hadji Djalaluddin*, p. 22. Influenced by Hamka's evaluation, Benda writes, "The reformist agitation finally succeeded in forcing the authorities to suspend the ordinance on the West Coast of Sumatra." *The Crescent and the Rising Sun*, p. 76. Deliar Noer is more cautious, say-ing only, "The Government indeed withdrew its plan for the promulgation of the ordinance in the Minangkabau area." "Rise and Development," p. 290. Bouman mentions only that the ordinance encountered strong opposition. *Enige Beschouwingen*, p. 82.
28 The legal basis for the arrest was a file left by the former Assistant Resident of Agam which listed Sjech Thaher as one of the "communist conspirators." *Verbaal* September 14, 1927, X 14. The fact

Gonggrijp proposed that the old ulama be exiled to Digul in New Guinea. Sjech Thaher's arrest created a legal problem because he was a British protected subject. It also particularly offended the majority of Minangkabau religious teachers. Although he had never concealed his distaste for the Dutch government, Sjech Thaher strongly opposed the communist movement. The ulama saw Thaher's arrest as proof positive that the government was out to persecute Islam. After the Office for Native Affairs refuted the charges against Sjech Thaher, the Attorney-General ordered his release on August 22, three days after the ulama conference. But he had to leave Minangkabau immediately. It was his last visit to his birthplace.

While the movement against the Guru Ordinance was rapidly gaining strength, the local administration confiscated the Quranic commentary written by Sjech Thantawi Jauhari (*Al Jawahir fi Tafsir Al Quran Al Karim*) and his book on the Quran and modern science (*Al Quran wa'l'ulm Asjryiah*). According to de Vries, these books, particularly the first one, were very nationalistic and anti-Western in tone. Since the Guru Ordinance was not yet in force, continued circulation of these books might cause an unchecked growth of anti-Western feeling among the people. The seizure instantly caused an uproar among the Kaum Muda followers. Although the books were in fact not used as texts in religious schools, their confiscation brought accusations that the government wanted to "poison the ummat Islam."[29] Again the central government had to intervene. Van der Plas argued that the confiscation was unwarranted and even tarnished the Dutch image in the Middle East. The central government instructed the local administration to cease confiscations.

Against the background of Sjech Thaher's arrest and the confiscation of religious books, it is no wonder that news about the victory over the Guru Ordinance caused a sensation. But a feeling of anxiety that Islam might still be in danger persisted and was clearly expressed in a meeting on November 4, 1928, in Sjech Djambek's surau. Attended by more than 1,500 persons, the meeting was under the chairmanship of Saalah Sutan Mangkuto, the Muhammadijah leader. The anti-Guru Ordinance

---

that Sjech Thaher had helped any Minangkabau who came to Malaya, even if they were political fugitives, heightened government suspicions of him. The correspondence on his case is contained in: *Mailrapport* 573x/'28, 674x/'28 and 906x/'28.

29 *Kemaoean Zaman*, September 1928.

movement had shown those present that, in the face of the anti-Islamic policies of the government, Minangkabau unity could be a major force. Hadji Djalaluddin Thaib, a leader of the Sumatra Thawalib, warned the audience that "the real intention of the government," no matter what its form, worked always "to the detriment of Muslims." Unity among religious teachers, Western-educated persons and "the custodians of original adat" was therefore essential. The meeting decided to form a federation embracing all social groups and organizations in Minangkabau.[30]

The idea of unity was based on a realization that the Minangkabau scene was characterized by an unhealthy competition among the numerous organizations. In order to achieve a concerted effort in the fields of "religion, adat, education and social welfare," the delegates decided to form a strong unified body. The attempt to create this unified body, however, proved anti-climactic after the mood of unity which had prevailed in the latter half of 1928.[31] Neither the campaign against the Guru Ordinance nor the rising feeling that Islam was being threatened could end the fragmentation of organizational life. On the contrary, they encouraged the radical tendencies in the Islamic nationalist movement. The Guru Ordinance and other religious issues contributed to the expansion of Muhammadijah, to the emergence of the PSII branch, and the reunification of the Sumatra Thawalib.

The Establishment of the PSII

The opposition to the Guru Ordinance released the hitherto suppressed anti-government feelings created by government persecution of the remnants of the communist movement. On their visit to Java, Hadji Abdul Madjid and Datuk Singo Mangkuto observed the growing success of the non-cooperative parties in the popular movement. The Partai Nasional

---

30 *Peringatan "Madjelis Permoesjawaratan,"* p. 31; Politieke Politioneel Overzicht, 1928, *Mailrapport* 316x/'29.
31 Between November 1928 and March 1929, three attempts were made to organize a federation. The first was the Persatuan Ummat Islam, followed by the Persatuan Minangkabau. In January the name was changed to Persatuan Kebangsaan Minangkabau. This last change weakened the organization by giving rise to the accusation that it was looking backward toward regionalism rather than forward to an emerging "Indonesian unity." *Tjaja Soematra*, March 25, 1929; *Radio*, March 6 and 16, 1929; Politieke Politioneel Overzicht, lste kwartaal, *Mailrapport* 570x/'29; and (particularly on Persatuan Kebangsaan) Hamka, *Sedjarah Minangkabau*, p. 45.

Indonesia (PNI, Indo-nesian Nationalist Party), which was formed in July 1927, had just held its successful first congress under Sukarno. With a declared prime objective to "end the Netherlands government in Indonesia," the PNI was growing into a mass party. The Partai Sarekat Islam (PSI) represented a continuation of the first Indonesian mass party, the Sarekat Islam, which had competed with Muhammadijah to become the leader of the Islamic movement. The PSI was now a radical political party. After the failure of the Islamic World Congress, planned for Mecca in 1927, the PSI rapidly abandoned its political pan-Islamist direction and began to emphasize an Indonesian unity based on Islam. In October 1928, Minangkabau delegates attended a PSI-sponsored ulama congress in Kediri. Although the congress itself failed to achieve its goal of establishing a unified forum for religious teachers throughout Indonesia, Datuk Singo Mangkuto and Hadji Abdul Madjid had an opportunity to study the PSI. Soon after their return to Minangkabau, they began planning for the establishment of party branches there.

Datuk Singo Mangkuto was chairman of the Persatuan Adat of Sungai Batang, and he used this party as his first forum. He began to introduce the PSI's political views to the adat party in his reports of December 2nd and 3rd. In these sessions, Datuk Singo Mangkuto discussed the vices of colonialism and imperialism and proclaimed that Indonesia could not attain progress until it was liberated from the Dutch.[32] The meetings were only a first step. On December 22, Datuk Singo Mangkuto and Hadji Abdul Madjid organized the first PSI branch in Sungai Batang. Its members were mostly former students of the Sumatra Thawalib schools in Padang Pandjang and Manindjau. Datuk Singo Mangkuto became the chairman and Hadji Abdul Madjid was elected as the adviser.[33] On the

---

32 Politieke Politioneel Overzicht, 1928, *Mailrapport* 316x/'28.
33 Members of the executive board were:

Chairman:	Datuk Singo Mangkuto
Vice-Chairman:	H. Uddin Rahmany
Secretary I:	Datuk Putih
Secretary II:	Darwis Thaib
Commissioner:	Sutan Bagindo
	Habladin Sutan Maaruf
	Sutan Sulaiman
Adviser:	Hadji Abdul Madjid

same day, Hadji Uddin Rahmany, director of the Sumatra Thawalib in Manindjau, formed a boy scout section of the party, called the Sarekat Islam Afdeling Pandu (SIAP).

The emergence of the PSI branch in Sungai Batang, however, resulted in the demise of the Persatuan Adat. Datuk Singo Mangkuto, the founder of the adat party, lost interest in it because he had more freedom for his political activities through the PSI than through the adat party, which gave priority to social harmony. Even though the PSI tried to recruit its cadres from the same social group to which the Muhammadijah appealed for support, that is, the Kaum Muda educated group, the relationship between the two organizations was initially very good. The inclusion of Datuk Singo Mangkuto as a member of the Muhammadijah delegation to Java and the organization's effort to form a federation of Minangkabau organizations had healed the wounds caused by the conflict over the election of the nagari chief of Sungai Batang. This good relationship enabled the two groups to remain aloof from the controversies between the Muhammadijah and the PSI central boards which occurred in Java.[34] The cordiality, however, began to deteriorate with the worsening of relations between the organizations on Java. In January 1929, Datuk Singo Mangkuto and the secretary of Muhammadijah in Sungai Batang went together to Java to attend the national congresses of their respective organizations. The PSI Congress, held in late January in Batavia, decided among other things to change the name of the party to Partai Sarekat Islam Indonesia (PSII) in order to indicate its fuller commitment to the Indonesian struggle. The Congress also determined to enforce "party discipline"; this forbade PSII members from membership in the Muhammadij ah. This measure ended the chance for resolving disputes between the Muhammadijah and the PSII amiably. In Sungai Batang, it not only ended the double membership which some members of the PSII had enjoyed, but it also reopened direct competition between the two organizations.[35]

Tjaja Soematra, January 16, 1929, and *Warta Hindia*, January 23, 1929.

34 The cordial relationship between the Muhammadijah and the PSI in Sungai Batang caused Saalah Sutan Mangkuto, the Muhammadijah leader in Padang Pandjang, to warn the Sungai Batang branch to avoid further joint activities. Politieke Politioneel Overzicht, 1st halfjaar, 1929, Mailrapport 793x/'29.

35 van der Plas, "Gegevens," p. 34.

In order to expand the PSII, Datuk Singo Mangkuto effectively manipulated the anti-government feelings held by the Manindjau people. His fiery nationalist speeches attracted wide audiences, and, at the same time, also provoked the authorities. In June 1929 he was indicted for sedition and subsequently sentenced to two years imprisonment. Shortly after his arrest, five penghulu from Sungai Batang who were members of the PSII were also arrested.[36] These arrests paralyzed the PSII, then only in its initial stage of expansion. Hadji Abdul Madjid, recently elected adviser to the newly reunited Sumatra Thawalib, shifted his attention to Thawalib activities. Other PSII leaders also joined the Sumatra Thawalib, leaving the PSII under the leadership of Hadji Uddin Rahmany.

Despite these blows, the PSII in Sungai Batang was not completely crippled and it remained a forum for political activities. On May 19, 1929, Duski Samad, a Thawalib graduate, took the initiative in organizing the Danau perantau in Lampung.[37] By the time of the arrests of the PSII leaders, the Lampung group was dominated by the members of that party. In January 1930, branches of the perantau organization, the Pembela Negeri (PN, Protectors of the Country), were formed in Padang and Bukittinggi.

PSII influence in the PN was manifested at the first PN Congress held in Manindjau, in March 1930, the same time as the Muhammadijah National Congress. Hadji Abdul Madjid presided over the PN Congress, which designed an economic program and discussed the causes of "retarded social development." One speaker compared the PN's objectives with those of Gandhi's swadeshi movement in India. Another lectured on the politics of non-cooperation, while others discussed the possibilities of boycotting European imports.[38]

Until the end of 1930, when it began to concentrate its activities on purely economic matters, the PN served as a channel for the political activities of PSII members. By the beginning of 1931, the PN had developed weaving and cooking oil industries, and its leadership was no longer dominated by PSII members. With the advent of the economic

---

36 *Warta Hindia*, September 7, 1929, and *Tjaja Soematra*, September 4, 1929. Datuk Singo Mangkuto was convicted for sedition and accused of violating Articles 154 and 156 of the *Wetboek van Strafrecht*. Politieke Politioneel Overzicht, 3de kwartaal, 1929, *Mailrapport* 1099x/'29.
37 Sutan Maaruf, *Riwajat X Koto Manindjau*, p. 1.
38 Politieke Politioneel Overzicht, lste kwartaal, 1930, *Mailrapport* 477x/'30.

depression, the PN was forced to concentrate its efforts on the economic situation. In the meantime, the PSII had overcome its internal crisis and Permi also was rapidly expanding its influence.

The Emergence of Permi

The existence of Thawalib schools in various parts of Minangkabau was a major factor behind the success of Hadji Rasul and his associates in organizing the religious teachers into a unified opposition to the Guru Ordinance. Some early proponents of the anti-ordinance movement, for example, Hadji Djalaluddin Thaib and Ali Emran Djamil, were teachers or former students of the Thawalib schools. During the campaign against the Guru Ordinance, these leaders had the opportunity to intensify their drive to unify the Thawalib organizations. In January 1928, in a preparatory meeting, several leaders of the Thawalib of Padang Pandjang and Parabek agreed to unite the Sumatra Thawalib schools in one organization. As in 1922, when five Sumatra Thawalib schools had temporarily united their student organizations, the new unification plan was motivated by the desire for a uniform school system and a drastically revised curriculum. The Sumatra Thawalib Union (Persatuan Sumatra Thawalib) was formed at a conference held on November 17-19, 1928, in Padang Pandjang. According to its provisional statutes, the new association would strive "for the expansion of Islamic learning in order to nurture and vitalize the Islamic soul and spirit." In addition to standardization of curriculum and textbooks, its programs were directed toward "establishment and aid to schools offering Islamic subjects, and advice on subjects useful for [economic] welfare to be included in the curriculum."[39] The conference decided to study the possibility of including practical subjects, such as agriculture, commerce and carpentry, as well as other secular subjects, such as health education, geography and world history, in the curriculum.

The recognition that such a program required a broad base of support was clearly reflected in the composition of the Union's board of advisers. It consisted of some prominent Western-educated intellectuals,

---

39 *Perdamaian*, 1, No. 1 (January 10, 1929). Conference speeches contained many appeals for unity among the three Minangkabau "elites," namely, the Western-educated intellectuals, the religious leaders and the guardians of adat. *Perdamaian*, 1, No. 4-5 (February 20, 1929).

Kaum Muda and Kaum Tua ulama, and Basa Bandaro, the leader of the Minangkabau trading community in Padang.[40] One of its advisers was Abdul Aziz Sutan Kenai-kan, the director of the Kweekschool Islamijah, a modern teachers' training school in Bukittinggi, whose students included graduates from Thawalib, Dinijah and Dutch-Native Schools. A former government agricultural inspector, Aziz was the first Western-educated intellectual who acted to correct the weakness of the existing religious school curricula with their overemphasis on theological and legal literature. His students received not just religious and secular instruction but also practical agricultural training.[41] Aziz hoped that, through this program, he would produce not only teachers but also promoters of economic independence.[42] Another Western-educated intellectual who worked closely with the Thawalib, though he preferred to stay outside the organization, was Muhammad Sjafei, founder of the Indonesisch Nederlandsch School (INS) in Kaju Tanam.[43] Convinced that the existing educational system was basically uncreative, Sjafei emphasized the harmony of intelligence, skill and art, a harmony which would encourage

---

40 The conference elected: Dr. Achmad Saleh, a government physician; Muhammad Sjafei, founder-director of the INS; Abdul Aziz Sutan Kenaikan, founder-director of the Kweekschool Islamijah; Sjech Djamil of Djaho, a Kaum Tua ulama; and Sjech Ibrahim Musa of Parabek, a Kaum Muda ulama. Most were unable to accept appointment, however, and in early 1929, a new board was selected, consisting of: Sjech Ibrahim Musa; Sjech M. Djamil Djambek; Sjech Abbas of Padang Djapang; Hadji Abdul Madjid; Abdul Aziz Sutan Kenaikan; and Basa Bandaro. It is noteworthy that the young leaders chose Hadji Abdul Madjid, a moderate Kaum Tua ulama rather than his longtime opponent Hadji Rasul.
41 In 1925, the school was located in Lubuk Sikaping, in the northern part of West Sumatra. "Het Moehammedansch Lyceum te Loeboek Sikaping," *Koloniaal Weekblad*, 4 (1926), p. 8, and Parada Harahap, *Dari Pantai Kepantai: Perdjalanan ke Soematra* (Weltevreden: n.p., 19 26), pp. 110 ff. In 1927 the school was moved to Bukittinggi. Van der Plas termed Aziz a very promising "young idealist, who should be supported by the government." "Gegevens," pp. 51-53 and 55.
42 Aziz wrote that economic dependency had been a factor in the spread of communism in Minangkabau. It was the duty of Islamic leaders, therefore, to realize that "in addition to improving the spiritual life of the Islamic community, we must also work for the betterment of their economic life." *Tjaja Soematra*, November 1928.
43 Muhammad Sjafei (1897-1969) was born in West Kalimantan. He was the adopted son of Marah Sutan. He attended Sekolah Radja in Bukittinggi from 1908 until his graduation in 1914, and later served as the first teacher at the Batavia Kartini School. Along with his father, he participated actively in the Budi Utomo and later the nationalist In-dische Partij. The two men were the chief promoters of that party in the Outer Islands. In 1922, he used the royalties gained from his various books and translations to travel to Holland. He and his father believed that their political aspirations could best be gained through education. On his return from Holland in 1926, Sjafei put his ideas on education into practice and opened a school in Kaju Tanam. The speech he gave on this occasion, outlining his thoughts on the role of education, is contained in *Soeara Boemipoetera*, 2, No. 21 (November 7, 1926).

self-confidence and instill a strong sense of purpose in the children.[44] Using their relationship with Westernized educators, such as Aziz and Sjafei, the Sumatra Thawalib leaders worked to modernize their own school system and at the same time to bridge the gap between the young Islamic modernists and Western-educated intellectuals.

The executive board included Hadji Djalaluddin Thaib as chairman, Ali Emran Djamil as vice-chairman, and representatives from the various Thawalib schools, the Dinijah school association and the Muhammadijah.[45] In general, these leaders, according to van der Plas, represented the moderate elements. The board planned to seek government recognition as soon as the statutes of the Union had been completed, and some favored asking for a government subsidy.[46] Van der Plas' impression of the early development of the Sumatra Thawalib Union was that it:

> ...Represents the Islamic-Arabic orientation. It forms a spiritual power, which must be taken into account. Its educational quality is very high. It is predominantly a *thinking* education [*denkonderwijs*]. Its leaders feel the need for a formation of a more orthodox society ...The Sumatra Thawalib Union is under a moderate leadership.[47]

While working to expand the school network, however, leaders of the new Union became increasingly involved in a far larger program of social reformation based on Islam. This widening scope of interest was a logical development, because the Union was partially influenced by PSII and Muhammadijah leaders.

---

44 Sjafei, *Arah Aktif* (Djakarta: J. B. Wolters, 1953), and Ag. Sujono, *Aliran Baru dalam Pendidikan dan Pengadjaran* (Djakarta: Harapan Masa, 1965), pp. 142-152.
45 The first executive board of the Sumatra Thawalib Union was:

Chairman:	Hadji Djalaluddin Thaib (PGSA)
Vice-Chairman:	Ali Emran Djamil (Thawalib of Parabek)
Secretary:	Hadji Sjoeib (Thawalib of Padang Pandjang)
Treasurer:	Thaher Bey (Dinijah School)
Commissioners:	H. Alauddin (Thawalib of Manindjau) Saalah Sutan Mangkuto (Muhammadijah) Duski Samad (PSI of Manindjau)

46 van der Plas, "Gegevens," p. 17.
47 *Ibid.*, p. 54.

The second Union conference, held in Batu Sangkar on May 20-21, 1929, demonstrated the new, enlarged interests. Specific plans were made for the improvement of the religious school system and the subjects to be included in the new curriculum. The conference also explored the proper place of the Union in Minangkabau and in Indonesia as a whole. In assessing the possibilities for transforming Minangkabau society, the young leaders of Sumatra Thawalib realized that they would face opposition from adat elements. In closed meetings, the "social reformers" began to discuss the problems of a colonial government which supported the adat authorities.[48]

These deliberations were reflected in the speeches given subsequently at a mass rally held on May 22. Basing his claim on the prime function of the penghulu as the protector of religion, Hadji Djalaluddin Thaib, a penghulu himself, urged adat guardians to join with the Sumatra Thawalib Union. He reminded them of the ongoing threats to Islam in Minangkabau. Another speaker, Duski Samad, stated openly that the goal of the Union was to become an organization for the whole Indonesian people. Although the Sumatra Thawalib would not be involved in politics, it strove toward a unity based on race and religion. Furthermore, according to Samad, the Thawalib schools intended to edu-cate the youngsters in a spirit of friendship and nationality. Ali Emran Djamil elaborated the economic plan of the Sumatra Thawalib and its effort to improve the people's welfare.[49]

In retrospect, it can be seen that the ambivalent nature of the Sumatra Thawalib Union dated from its first conference. Conference speeches demonstrated the growing strength of the notion of Indonesian unity, but, at the same time, they also reflected a deep concern for Minangkabau matrilineal society. These overlapping ideological problems continued to characterize the activities of the Sumatra Thawalib and its successor, Permi.

The expanding scope of its interests forced the Sumatra Thawalib to change its organizational structure. At the first conference, twenty of the existing 39 Thawalib schools became provisional branches of

---

48 Roesad, "Nota over de Godsdienstig-Politieke Beweging."
49 de Vries' report on the public meeting of the Sumatra Thawalib, Fort van der Capellen, Wednesday May 22, 1929, *Mailrapport* 582x/'29.

the organization. By the time of the second conference, only fifteen branches remained. In some places, such as Pajakumbuh, the branch was established before there was a school. In other places, such as Batu Sangkar, the promoters of the organization were teachers at the Dinijah schools.[50] The core of the organization was formed by the Thawalib of Padang Pandjang and Parabek, from which many of the leaders had graduated. In Padang Pandjang, the majority of the local leaders were also teachers at the school.

In spite of the enlarged program, until early 1930, the main activities of the Sumatra Thawalib association were directed toward education.[51] It worked closely with the Muhammadijah and the organization of the Dinijah schools. The Thawalib school in Bukittinggi, under the leadership of Ali Emran Djamil, began to introduce practical subjects, such as agriculture and economics, into its curriculum. Abdul Aziz, the director of the Kweek-school Islamijah, was also a part-time teacher at the Thawalib school. In the meantime, the Thawalib leaders continued their attempts to gain support from the penghulu.[52] New forces, however, were beginning to affect the Union.

At the end of 1929, Hadji Djalaluddin Thaib (a "conciliatory figure") went to Java for medical treatment, leaving the Thawalib Union to the leadership of the more aggressive Ali Emran Djamil.[53] Also in this period, a Minangkabau perantau ulama, Pakih Hasjim, returned home. He had been active in the famous Indonesische Studieclub in Surabaja, and he came as the personal emissary of Dr. Sutomo, founder of the club. He wanted to promote the establishment of a national bank and a national

---

50 Politieke Politioneel Overzicht, 3de kwartaal, 1929, *Mailrapport* 1099x/'29, and *ibid.*, 1ste halfjaar, 1929, *Mailrapport* 793x/'29.
51 The government remained suspicious of the Union's true intentions, and in August 1929, the Assistant Resident of Lima Puluh Kota and the controleur of Suliki investigated the madrasah in Pandang Djapang. They found nothing to substantiate their suspicions. Sinar Soematra, August 9, 1929.
52 Politieke Politioneel Overzicht, 3de kwartaal, 1929, *Mailrapport* 1099x/'29.
53 Ali Emran Djamil had just broken with his former mentor, Sjech Ibrahim Musa of the Parabek Thawalib. Djamil had been a graduate of and then a junior teacher at the Thawalib, but, in early 1929, he had proposed that the three highest classes be transferred to Bukittinggi in order to add more secular subjects to the curriculum. Sjech Ibrahim and some other junior teachers objected, believing it might lead to a decline of the Parabek school. Ali Emran Djamil left along with several of his students and established a new independent Thawalib in Bukittinggi. Tamar Djaja, "Islam di Indonesia," unpublished manuscript; Politieke Politioneel Overzicht, 3de kwartaal 1929, *Mailrapport* 1099x/T29.

fund. Although his efforts failed to attract the individualistic Minangkabau merchants, Pakih Hasjim did achieve a close cooperation with the Thawalib leaders. By the end of 1929, several Minangkabau student activists from Cairo and Mecca had arrived, and they also joined the Sumatra Thawalib. In February 1930, Iljas Jacub, whose activities in the Middle East will be discussed later, arrived in Padang. Meanwhile, the Sumatra Thawalib had supposedly been purified by the Muhammadijah, which it-self was experiencing increasing hostility by the local administration. In the same period too some Minangkabau perantau traders who were members of Sukarno's Nationalist Party attempted to establish local branches of that party.[54]

Internal developments in the Sumatra Thawalib Union reached a climax at the third conference of May 20-21, 1930. It was the biggest and also the last conference of the Sumatra Thawalib. Its major decision was the transformation of the Persatuan Sumatra Thawalib into the Persatuan Muslim Indonesia (initially abbreviated as PMI, but better known as Permi, Association of Indonesian Muslims). Membership was open to the public, and a women's section was established. Unlike previous Thawalib con-ferences, this one (later called the First Permi Congress) decided not to seek government recognition.[55]

The influence which the newcomers from Java and the Middle East exerted on the congress was clearly shown in the major themes of its platform and their emphasis on the people's economic and spiritual development. Pakih Hasjim, for example, popularized the idea of economic self-help and the formation of a national bank. An Al-Azhar graduate spoke about the different kinds of cooperatives. Duski Samad, a PSII leader, focused on the direct connection between the people's economic backwardness and the existence of a colonial power. But it was Iljas Jacub, a newcomer from Cairo, who first formulated the ideological foundation of Permi. He stated that the progress of life (*kemadjuan kehidupan*) could be fully attained only by simultaneous economic, spiritual and moral development. He believed these paralleled the three essential aspects of man's social life—as an adherent of a religion, a member of a nation, and a

---

54 Politieke Politioneel Overzicht, 1ste kwartaal, 1930, *Mailrapport* 477x/'30.
55 Politieke Politioneel Overzicht, 2de kwartaal, 1930, *Mailrapport* 812x/'30.

son of a *tanah air* (homeland).[56] Grounded in this awareness of the direct relationship between the goal, the progress of life and the inseparable aspects of social life, Permi based its struggle on the slogan "Islam and *kebangsaan* [nationality]."

At its first conference, held on August 5-9 in Pajakumbuh and attended by six branches, Permi formulated its final statutes. The preamble to these declared the membership's determination to "catch up" with the Western World and to participate in the renaissance of the Eastern World.

> Indonesia, which consists of many islands, with its eighty per cent Muslim population, is a part of the Eastern World. Basing their struggle on the principle of Islam and their nationality, they [the Indonesian Muslims] are striving for progress in order to fight for [their] *human* rights [which] are expressed in their social order and welfare and *dignity*.[57]

In order to implement its programs, Permi formed departments for education, enterprises, Islamic propagation and the boy scouts. It was decided to establish branches throughout Indonesia.

Under the chairmanship of Hadji Abdul Madjid, the Kaum Tua ulama and adviser to the PSII, the first Permi central board consisted of persons from different backgrounds. Three of them, Iljas Jacub, Mansur Daud and Hadji Rasul Hamidy, were new arrivals from the Middle East; two had already been active in the PSII; and one was a member of a nationalist party in Java. The rest were teachers at Thawalib schools. Except for Hadji Abdul Madjid and Pakih Hasjim, all belonged to the Kaum Muda educated group and were young men in their late twenties and early thirties.[58]

---

56 *Pompai*, 11 (May/June 1930).
57 *Anggaran Dasar dan Anggaran Tetangga dari Persatoean Moeslim Indonesia* (Padang: PMI, 1930). The emphasis is in the original.
58 The first executive board of Permi consisted of:

Chairman:	Hadji Abdul Madjid (PSI of Manindjau)
Vice-Chairman:	Iljas Jacub (from Cairo)
Secretary:	Mansur Daud (from Turkey)
	Darwis Thaib (PSI of Manindjau)
Treasurer:	Hadji Sjuib el Jutusy (Thawalib of Padang Pandjang)

One direct consequence of the dissolution of the Sumatra Thawalib Union and the formation of Permi was a break with the leaders of the Muhammadijah and the Dinijah associations. Whereas the Muhammadijah was striving to eliminate its politically oriented leaders, Permi was on its way to becoming a political party. The Dinijah maintained its original course as a purely educational and school organization. Some of the Thawalib's influential advisers also opposed the transformation to Permi. Basa Bandaro, a financial backer and key adviser of the Thawalib, initially opposed its dissolution. Some Kaum Muda ulama, such as Sjech Ibrahim Musa of Parabek, threatened to cut their ties with the new organization. Nevertheless, in spite of their generally negative response, the Kaum Muda ulama did not openly criticize Permi until the middle of 1931. Even Hadji Rasul, who was known to be very critical about its ideology of "Islam and kebangsaan," considered it one of "three major Islamic organizations, which are striving as best they can to attain progress in accordance with the times."[59] The neutral attitude of the Kaum Muda ulama proved a great advantage for Permi, for it permitted the organization to pursue its plans. Criticism from the widely respected ulama would have been a major hindrance.

In its expansion drive into the rural areas, Permi often confronted problems similar to those faced by the Muhammadijah. Its success in the nagari depended upon its local promoters, most of whom belonged to the Kaum Muda educated group. Unlike the Muhammadijah, Permi could use the scattered Sumatra Thawalib schools as a base of operations. In the towns of the interior, its influence was spread through public meetings, tabligh, participation in various social activities, and infiltration of the locally based mutual assistance organizations. Similar methods were also used in towns where the Thawalib did not have schools .

Dating from its first congress, Permi determined to make Padang, the Residency capital, the seat of its own headquarters. This was in line with

Department of Education:	Ali Emran Djamil (Thawalib of Bukittinggi)
Department of Enterprise:	Pakih Hasjim (Indonesische Studieclub-Surabaja)
Department of Islamic Propaganda:	Hadji Rasul Hamidy (a former activist in Mecca)
Department of Boy Scouts:	A. Gaffar Ismail (Thawalib of Parabek)

[59] The other two were Muhammadijah and the PGAI. From his book *Pedoman Goeroe* (1930) as quoted in "Kaoem Moeda di Minangkabau," *Pandji Islam*, 11 (March 1941), p. 8896.

party desires to achieve a national, rather than merely local, status. By establishing headquarters in Padang, the party would also transfer the center of Minang-kabau political activities from the interior to the coast. As a first step in this direction, Permi participated in the activities of existing Padang organizations. In June 1930, for example, Permi joined in a protest meeting initiated by the government teachers' association (PGHB) against a plan to halt expansion of the HIS.[60] Permi's next move was to promote cooperation in the activities of the several trade unions, religious organizations and merchant associations in Padang. In September, therefore, Permi sponsored the establishment of a Committee for the Creation of Unity, with the immediate goal of building a permanent national meeting hall. This failed because the Padang traders proved uninterested given the deepening impact of the economic depression. Permi tried another approach through individual efforts by its leaders. In the same month, Chairman Hadji Abdul Madjid tried to build a surau for the non-Padang settlers. But because he started collecting contributions without first getting the necessary government approval, he was forced to abandon the plan and pay a fine. Another unsuccessful individual approach was that of Iljas Jacub and Pakih Hasjim who attempted to form a cooperative.

At first Permi could only indirectly influence the Padang Western-educated youth, who were organized into the Jong Islamieten Bond (Young Muslims' Union). At the end of September, however, Permi announced the establishment of a Padang branch and it began a massive effort to assert its influence by holding a series of mass rallies and issuing publications. Major figures of Permi addressed almost every rally. The effort culminated in the formation of a Committee for Islamic Celebrations under Permi domination. In December 1930, before the celebration of the Prophet's Ascension, Permi seized the initiative and

---

60 In 1927, Governor-General de Graeff had established a Hollandsch-Inlandsche Onderwijs Commissie under the chairmanship of Prof. Schrieke. Their report, submitted in 1930, recommended the suspension of plans to expand the HIS system. The PGHB viewed this as an obstacle to further educa-tional development and also saw that in practice the freeze would hamper job and promotion opportunities for its own members. Muhammadijah, on the other hand, supported the commission's recommendations because it believed they would benefit the organization's own "secular" school system. The Taman Siswa likewise favored the suspension, believing it would stop the "denationalization process" of Indonesian youth carried out in the HIS. Politieke Politioneel Over-zicht, 2de kwartaal, 1930, *Mailrapport* 812x/'30.

organized a permanent committee for religious celebrations. By so doing, Permi managed to surpass Muhammadijah, the biggest Kaum Muda organization. The Muhammadijah did not have a representative on the Committee, but, as a Kaum Muda organization, it could not keep aloof from it. The domination of Permi over the Committee enabled that organization to have the decisive word in the selection of speakers, design of the agenda, etc., for the approaching celebrations. Permi had taken its first important step toward leadership of the Kaum Muda in Padang.

This success was reinforced by Permi's ability to win the support of the important Minangkabau merchants in the Pasar Gadang, Padang. Through Basa Bandaro, the most influential figure in the trading community, Permi was able to forge a close relationship with the leadership of the Himpunan Saudagar Indonesia (HSI, Indonesian Merchants' Association). This enabled Permi to fund its educational program, particularly the establishment of a modern Islamic college.

By the beginning of 1931, Permi's development had passed the critical stage. It had successfully established itself in Padang, and,meanwhile, in the interior it benefited from the "purification process" in the Muhammadijah. In Pariaman, a northern coastal town, Permi managed to infiltrate the Kaum Tua.

Administratively and financially, the Thawalib schools remained independent units, but their school programs and their extra-curricular activities came under the direct control of the Permi department of education. These numerous Thawalib schools provided Permi with local leaders and new cadres. In his annual political report for 1930, the Resident concluded that: "Permi has become more and more predominant."[61] At the same time, by its slogan "Islam and kebangsaan," Permi had enlarged its split with the Kaum Muda ulama. Its attempt to reconcile the two different ideologies, Islam and nationalism, was to make it a target for attacks by other Indonesian Muslim organizations.

The Regrouping of the Kaum Tua Schools

On May 20, 1930, a week before the Persatuan Sumatra Thawa-lib was

---

61 Politieke Politioneel Overzicht, 4de kwartaal, 1930, *Mailrapport* 228x/'31.

transformed into Permi, the prominent Kaum Tua ulama finally succeeded in uniting their schools or madrasah under a single organization, the Persatuan Tarbijah Islamijah (PTI, Association of Islamic Schools). This represented the climax of a two-year effort to unify the school system and establish a common front against the increasingly active Kaum Muda organizations. Through the formation of the PTI, the Kaum Tua ulama managed to revive their old organization, the Ittihadul Ulama, which had rapidly declined since the slackening of the religious conflict.

On May 5, 1928, five months after the promoters of the Sumatra Thawalib unification held their conference in Parabek, Sjech Sulaiman Arrasuli of Tjandung, a prominent Kaum Tua ulama, took the first step toward the reformation of Kaum Tua religious schools by copying the Kaum Muda system. He introduced a "modern" graded school system into his traditional madrasah and changed the name to Tarbijah Islamijah (Islamic Education). At the same time, he made the first move toward a unification of the Kaum Tua schools. In the face of the expanding Muhammadijah school network and the unification of the Sumatra Thawalib schools, Sjech Arrasuli believed the Kaum Tua schools needed a common system and curriculum. His attempts toward the unification of the Kaum Tua schools received strong endorsement from the local administration.[62] The effort was intensified after the campaign against the Guru Ordinance and the emergence of the Persatuan Sumatra Thawalib. In January 1929, Sjech Djamil of Djaho, the former leader of Muhammadijah, also renamed his school Tarbijah Islamijah. From that time on, Sjech Djamil and Sjech Arrasuli worked closely together. Their cooperation finally resulted in the convocation of a Kaum Tua conference and the formation of the PTI.

At the Kaum Tua conference, held in Tjandung (near Bukit-tinggi), the Kaum Tua ulama declared a determination to continue their struggle on behalf of the Shafiite school of law. They would base their educational program on the preservation and the strengthening of harmony between

---

62 Abdul Rusli A. Wahid (son of a prominent Kaum Tua ulama of Suliki and himself current chairman of the Kaum Tua party, Perti) told me that in 1928, he, Sjech Arrasuli and Sjech Djamil of Djaho were summoned by Assistant Resident Groene-veldt,who urged them to organize the Kaum Tua and check the spread of the Kaum Muda activities, particularly the Thawalib. But the official warned them about involvement in politics. (Interview, Djakarta, November 1968.)

"the eternal adat and the obligatory religious law" (*adat nan kawi, sjarak nan lazim*). The promoters of the PTI comprised the last generation of "the grand tradition" of the Minangkabau madrasah. Each was the personification of his respective school and the most prominent Kaum Tua ulama in his region. Because of their prestige, their close cooperation with the adat authorities, the friendly attitude of the local administration, and the already numerous Kaum Tua oriented schools, the PTI already included 36 schools by the end of 1930. By early 1931, it had 30 branches and about 4,000 members.[63]

The Muhammadijah and Permi leaders were former students of the Kaum Muda ulama, that is, the second generation of modernists, but the PTI leaders were prominent Kaum Tua ulama themselves. The personal influence of an ulama in his respective region determined the success of the PTI in that area. The character of the PTI as an organization, therefore, was largely personal and parochial. In his own sphere of influence, the ulama had remained a key figure to whom minor Kaum Tua religious teachers and local tarekat leaders owed deference. This personal and rather authoritarian character of the PTI, however, weakened its ability to compete with the Kaum Muda organizations and eventually led to its downfall.

Conclusion

The determination which the Kaum Muda ulama and their associates and students displayed in their opposition to the Guru Ordinance reveals the central position of religious schools in their lives and activities. The Guru Ordinance issue contributed to the expansion of the Kaum Muda school network and to the process of modernization of the religious schools. The campaigns against the Guru Ordinance provided the Muhammadijah with a good opportunity to expand its own organization and increase the number of its schools. The Thawalib leaders used the campaign to establish an effective unity of their schools. The opposition movement accentuated the political side of the Kaum Muda schools and resulted in a re-emergence of nationalist political parties in Minangkabau.

---

63 Politieke Politioneel Overzicht, 4de kwartaal, 1930, *Mailrapport*, 228x/'31; Gonggrijp, "Memorie," p. 19.

The Guru Ordinance campaign, however, divided the heretofore united pioneers of the Kaum Muda movement and threatened to revive the conflict between the Kaum Muda and Kaum Tua ulama. Hadji Abdullah Ahmad, the most modernist Kaum Muda ulama, believed in the government's good intentions because he had had a close relationship with the authorities since the 1910's. He, therefore, approved the Guru Ordinance. His acceptance separated him from his closest friend, Hadji Rasul, the spiritual leader of the opposition movement, and particularly from the politically oriented Islamic modernists. The erosion of Hadji Abdullah Ahmad's influence among the graduates of the Kaum Muda schools became obvious when the latter began preparations for their Islamic College. Hadji Abdullah Ahmad had collaborated with the Dutch in establishing his Normal Islam, but the young Islamic modernists, particularly those who belonged to Permi, preferred to set up their own school without government help.

The political and divisive character of the Guru Ordinance was an important factor precipitating the separation. Hadji Abdullah Ahmad and the "loyal" Kaum Tua ulama believed that the ordinance would in no way hamper their activities. But Hadji Rasul and his colleagues along with the young Islamic modernists did not and could not trust the government, and, in their view, the ordinance could mean nothing less than a direct assault on their schools and on their profession as religious teachers and preachers. They perceived the ordinance as a means to obstruct them in the pursuit of their religious and social obligations. Their distrust of government intentions was intensified by various government actions which were interpreted as signs that the Dutch were, indeed, trying to persecute Islam.

After the Guru Ordinance campaign, the Kaum Muda organizations continued to follow similar educational programs, but each organization displayed its own particular political activities and views. By the end of 1930, these could be divided into three categories. First was the PGAI, under the leadership of Hadji Abdullah Ahmad. It was not involved in politics and it was considered by the government to be a "loyal organization." As far as the government was concerned, the PTI of the Kaum Tua ulama also belonged to this group. Second was the increasingly moderate Muhammadijah. Supervised by the Central Board in Java and led by Sutan Mansjur, the organization concentrated its efforts on "purely" educational and religious matters. Third was Permi, which rapidly expanded from an educational to a politically oriented socio-economic organization. Also in this group was the non-cooperative PSII.

The next period, that between 1931 and the middle of 1933, includes a continuing search for suitable ideological bases for struggle among the Kaum Muda educated group as well as a time of increasing fundamentalist attitudes among the Kaum Muda ulama. The period is characterized by a proliferation of types of political activities, an expansion of private schools and the modernization of religious schools. In this period, Western-educated intellectuals who had been active in the nationalist political movement in Java tried to extend their influence in Minangkabau. Permi meanwhile spread its influence to other parts of Sumatra and to Java. In Minangkabau, the two and one-half year period was a time when the newcomers from the Middle East, particularly from Cairo, became leaders in the nationalist struggle and in educational development.

CHAPTER SIX
POLITICIANS AND EDUCATORS

The close relationship between schools and politics, both conceived as means to national independence, stemmed from the nature of orthodox Islamic modernism. The drive for a return to the original sources of religion and the appeal for rationality in religious belief led the students to question their own social and political environment. The Kaum Muda religious schools became the mechanism for establishing direct contact with the population at large. The success of an organization was very often dependent upon the number and quality of its schools. This mutual dependence between the schools and the social, religious or political reformers explains the easy transformation of a school organization into a political party and conversely the need for organizations to have their own schools.

Dissension among the Kaum Muda educated group was determined more by different senses of urgency rather than any doctrinal disagreements, by personal inclinations rather than conflicts of loyalties. The "purification" of Muhammadijah and the increasing politicization of Permi clearly illustrate the vague border separating the political and the educational activities of the Kaum Muda educated group. Similar characteristics marked the extra-curricular activities of the Indonesian and Malayan students (called *Jawah* by the Arabs) in Cairo in the 1920's. While pursuing their studies at the various educational institutions, particularly Al-Azhar University in Cairo, the students became involved in the politics of national independence. Most of the group, led by Mahmud Junus, a Minangkabau, and Faturrahman, a Javanese, prepared to return home as teachers and religious reformers. Muchtar Lutfi and Iljas Jacub were leaders of a group which planned to join the political nationalist struggle at home. They took part in the Egyptian independence movement as students in Cairo.

The interaction and competition between these two groups of students was influential in the course of Minangkabau political and educational development in the early 1930's.

Minangkabau Student Activities in Cairo

Iljas Jacub arrived in Cairo late in 1923. He was born in 1902, the son of a trader from Asam Kumbang, in the Painan district, on the southern coast of Minangkabau. He graduated from the second class school in 1916. For about a year, Iljas worked as an apprentice clerk at the Ombilin coal mine in Sawah Lunto. For three years afterward, he studied religion in a madrasah in Koto Merapak. In 1921, he went to Mecca where he studied for two years. He then continued his education at Al-Azhar. Iljas arrived in Cairo just after Djanan Thaib,[1] a Minangkabau student at the university, had organized the Indonesian-Malayan students into their own organization, the Djamiah el Chairijah el Djawah (Welfare Society of Jawah Students).[2] Iljas was elected as its secretary.

The Welfare Society was a mutual assistance organization designed to improve the living conditions of the students and to help them in their studies. Its establishment had been motivated by the poor conditions which prevailed at the *riwak al Jawah* (compound of Jawah students). Al-Azhar had allotted the compound to them but it proved unsanitary, dirty and generally unsuitable for study. Food was also far from adequate.[3]

---

1 Djanan Thaib was the first Jawah student to receive the highest degree offered by Al-Azhar. He was born in Sarik (near Bukittinggi) in 1891. He graduated from the second class school in 1904 and lived as a traveling urang siak until 1911 when he went to Mecca to study. In 1919, he was admitted to the seventh grade of Al-Azhar and he graduated in June 1924.

2 The Jawah compound established its first student organization, the Djamiah Setia Peladjar (Students' Association) in 1913. It was headed by Sjech Ismail, a Minangkabau ulama from Padang and the head of the student compound. Sjech Ismail (1870-1930) had been in Cairo since 1894. *Verbaal* January 5, 1915, no. 7, and February 1, 1915, no. 38.

The other members of the executive board included students from North Sumatra, Palembang, Sambas, Banten, Solo, Surabaja, Singapore and Patani. The Djamiah was shortlived. It suffered a profound crisis in January 1916 after a student from Palembang killed two others, from Minangkabau and Bandjarmasin. *Verbaal* May 12, 1926, and February 25, 1926.

3 In early 1900, Al-Azhar assigned a compound, called a *riwak*, to the Jawah students, where they could live and study under the guidance of a university-appointed supervisor. An Egyptian observer reported in a December 1924 issue of the Arabic journal *Hadramaut* (published in Surabaja) that conditions in the riwak were poor. Quoted by R. Kern, Adviser for Native Affairs,

The activities of the Society were greatly intensified in 1925 when a number of new students arrived, bringing the total membership to about two hundred.[4] The boom in rubber in Malaya and coffee in Sumatra plus a general economic improvement in the Indies undoubtedly enabled more students to come to Cairo.

One of the new arrivals was Mahmud Junus; unlike the majority of the Jawah students, he was already an experienced teacher and writer. Mahmud was born in 1900 in Sungajang (Batu Sangkar), the son of an adat religious functionary, *imam adat*. He studied religion as a child under the guidance of Sjech Thaib Umar, a pioneer of the Islamic modernist movement. His secular education was limited to attendance at the volksschool. In 1915, he had become an assistant to the teacher. After Sjech Thaib Umar died in 1920, Mahmud was one of three teachers appointed by the nagari. In 1922, he began to translate the Quran into Malay; he then published it in serial form. He wrote several elementary school textbooks, among them the *Hikajat Nabi Muhammad* (History of the Prophet Muhammad), and a guidebook for prayer. In the meantime, he served as an editor of *Al-Basjir*, a journal published by his madrasah. At the insistence of his maternal uncle, a rich merchant, Mahmud eventually continued his study abroad. He went to Cairo because his late teacher had told him that there was nothing new he could study in Mecca.[5] He en-rolled in Al-Azhar, and a year later he received the *alamiyah* degree, conferred on foreign students who fulfilled all the requirements except Arabic. In 1926 he was admitted to the Arabic Department of the Darul Ulum in Cairo, the first college to combine secular and religious subjects.

Soon after his arrival in Cairo, Mahmud Junus was elected one of the first editors of the Welfare Society publication, *Seroean Azhar* (The Call of Azhar), first issued in September 1925. The director of the journal was Raden Faturrahman, vice-president of the Society. The editor-in-chief was Djanan Thaib, the president of the Society. Other members of the editorial board included Iljas Jacub, founder of the journal, and

---

in a letter to the Governor-General, Weltevreden, June 20, 1925, no. 597, *Mailrapport* 76x/'25.
4 In 1925, another 27 Malay students came to Cairo, which brought the total to about 80. William R. Roff, *The Origins of Malay Nationalism* (Kuala Lumpur: Pustaka Ilmu, 1967), p. 88. The total number of Indonesian students registered at the Dutch consulate was about 150. R. Kern letter, Weltevreden, November 23, 1925, *Mailrapport* 1134x/'25.
5 Interview with Prof. Mahmud Junus, March 1968, Djakarta.

two Malay students, Abdul Wahab Abdullah and M. Idris al-Marbawi. The real brain behind the journal was Iljas Jacub, for after publication of the first issue, Djanan Thaib became only a figurehead. He left Cairo for Europe in order to contact the Indonesian students in Holland. Although he temporarily returned to Cairo, he soon moved to Mecca. He had been the first Jawah student to obtain the highest degree granted by Al-Azhar. In Mecca he founded the Sekolah Indonesia (Indonesian School). Iljas Jacub led *Seroean Azhar* until he resigned in 1927.

The objective of *Sevoean Azhar* was "to promote knowledge, progress and unity among Indonesian [and Malayan] students in Egypt." Its contents clearly reflected the mood of the students at that time. It appealed for progress, and displayed an anti-colonial nationalism. The incipient nationalist feeling was present already in the first editorial. Written by Mahmud Junus, it urged the students to concentrate on their studies for the benefit of the fatherland and to lay a solid foundation for unity among the people of Sumatra, Java, Borneo and Malaya.[6]

This same attitude was also reflected in the students' activities. Dutch consular reports indicate that almost all student gatherings from 1926 until 1929 were demonstrations of anti-Dutch sentiments combined to some extent with criticism of British colonial power.[7] At a *lebaran* (end of the fasting month) celebration on April 8, 1929, the Indonesian students used the occasion to introduce the newly approved national anthem. Mahmud Junus had translated the anthem, "Indonesia Raja," into Arabic and distributed it to the Cairo student community.[8] The meeting exuded a spirit of *wathan* and *wathaniah* (nation and nationalism). Like any other student gathering, it had a full complement of speeches. Some students even discussed the eventual independence of Indonesia. The Dutch consul reported that they acted like "the leaders of the [Egyptian nationalist] Wafd party."[9]

---

[6] William R. Roff, "*Indonesian* and Malay Students in Cairo in the 1920's," Indonesia, 9 (April 1970), pp. 73-88.

[7] van der Plas Report, Cairo, February 4, 1929, *Mailrapport* 142x/'29. In his memoirs, van der Meulen, a former vice-consul, recounts his first experience with the Indonesian students in Cairo. In 1926, he attended a lecture on Indonesian history by an Arab scholar. Though the lecture was moderate in tone, during the question period, van der Meulen was heavily attacked by the Indonesian students as a representative of the Dutch government. *Ik Stond er Bij*, pp. 83-87.

[8] Report of the Dutch consul in Cairo, *Verbaal* May 24, 1929, X 10.

[9] *Radio*, April 13, 1929.

Several factors influenced the attitude of the students. First of all, the Dutch consul took little interest in their welfare. Since the 1910's, Snouck Hurgronje had been arguing that a Dutch orientalist should be attached to the Consulate, because he could maintain a close relationship with the student community. But this proposal was considered too expensive by both the Ministries of Foreign and Colonial Affairs.[10] Study in Cairo was relatively expensive by Indonesian standards and also very difficult for those whose mother tongue was not Arabic. Only a handful of Indonesian and Malayan students could obtain the much coveted Al-Azhar diploma. So difficult were the examination procedures that non-Egyptian students were usually "protected" by their respective national representatives during the examination period. For years, the Indonesian students had been asking for such "protection" without result. Only after a famous Egyptian ulama, Sjech Thantawi Jauhari, established a committee to "protect" these students did the Dutch government take action. In August 1925, the Governor-General instructed the Consul in Cairo to act as the "protector" of the Indonesian students during the examination period.[11] The decision was finally made because the Dutch suspected Sjech Thantawi, a known radical, and they were concerned about the consequences of the students' obvious indignation at the Consul's indifference.[12] The Welfare Society to some extent also owed its initial establishment to the problem of the lack of communication between the students and the Consulate.

The political situation in Indonesia exerted an important influence over the Cairo students. Since the appearance in 1914 of the first Jawah journal, *Al-ittihad*, the Indonesians in Cairo had in general been sympathetic towards popular movements in Indonesia. The journal, for example, expressed its approval of the organizations being established in the Indies, including such different ones as Sarekat Islam and Budi Utomo.[13] The communist rebellions of 1926-1927 also had their impact on the minds of the students, particularly those from Minangkabau. The student community kept in touch with developments through its

---

10 *Mailrapport* 113x/'29; van der Meulen, *Ik Stond er Bij*, p. 84.
11 Extract from the Governor-General's decision, no. 2X August 1925, *Mailrapport* 746x/'25.
12 Report from the Dutch Consulate, Cairo, October 9, 1925, *Mailrapport* 1040x/'25.
13 Snouck Hurgronje, letters, *Verbaal* January 5, 1915, no. 7 and February 5, 1915, no. 48.

subscriptions to Indonesian nationalist newspapers.[14] The activities of the students in Cairo also received wide coverage in some Indonesian newspapers. No less important an influence on the Cairo students was that exercised by the Perhimpunan Indonesia (PI, Indonesian Association), the radical nationalist student organization based in Holland. In 1925, the PI introduced new radical principles emphasizing national mass action, and it began to point out the contradictions in the colonial situation. About this time, Djanan Thaib, the president of the Cairo Welfare Society, established direct contact with the PI.[15] In 1926, the PI under Hatta, a former leader of the JSB, was acknowledged by several political parties in Indonesia as a forerunner of the revolutionary nationalist movement. The Indonesian students in Cairo maintained a close relationship with the PI until 1929;[16] after that, the politically oriented students left Cairo and the PI in Holland fell into the hands of the leftist faction.

The political climate in the Middle East, particularly in Egypt, strengthened the students' nationalist feelings and inspired them with an ideology based on the slogan "Islam and nationality." The popular Egyptian Wafd party, which combined the religious fervor of Muhammad Abduh and the nationalist appeals of Mustafa Kamil, deeply influenced the students. The Egyptian students themselves had been active in politics beginning in 1909.[17] Even the most detached student could not fail to be attracted by the nationalist fervor in the air.

In spite of the unmistakable impact of nationalism, the Jawah students had a crucial problem. What would be the correct attitude for them to adopt? Should they get involved in politics or remain aloof? The students were forced to define their priorities and to conceptualize their future roles. The majority, under the leadership of Mahmud Junus and Faturrahman, thought that the first obligation of the students was the completion of their studies so that they could return to their country as educators and

---

14 Nawawi, a student from Palembang, was a correspondent of the nationalist paper *Pertja Selatan*, and Talut Mustafa, a Minangkabau, was a regular contributor to *Noeroeljaqin*, published in Batu Sangkar.

15 *Seroean Azhar*, 1, No. 1 (September 1925); Letter of R. Kern, Weltevreden, January 6, 1926, no. H/3, *Mailrapport* 59x/'26.

16 Report by van der Meulen, *Mailrapport* 113x/'29.

17 Jamal Mohammad Ahmed, *The Intellectual Origins of Egyptian Nationalism* (London: Oxford University Press, 1960), pp. 116-117; Christina Harris, *Nationalism and Revolution in Egypt: The Role of the Muslim Brotherhood* (The Hague: Mouton, 1964), pp. 71-79.

social reformers. Though not repudiating the majority's opinion, others, led by Iljas Jacub, insisted that students had an immediate obligation to liberate their country. For this reason, they should involve themselves directly in the politics of independence and prepare to become future political leaders as well as educators. The division within the student community was deepened by differences in personality, experience, Family background and local origin.

An actual split did not occur until 1928, but the seed was planted with the arrival of Muchtar Lutfi in 1926. Born in Balingka (near Bukittinggi) in 1901, Muchtar was a son of Sjech Abdul Latif, a maternal uncle of Hadji Djalaluddin Thaib. His father died when Muchtar was still very young, and he was raised and educated by the younger brother of his father, Sjech Daud Rasjidi. In 1911, Muchtar followed Sjech Daud to Mecca and studied there for three years. After returning from Mecca, he became a student of Hadji Rasul. From 1916 until 1919, while continuing his studies, he taught at the newly established Dinijah School in Padang Pandjang. In 1919, he began his adventurous career as a traveling religious teacher in Minangkabau and South Tapanuli. In 1922, after he had just settled down, Sjech Djambek, a friend of his late father, persuaded him to come to the Dinijah school in Bukittinggi. During the communist movement Muchtar, although not a communist himself, displayed increasingly anti-government sentiments. In 1925, using the pen-name Tarfish, he wrote an anti-government treatise, Hikmatul Muchtar (The Chosen Wisdom), in Arabic. The book was subsequently banned, but aided by relatives and his teacher, Muchtar escaped to Kuala Lumpur.[18] There he was assisted by Sjech Thaher Djalaluddin. Using a British passport,[19] Muchtar went to India, where he was joined by his cousin, Mansur Daud, a son of Sjech Daud.[20] They traveled to Mecca; Mansur then continued on to Turkey, while Muchtar went to Cairo.

---

18 Provincial Bureau of Investigation, Sumatra's Westkust, July 17, 1933, *Mailrapport* 934x/'33. Interview with Datuk Palimo Kajo (Mansur Daud), Bukittinggi, July 13, 1968. On Muchtar Lutfi's escape, see Hamka, *Ajahku*, pp. 132-133.
19 Am Am, "Kiai jang djadi Perkakas," *Pembela Islam*, 54 (1932), pp. 33-36.
20 Mansur Daud was born on March 10, 1909, in Balingka. He graduated from the second class school in 1917 and then studied religion at the Surau Djembatan Besi until 1923. Afterward he visited India, spending six months in Lahore and Qadian, centers of Ahmadyah factions. He then moved to Hyderabad where he studied Urdu and improved his knowledge of Arabic and English on a grant from the government.

After he arrived in Cairo, in early 1926, Muchtar became a close companion of Iljas Jacub, the secretary of the Welfare Society. Because the Society was non-political and also had Malay members, Muchtar and Iljas founded a new group to work for political goals. This organization, the Perhimpunan Pendjaga Indonesia (Association of Indonesian Defenders) was established on April 12, 1926 with Muchtar as chairman and Iljas as adviser.[21] Its members were all Indonesians, predominantly Minangkabau. Of the six members on the executive board, only one was not a Minangkabau. The total number of the Minangkabau students in Cairo, it should be noted, was no more than twenty.[22] The organization was not very active and it functioned as little more than a political discussion club.

Muchtar meanwhile gained a much wider exposure to the political movement in the Middle East when the Caliphate Congress (Mu'tamar al-khilafah) was held in Cairo from May 13 to 19, 1926. The congress had been called to discuss the feasibility of reviving the caliphate, and it was attended by Hadji Abdullah Ahmad and Hadji Rasul. Muchtar was elected the official representative of the Welfare Society and also served as private secretary to Hadji Abdullah Ahmad during the congress. Participation in the congress gave Muchtar opportunities to meet with many important Egyptian ulama. He himself was instrumental in persuading the Islamic World Congress to confer on the two Minangkabau ulama an honorary degree (*doktor al-fiddin*) in religion.[23] The congress itself was a failure. It took note of the already known fact that there were many colonized Muslim countries and that theoretically the caliph had no direct religious authority. But for Muchtar and his friends, the congress confirmed their view that political Pan-Islamism was impossible. In retrospect, the failure

---

[21] Other members of the executive board were: Rasul Telur, Abdullah al-Indonesia and Raden Faturrahman. *Bandera Islam*, August 5, 1926, cited in *Overzicht van de Inlandsche Pers*, 31/1926, p. 406.

[22] No exact figure is available, for the Consulate reported only the number of students using Dutch passports. According to a Minangkabau student, in 1928 there were thirteen Minangkabau students in Cairo. *Tjaja Soematra*, August 14, 1928. In early 1929, there were fifteen at Al-Azhar and other institutions. Netherlands Legation Report, Cairo, March 1929, no. 342, *Mailrapport* 244x/'29. But at the end of 1929, it was reported that only thirteen were left out of the total of 300 Jawah students. *Noeroelj* aqin, 25, 1929. Most of the students arrived in 1924. By 1930 there were sixteen. Junus, *Sedjarah Pendidikan Islam*, p. 88.

[23] Hamka, *Ajahku*, pp. 144-145.

of this and a later caliphate congress, held in June of that same year in Mecca, did make an important contribution to the notion of nationalism with a Muslim soul, which the Cairo students later introduced in Minangkabau.

Iljas Jacub had been able to separate his political activism from his position as the secretary of the Welfare Society, but he proved unable to restrain himself as the editor-in-chief of *Seroean Azhar*. Articles in the journal became increasingly political in tone, until it had in effect become a nationalist political organ instead of simply a forum for student debates.[24] The Dutch government still subscribed to the official myth of Pan-Islamism and thus viewed *Seroean Azhar* as a potential danger. On the advice of the Dutch Consul in Cairo, the Governor-General banned *Seroean Azhar* from the Netherlands Indies. Economically, the ban was not serious because the journal had only 300 subscribers in Indonesia, as compared with the 700 copies sent regularly to Malaya.[25] The ban, however, did shock the student community, because it suggested that the Dutch considered their school activities as part of a larger political effort. Such official opinions about their activities might prejudice the Cairo students' chances to continue their education. Fear of reprisal by the colonial government in Indonesia (or by the Sultans, in Malaya) could cause their parents to recall them. Consequently, in July 1927, Iljas Jacub was forced to resign from *Seroean Azhar*. Three months later, he and Muchtar began publication of *Pilihan Timoer* (Eastern Choice), which was independent of the Welfare Society.

In September 1927, the Welfare Society celebrated the second anniversary of *Seroean Azhar*, and Mahmud Junus was elected its editor. In his acceptance speech, Mahmud declared that he would not tolerate any political writing in the journal. But certainly drawing a clear distinction between political and non-political writing was not easy. The major factor which divided the student community was their sense of urgency and expedience rather than any conflict of ideology. Seroean Azhar remained banned in Indonesia. Mahmud's tenure, furthermore, was very short. In January he went to the Consulate to protest against continuation of the

---

24 Roff, "Indonesian and Malay Students."
25 Netherlands Legation Report, Cairo, January 28, 1928, no. 181, *Mailrapport* 562x/'28.

ban. In February he informed the Consul that he was resigning from the journal because he was overburdened by work.[26] He was succeeded by Raden Faturrahman, who was also the director of the journal. In April, the Egyptian government delivered a strong warning to *Seroean Azhar*. The new editor agreed to let the Dutch Consul censor manuscripts before publication. The journal, however, also suffered from a lack of funds, and it soon ceased operations.[27]

Pilihan Timoer, unlike *Seroean Azhar*, was, from its inception in October 1927, clearly political in content. The journal, whose motto was "for the land and the people of Indonesia and Malaya," covered many areas. Besides Quranic commentaries and religious subjects, it also contained sections on history, women, and more general problems of civilization, for example, questions of the relationship between East and West or the backwardness of nations. But its editorials caused the journal to be banned from Indonesia. The editorial of December, written by Iljas Jacub and entitled "A way toward progress," was a bold political treatise. It began with criticism of the so-called rust (tranquility) policy pursued by the Dutch government in the wake of the tumultuous political activities of the 1920's. "Tranquility," according to Iljas, did not always mean peace, for it could also be found in the jungle:

> where everything is quiet. There is neither farmer nor wood-collector around; not even a deer can be found. There, wild beasts rampage ferociously; little animals and men are forced to run for their lives.

The analogy referred to the unjust relationship between ruler and ruled. The editorial complained about the gulf that existed between the intellectuals, who were supposed to be the leaders, and the mass of the population. As a. result, an intolerable impasse had been reached in the movement toward progress. A way to break up this impasse was to build a people's organization, holding regular congresses for representatives of the people. The congress would be a forum where the voice of the people

---

26 *Ibid.* and February 1928, *Mailrapport* 562x/T28.
27 *Ibid.*, and April 13, 1928, no. 500, Mailrapport 562x/'28.

could be heard. Every district should have its own chapter of the people's organization, as the representative of the central board. The members of the executive board of the people's organization and of the congress would represent all indigenous organizations. In the congresses and other meetings, either at the local or national levels, other leaders and intellectuals should be invited to participate. By working through such congresses, an overall plan of action for Indonesia could be designed. The congress could also act as the representative of Indonesia in any world congress.[28]

"The way toward progress" suggested in this editorial was a challenge to the Dutch-instituted Volksraad and represented in effect a proposal to establish a "shadow government." *Pilihan Timoer* was soon banned in Indonesia. The Dutch Consul in Cairo warned the British High Commissioner in Egypt about "the revolutionary character" of the journal and advised that it should also be banned in Egypt and Malaya.[29] In April 1928, at the suggestion of the British High Commissioner, the Egyptian government banned the publication of *Pilihan Timoer*.[30] The journal had lasted only six months. But the political views of its editor-publishers, Iljas and Muchtar, including the idea of a people's organization, the notion that a political movement should be carried out on a national basis and the need for participation of the intellectuals in a popular movement were later adopted by Permi.

Iljas and Muchtar were under the spell of the nationalist movement in Egypt. They not only observed it but also had personal contact with its leaders. "Their activities," according to van der Meulen, the former Dutch vice-consul, "brought excitement not only within the walls of the Muslim university [Al-Azhar] but also outside, in the Egyptian press and in the anti-British organizations."[31] According to several dispatches from the Dutch consulate, after *Pilihan Timoer* ceased, Iljas became a close companion of Dr. Abdul Hamid Bey, the president of the radical Islamic Youth Congress and an influential Egyptian parliamentarian. Iljas was

---

28 *Pilihan Timoer*, 3 (December 1927).
29 Netherlands Legation, Report to the Foreign Minister, Cairo, March 30, 1928, no. 503/185, *Verbaal* April 18, 1928, Kabinet Letter S6.
30 *Ibid.*; and Legation Report, April 14, 1928, no. 57a, *Verbaal* August 22, 1928, Kabinet Letter A14.
31 van der Meulen, *Ik Stond er Bij*, p. 90.

reportedly also good friends with Sjech Mahmud Abouel Ayoum, the inspector of Al-Azhar and an important leader of a radical non-communist Egyptian organization.[32] Throughout the latter part of 1928 and early 1929, both Iljas and Muchtar were frequent visitors at the "House of the Nation," the headquarters of the Wafd, the Egyptian nationalist party.[33] Their political activities generally and their participation in the Egyptian nationalist movement annoyed the Cairo government, and, according to van der Meulen, it asked the Dutch consulate to send the two students back home or else they would be put in an Egyptian prison. The Consul helped them to go to Mecca under the pretext of continuing their studies, "so that they did not have to be ashamed when they returned to the West Coast of Sumatra" without an Al-Azhar diploma.[34] Later in Minangkabau, Muchtar used his acquaintance with important leaders in the Muslim world as propaganda on behalf of Permi.

Muchtar and Iljas, though they left Cairo without completing their studies, were full of ideas about future activities. At the time of their departure in April 1929, the unity among the Jawah student community had greatly eroded. The resignation of Iljas as the editor-in-chief of *Seroean Azhar* had been the first outward sign of internal dissension in the student community. The subsequent publication of *Pilihan Timoer* exacerbated the situation. The Welfare Society itself lacked money. The decline in donations from Indonesia and Malaya was apparently considered by some non-Minangkabau students a direct consequence of the political activities of Muchtar and Iljas. The controversy became so intense that on July 28, 1928, all the Minangkabau students, following the lead of Muchtar and Mahmud Junus (who in fact opposed Muchtar), resigned en bloc from the Welfare Society.[35] The split did not long remain a purely

---

32 Sjech Ayoum strongly opposed the Egyptian student organization which was being influenced by the leftist Berlin League. Attorney-General's office, April 2, 1928, no. 644/H, *Verbaal* August 22, 1928 A/14.
33 Netherlands Legation, Cairo, April 13, 1929, *Verbaal* May 24, 1929 X/10.
34 van der Meulen, *Ik Stond er Bij*, pp. 90-91. After his arrest, Iljas told the police that he had left Cairo because he wanted to go home. He stopped at Mecca because he wanted to make the *hadj*. *Mailrapport* 861x/'34. Both Muchtar and Lutfi were soon elected to the executive board of the Indonesian organization in Mecca led by Djanan Thaib. The Jeddah consulate reported that their transfer to Mecca created some misgivings among the Indonesiam *mukim* settlers because it was feared that they might threaten the hitherto cordial relations between this community and the Dutch consulate.
35 *Tjaja Soematra*, August 14, 1928.

ethnic one. Mahmud intensified his appeal: "You come to Egypt to study and while you are in this country you should refrain of all activities except seeking knowledge."[36] Another Minangkabau student, Talut Mustafa, the son of an important Kaum Muda ulama, echoed Mahmud's warnings in student gatherings and urged his colleagues to avoid politics. Although the departure of Iljas and Muchtar reduced the anti-colonial activities of the students,[37] the Welfare Society by 1929 was already too divided by internal dissension to recover. Some students had already been recalled by their parents, who feared reprisals by the authorities.

While Muchtar and Iljas were busy writing political treatises, Mahmud was preoccupied with designing educational reforms for Minangkabau. Inspired by his experience in Darul Ulum, Mahmud proposed a tentative plan for a reformed religious school. It divided religious schools into three levels—elemen-tary, intermediary, and advanced. The advanced school would be organized in several departments following the system used at the Darul Ulum. Curricula in the elementary religious schools would include secular subjects, such as world history and geog-raphy. At the intermediary level, some branches of science, such as physics, geology and botany, would be added.[38] Mahmud refined this plan later after he returned to Minangkabau, but while still in Cairo he kept himself busy by writing the elementary textbooks which such a system would require. Together with Kasim Bakri, he co-authored a book on pedagogy and an Arabic-Malay dictionary, *Kamus Keemasan* (The Golden Dictionary). Mahmud himself wrote several textbooks for elementary religious schools on Quranic exegesis and fikh (law), and also produced the first illustrated Arabic textbook. All were published in Cairo. In early 1930, Mahmud also published a textbook on chemistry and one on health education. These were the first elementary books on modern sciences written by a religious teacher for religious schools. In his introduction to the chemistry book, Mahmud approvingly quoted an Egyptian ulama, who stated: "The Muslims have committed a sin because they ignore several religious obligations which were imposed on the community as a whole (*fardhu*

---

36 "Kaoem Moeda di Minangkabau, XV," *Pandji Islam*, 19 (May 12, 1941); and interview with Mahmud Junus, Djakarta, March 1968.
37 Netherlands Legation, Cairo, October 18, 1929, no. 1190, *Mailrapport* 1107/'29.
38 *Noeroeljaqin*, 24 (1929).

kifajah). They let the Europeans produce their necessities, although religion urged them to do their utmost." This appeal was not new. It dated from the early period of Islamic modernism and in Minangkabau itself a similar appeal can be found in the writings of the Kaum Muda ulama in *Al-Moenir*. But in religious schools, except for some modernization in the teaching system, no substantial advances had been made towards the incorporation of elementary science subjects into the curriculum. Mahmud urged the religious teachers in Minangkabau to catch up with the modern world.

> [According to religion] no true Muslim should give up hope, no matter how impossible the situation is. And if we cannot make it in our generation, with God's blessings, we are doing it for our offspring. It is then obligatory for us to provide our children with the foundation of sciences...so that our offspring can expand and develop [the sciences] as high as pos-sible.[39]

By this program, Mahmud hoped not only to bridge the gap between the secular and religious schools but also to provide the religiously educated youngsters with the tools for competing with others. His program presented the Thawalib and the Dinijah schools with valuable suggestions for use in their efforts to modernize their religious schools. Later, in 1931, Mahmud Junus himself became directly involved in the modernization of religious schools.

In order to pursue this educational reform program, Mahmud and his friends founded the Sidang Pengetahuan (Council of Knowledge) in December 1929. Its purpose was to disseminate knowledge by publishing books in Malay and Arabic for use in religious schools throughout Indonesia and Malaya. The Council also hoped to assist its members in their studies. Some of the elementary textbooks written by Mahmud Junus were published by this organization. It was quite a profitable business, and, by the end of 1930, a few textbooks had already been reprinted three times. Almost all Kaum Muda elementary religious schools in Minangkabau used them as textbooks. Unlike prior student organizations in Cairo, the

---

39 Quoted in "Kaoem Moeda di Minangkabau," pp. 9071-2.

Sidang Pengetahuan had exclusively Minangkabau members. Mahmud himself served as its first chairman. Most of the members played an important role later during the religious school reform of the thirties.

In July 1930, Mahmud became the first Jawah student to obtain a degree from the Darul Ulum. Mahmud had also emerged as one of the best students. It was a great moment for the Sidang Pengetahuan. On August 23, the organization held a big celebration to honor him. The celebration was attended by the Jawah students along with several Egyptian professors and ulama, such as Sjech Rasjid Ridha and Sjech Thantawi Jauhari, and several political leaders. It was, indeed, a great moment for Mahmud Junus, since most of the Egyptian ulama and professors who praised his performances were highly respected among the Kaum Muda circles in Minangkabau and in other parts of Indonesia. The Sidang Pengetahuan published a booklet, *Haflah Takrim* (Glorious Celebration), written in Arabic, to commemorate the occasion.[40] In the meantime, in Padang, a special committee was organized to give Mahmud a hero's welcome. But Mahmud took the eastern route from Singapore via Pekan Baru. In October he arrived in his nagari, Sungajang.[41]

Iljas Jacub, for his part, discovered on arrival that he was considered an undesired person by the Dutch government. When he arrived in early July from Mecca, the government had already imposed a travel restriction and he was arrested. Muchtar Lutfi, who was still on the government list as a "commu-nist fugitive," had to wait for another year in Mecca, until

---

[40] The highlight of the party came when the honored guests gave their speeches. *Haflah Takrim* described the scene as follows:

"The first opportunity was given to Mahdi Bey Allah, an instructor of pedagogy at Darul Ulum and a private tutor to the present King Farouk. After praising his student Mahmud, he said enthusiastically, 'We should not be sad, because it is your duty, Indonesians, to send one Mahmud every year.' Sjech M. A. Muthalib, the Arabic instructor, rose, followed by Sayyid Muhammad Rasjid Ridha, the editor of the famous *Al-Manaar*. He said that he hoped Indonesia, a rich and prosperous country, would be able to take care of itself and defend itself from the incessant attacks by Christian missionaries. Sjech Thantawi Jauhari, author of a famous Quranic commentary, announced his happiness, saying Indonesia was already as a second fatherland for him because of his love for the country and his correspond-ence with Indonesians. Prof. Shaleh Bey Hasjim also contributed valuable advice. And finally, Dr. A. Hamid Said, president of Sjubhanul Muslimin and a member of parliament, arose and enlivened the party with his famous oratorical skill, full of zest and enthusiasm. At the close of the party, Mahmud Junus replied to all the speeches addressed to him."

Politieke Politioneel Overzicht, 4de kwartaal 1930, *Mailrapport* 228x/'31.

[41] The excerpt is contained in *Pandji Islam*, 21 (May 26, 1941), pp. 9096-9097.

his name was cleared by the government. In July 1931, he arrived in Bukittinggi as a free person.

Influence of the Middle East Perantau

Beginning in the early 1920's, the Kaum Muda followers in Minangkabau proudly called their schools "the gates to Egypt." The schools were being designed not only to produce qualified religious teachers but also to train candidates for higher educational institutions in Egypt, a center of Islamic modernism. The prestige of Cairo stemmed from the influential Al-Azhar and the fact that the famous modernist journal, Al-Manaar, was published there. Edited by Sjech Rasjid Ridha, the journal had been likened to "a beam in the darkness," which had enlightened the Muslim world. "The call of Egypt" was, indeed, an important incentive for the religiously educated Minangkabau youth to pursue their studies.[42]

But few students could continue their education in Egypt. Only those who belonged to well-to-do families and a few student adventurers, such as Muchtar Lutfi, were able to go to Cairo. This wider exposure to the outside world, combined with their advanced education, gave the Cairo returnees an advantage in the contest for leadership among the Islamic modernists. Moreover, the already influential position held by the Kaum Muda educated group in various educational and political organizations provided the Cairo returnees with a strong base of support for carrying out their ideas.

Unlike most of the Western-educated perantau intellectuals, the Islamic modernists came home. They went to the rantau, Cairo or Mecca, in order to prepare themselves to succeed their teachers as reformers and educators. On their return, they participated and often led in the reform of the religious schools. Mahmud Junus established a school which soon became a model for the Dinijah and Thawalib schools. He was appointed director of the newly founded modern teachers' training school or college, the Normal Islam. Iljas Jacub was active in developing Permi's Islamic College, and Muchtar Lutfi became the director of a politically oriented teachers' training school for girls and an intermediate religious school,

---

42 "Kaoem Moeda di Minangkabau,XV."

the Tsanawijah. It was Mahmud Junus and his "non-political" colleagues, however, who concentrated their full effort on educational programs, and his influence in Minangkabau religious and educational circles increased after the exile of Iljas and Muchtar.

Iljas and Muchtar, who had been exposed to the Egyptian nationalist struggle, joined Permi and became important leaders of the rapidly growing radical party. Drawing on their Egyptian experience, they guided the radicalization of political activities in Minangkabau and the search for a suitable political ideology. Under their influence, Permi with its ideology "Islam and kebangsaan" initiated an ideological controversy among the Kaum Muda educated group. Desiring to influence the political movement, Permi introduced a new aspect into the ideological controversies between the Islamic and the kebangsaan ("secular" nationalist) groups. The Permi version called for a new examination of the Minangkabau concept of its world, its alam.

CHAPTER SEVEN
THE SEARCH FOR AN IDEOLOGY

In the editorial of the first issue of *Medan Rakjat* (People's Forum), published in February 1931, Iljas Jacub lamented the crisis in the Indonesian popular movement. He particularly referred to the split between the Islamic and the kebangsaan ("secular" nationalist) parties. The Islamic group condemned the ideas propagated by the secular parties as "forbidden by religion" (haram). The kebangsaan group regarded Islam as "worthless" in the nationalist movement. This, said Iljas, was a "tragic situation."

> In our opinion, there is no difference or conflict between the goals of these two groups. Although they base [their struggles] on two different principles, they both want to lead and to direct our people toward the achievement of progress and human dignity.

Iljas appealed for unity as a sign of maturity: "No one will recognize your maturity unless you demonstrate it yourself." In his view, the crisis could be solved by incorporating Permi's slogan of "Islam and nationality" into the political movement.[1]

During 1930 a gradual breakdown occurred among the regional nationalist parties, such as Budi Utomo and Sarekat Sumatra, and many regional youth organizations were dissolved. It was a time when the notion of political Pan-Islamism lost its significance as a basis for the anti-colonial struggle. The idea of *Indonesia Raja* as the basis for national unity and a political entity had grown beyond either local nationalist or

---

1 *Medan Rakjat*, 1, No. 1 (February 1931).

Pan-Islamist aspirations. But at the same time, ideological differences among the nationalist parties had come to the surface. The Permufakatan Perhimpunan Politik Kebangsaan Indonesia (PPPKI, Consensus of Nationalist Political Associations of Indonesia), initiated by Sukarno in December 1927, had to some extent reduced the dissension between the cooperative and non-cooperative political parties by emphasizing the need for unity. This loose federation, however, had failed to tackle the basic differences in political ideologies and strategies. Ideological issues separated the Islamic from the "secular" nationalist groups; questions of strategy and the tactics of struggle divided the radical groups into "mass-oriented" and "social-pedagogic" parties.

Ideological conflict between the Islamic and the kebangsaan groups was particularly intense after the secular nationalists, led by Western-educated intellectuals, had gained more prominence in the popular movement. The secular nationalists suffered major setbacks, such as the temporary arrest of Sukarno in 1929 and the split among the radical leaders which followed the dissolution of the National Party, but the ability of the Western-educated leaders to articulate political issues and employ modern methods for spreading their influence enabled them to seize the initiative in the independence movement. The Dutch reaction tended to magnify the potentialities of the Western-educated intellectuals as anti-colonial leaders, and this too worked to the advantage of the secular nationalists in their competition with the Islamic group.

The Islamic political parties lost the initiative in the middle 1920's following the break of the communists from the SI, the first Indonesian mass party. The PSI, successor of the SI, gradually declined in influence even among its Islamic clientele. Its several attempts to unite all Muslim organizations on the basis of political Pan-Islamism ended in failure. In its effort to retain political leadership among Muslims, the PSI was in competition with the rapidly growing but non-political Muhammadijah. In 1930, certain factors helped minimize the open conflict among Muslim organizations. Mussolini's attack on Muslim Tripoli awakened a feeling of Islamic solidarity. Criticism by secular nationalists about the inadequacies of Islam as a basis for nationality put all the Muslim parties in one category separate from the "nationalists." Dr. Sutomo's criticism of the pilgrimage to Mecca on the grounds that Digul, the place to which political leaders were exiled, was a more honorable place than the Holy City increased the

Islamic distrust of the intention of kebangsaan leaders.

Both the Islamic and the kebangsaan groups agreed on the need for supra-ethnic unity and for the liberation of Indonesia from the colonial power. In their international orientation, however, the secular nationalists, particularly those under Sukarno's influence, looked to cooperation among Asian nations. The Islamic group, on the other hand, insisted on the need to realize the concept of "Islamic Brotherhood." The fundamental issues centered around the nature of Islam as a perfect and all-embracing religion, the basis for Indonesian unity, and the goal and substance of independence. The orthodox Muslims assumed that Islam should not only be concerned with the world hereafter but also with guiding man in his earthly life. Since Islam was not invented by man but rather given by God, it was by definition perfect. The purpose of life, therefore, should be to realize the teachings of Islam. Nationalism, on the other hand, originated from man's own mind and desires. As such, it was inherently defective for use as a guide. Moreover, the idea of kebangsaan came from Europe where it had divided humanity into hostile nations and had inspired nations to oppress each other. From the Islamic point of view, nationalism as promoted by the secular nationalists was a faulty and even forbidden basis for struggle. An Islamic publicist pointed out:

> A kebangsaan [person] who dies in the struggle for the independence of Indonesia, dies "in the name of the nation." The death of a Muslim in his fight to liberate Islam is the death which is called in the Quran "*fi sabillillahi*," "in the path of God."[2]

The attempt by Permi leaders to rationalize Islam and nationalism stimulated a heated ideological conflict among the Islamic modernists. The Permi leaders created a split within the Kaum Muda educated group and widened the gap between them and their former mentors, the Kaum Muda ulama. Educated in the spirit of idjtihad which emphasized freedom of thought and the need for reform, the Kaum Muda educated group saw themselves as engaged in the search for a suitable ideology needed for their role as social reformers. In addition to determining a philosophical

---

2 "Nasionalisme tiada Bertentangan dengan Islam," *Pembela Islam*, 60 (1932), pp. 3-4.

basis for struggle, the younger generation of Islamic modernists were involved in controversies over strategy and tactics. The controversies were intensified by the desire of Minangkabau political leaders to expand their influence to other parts of Indonesia and by the intrusion of secular nationalist parties into the political movement in West Sumatra.

Islam and Kebangsaan

"The ideological bases of this organization," according to the Permi constitution, "are Islam and nationality (kebangsaan)."[3] When Iljas Jacub stated this slogan at the First Permi Congress in October 1930, he introduced a new ideological issue in Minangkabau. Still fascinated by his experience with the Egyptian nationalist movement, Iljas wanted to formulate a more definitive ideological basis for the Kaum Muda political movement and to help solve the crisis in the Indonesian popular movement. His experience in Egypt inspired him to seek a workable ideology which could accommodate both of the important strands in the Indonesian independence movement. Iljas, supported by his colleagues who had just returned from Cairo, managed to persuade the congress to accept his slogan for the new organization. In the middle of 1931, Muchtar Lutfi returned and he soon became the most effective spokesman for "Islam and kebangsaan" and Permi.

The new slogan was initially rationalized on the grounds that religious feeling and the awareness of belonging to one nation (*bangsa*) were both part of human life. One Permi publicist wrote:

> Men, no matter in whatever age or place they live, always have the feelings of *religion* and *nationality*. Religion is a spiritual feeling in our heart. It is called iman or belief. Nation is a group of people who are bound together by various social and cultural ties, such as language, morality, fate, destiny, etc...[4]

Islam itself recognized the idea of nationality. The religion stressed that its

---

3 *Anggaran Dasar dan Anggaran Tetangga Permi*, Article #3.
4 *Medan Rakjat*, 1, No. 2 (February 15, 1931).

adherents should give priority to their relatives before considering other people. In political terms, "relatives" could be equated with "nation." In its relation with people, a nation could be considered as one large family. Dedication to one's own nation, therefore, was also a religious duty (*ibadah*). In the words of the publicist:

> Allah demands that we work as hard as possible for the sake of Islam and for the spread of religion. But [we] should do more for our kebangsaan.[5]

The early attempts of Permi to find a generally acceptable ideology, however, aroused the suspicion of other parties. Some secular nationalist leaders were emphatic in their belief that religion should remain a purely individual matter, and they voiced their pessimism concerning Permi's "inherently inconsistent ideology."[6] Some Muslim leaders accused Permi leaders of joining the kebangsaan group. These Muslims could not accept the idea that religion and nationality were equal entities. As orthodox Muslims, they believed that Islam was at once religion, nationality and fatherland. They believed that Permi leaders, though raised and educated in the Islamic tradition, had corrupted the perfect nature of Islam and thereby weakened the Islamic group in its ideological conflict with the secularists.

In self-defense, Permi redefined its concept of Islam and kebangsaan. Its first political brochure, published in July 1931, stated:

> Permi is based on Islam and kebangsaan. These principles, however, are based on one fundamental principle, that is, "the Benevolence of God." If we look at the ideas that dominate the [popular] movement in the present day, [Islam and nationalism] form two distinct principles with two different spirits. The spirit of religion is very refined and pure, because it is based on tauhid. Its refinement and purity cannot be corrupted. No matter how harsh the suppression and how bitter the suffering, iman can never be

---

5 *Ibid.*
6 Politieke Politioneel Overzicht, 2de kwartaal, 1930, *Mailrapport* 812x/'30.

changed. The spirit of nationalism is also refined and pure, but, since it originates in human minds, it can sometimes be influenced by hawa nafsu. Under strong suppression, it can also be easily corrupted.[7]

Permi hoped that this explanation would prevent division within the Indonesian independence movement and help it to work toward the common ideals.

Muslim critics charged that this new formulation confused ideology with practical objectives and implicitly conceded the deficiency of Islam as the sole principle for national struggle. Since Permi had acknowledged that the love of nation and the urge for unity were recognized by Islam, why, then, should it add kebangsaan to its ideology? Muhammad Natsir, a Minangkabau perantau intellectual and a leader of the Persatuan Islam[8] based in Bandung, argued:

It seems that they [Permi leaders] are not satisfied with their Islam. They seem to feel that Islam is not enough, that they deem it necessary to add [something else] .

Islam, which they acknowledged as the essential foundation, according to Natsir, in practice would be superseded by kebangsaan, which was supposed to be merely a supporting idea.[9]

By emphasizing Islam as the basic foundation of its ideology, Permi wanted to condemn the secularist deification of the nation, the tanah air (home country), the beautiful *"Ibu Indonesia"* (Mother Indonesia). In practice, however, by using kebangsaan as a pillar of its ideology, Permi created misunderstandings among its own group, the Islamic modernists. Within the Minangkabau adat system, moreover, bangsa had an additional meaning; the *bangso* referred to the adat aristocracy, the original settlers of the nagari. Islamic modernists feared kebangsaan

---

7 *Semangat*, 1 (July 1931).
8 For more about Persatuan Islam, see Howard M. Federspiel, *Persatuan Islam: Islamic Reform in Twentieth Century Indonesia* (Ithaca: Cornell Modern Indonesia Project, 1970) .
9 Is [pseud. M. Natsir], "Koerang Tegas jang Meragoekan," *Pembela Islam*, 35 (November 1931), pp. 2-7.

could thus be interpreted as the personification of traditional adat glory. In this sense, promotion of kebangsaan could be an attempt to intensify Minangkabau "group pride and narrow minded-ness." Some Kaum Muda ulama argued that kebangsaan would eventually undermine the Islamic concepts of tolerance and open-mindedness and its condemnation of group pride (*assjabiah*).[10]

In Java, Islamic leaders feared that the idea of kebangsaan would be used to revive a pre-Islamic, Madjapahit type of unity. The so-called cultural nationalists had been spreading this myth, and the Islamic leaders feared they wanted to repudiate the contribution of Islam in breaking up ethnic boundaries and to revive the pre-Islamic way of life. Islamic leaders charged that such nationalism was no more than a kind of "modern *djahiliah*," an unenlightened idea in modern form. Islam had been revealed to man in order to abolish djahiliah ideas and practices, therefore, how could Permi hope to reconcile such antagonistic ideologies?

The orthodox exposition of the basic contradictions between Islam and kebangsaan forced Permi onto the defensive. At its Second Congress, in November 1931, the party defined "nationalism" as a "way of action," a strategy with specific goals and not as "a state of mind." "Kebangsaan," said Muchtar Lutfi, "is a way toward the achievement of Indonesian independence," and the meaning of Islam in Permi's slogan should be understood as the determination to attain "Islam in Honor." Man's responsibility to his community is a religious duty and his willingness to make sacrifices for the betterment of his nation is a kind of religious merit (*amal*).[11] On other occasions, Muchtar stressed that the struggle for national independence and for the improvement of social conditions should not be seen as ends in themselves. Although these efforts would benefit society, their ultimate goal was service to God. The fight for independence had to be carried out "in the name of Allah." Permi's idea of kebangsaan should not be considered the basis of its struggle but rather

---

10 Noer, "The Rise and Development," pp. 433-436. Praising Permi ideology, a young Kaum Tua leader of the PTI said: "In Minangkabau we call a man berbangsa if he has lands and forests, sawah and dry fields, and followers, but now..., where is our kebangsaan?" Politieke Politioneel Overzicht, February 1932, *Mailrapport* 415x/'32. In this context, *berbangsa* means the adat aristocracy and kebangsaan the symbol of traditional glory.

11 Tamar Djaja, "Islam di Indonesia."

an expression of "the demand for human rights."[12] In his debate with the Persatuan Islam, Muchtar called national-ism an ideological blueprint for changing the nation's destiny. Had not Allah stated in His Book (surah 13:11) that "Allah changes not the condition of a people until they change their own conditions"?[13]

Muchtar and other Permi leaders argued that kebangsaan was "a way of action" which worked externally to eliminate imperialism and capitalism and internally to break down provincialism, ethno-centrism and insularism. Kebangsaan "should be seen as the desire to make our nation equal with other nations." Nationalism as promoted by Permi implied the achievement of democracy, the eradication of all remnants of feudalism, and a declaration of war "against all suffering."[14]

In their desire to resolve the conflict between Islamic and kebangsaan groups and to make their party into a kind of "national catalyst," the Permi leaders failed to see that the issues of the early 1930's were no longer confined to questions of the proper philosophical basis for struggle. Permi leaders emphasized the immediate goal, the independence of Indonesia, and avoided involvement in the controversy about how an independent Indonesian state would be constituted. By doing so, they hoped to reduce the growing gulf between Islamic and kebangsaan groups. Unfortunately for the Permi leaders, the main themes of controversy had increasingly shifted to the very issues which they wanted to ignore. A leader of the Persatuan Islam wrote:

> The kebangsaan movement works with Indonesian people in the name of "Mother Indonesia" and for the sake of the Indonesian *marhaen* [little people]. The Islamic movement in this country works with the Indonesian Muslims in the name of Allah and for the independence of Islam.[15]

"The independence of Islam" meant nothing less than the creation of an

---

12 *Tjaja Soematra*, October 22, 1932.
13 *Pembela Islam*, 54 (1933), pp. 3-7.
14 The speeches of the Permi leaders, such as Muchtar Lutfi, Iljas Jacub and Ali Emran Djamil, are contained in: *Tjaja Soematra*, October 22, 1932; Politieke Politioneel Over-zicht, February-August 1932, *Mailrapport* 415x/'32, 777x/'32, 952x/'32, 1017x/'32.
15 "Marhaenisme dan Islam," Pembela Islam, 56 (1932), pp. 2-6.

Islamic state which would protect and propagate the Islamic religion. Though acknowledging the legal rights of non-Muslims, the state would strive for the realization of Islamic ideals. Its democratic system and its social justice would not be copies of Western concepts but rather correct manifestations of Islamic doctrine. The future state would apply Islamic laws and maintain Islamic morality.[16]

The Permi leaders found themselves in an ideological dilemma. Debates on the future of an independent Indonesia required them to formulate the substance of their concept, "Islam in Honor." But such a formulation might alienate the secular nationalists, who constantly argued that Islam was an inadequate foundation for a modern national state. The attempt by the Permi leaders to avoid these issues was seen by some Muslim leaders as a betrayal. They accused Permi leaders of compromising Islamic principles for the sake of political expediency.

Iljas Jacub, Muchtar Lutfi, as well as other Permi leaders, such as Hadji Djalaluddin Thaib, had had sound credentials for introducing the concept of "Islam and kebangsaan." They had already proved themselves both as true patriots and as men educated in the Islamic tradition. Along with other Cairo returnees, they were convinced that an appeal for kebangsaan could minimize the distrust existing between the Islamic and the secular nationalists. They were not very successful in attracting the Islamic modernists in Java, for these men had begun to formulate their own conception of an Indonesian Islamic state. Permi did, however, establish a close relationship with Sukarno and his Partai Indonesia (Partindo). Sukarno, who had launched the idea of a cooperation of Islam, Nationalism and Marxism,[17] saw Permi as a step toward the realization of unity in the Indonesian independence movement. Although Sukarno and the Permi leaders defined the relationship between Islam and nationalism in different ways, both desired unity between the Islamic and the kebangsaan groups and both acknowledged the need for mass political parties. Sukarno viewed cooperation between Islam and Nationalism as that between two political ideologies; Permi posited an all-embracing Islam in which nationalism had its legitimate place. But the two had a

---

16 Amelz, *H.O.S. Tjokroaminoto: Hidup dan Perdjuangannja* (Djakarta: Bulan Bintang, [1952?]).
17 Sukarno, *Nationalism, Islam and Marxism* (Ithaca: Cornell Modern Indonesia Project, 1969), pp. 35-62.

common ground in their obsession with national unity.[18]

Permi's failure as a "national catalyst" did not prevent it from becoming the largest party in Sumatra. It was able to mobilize young Minangkabau Islamic modernists. They were attracted by the slogan "Islam in Honor," for they conceived of Islam as a part of their own alam and a cultural treasure. The Permi idea of kebangsaan defined Islam more specifically as a nationalist political slogan. The appeal of kebangsaan based on Islam masked a determination to oppose the colonial power. At a time when opposition to the government was mounting, the slogan of "Islam and kebangsaan" became an attractive call to political action.

A consequence of Permi's attempts to rationalize a philosophical foundation with political objectives was further dissension among the Islamic modernist leaders in Minangkabau. The Permi slogan was not only a political ideology but also a strategy and a political program. Controversy over the strategies and goals of struggle contributed to numerous conflicts and on a scale that threatened to prevent cooperation even among Kaum Muda organizations.

Conflict between Permi and Other Parties

At a conference in July 1932, Permi announced that it would become "a radical, non-cooperative political organization working for the independence of Indonesia."[19] This decision was a culmination of internal developments and increasing participation by Permi in national politics. Since early 1931, party leaders had consistently cultivated the notion of "bravery." Bravery (*keberanian*) was lauded as the only way to erase the shame "etched on [our] foreheads" as the result of humiliation inflicted by a foreign power. A traditional sense of communal shame thus

---

18 Sukarno retained his close feelings for the Permi. In a 1953 speech on Islam and the national state, he said:
>"The Permi, my brothers, clearly said that 'Islam recognizes nationality, Islam acknowledges nationalism. It is true what Bung Karno has said. It is also true when Bung Karno warned: Beware of chauvinist nationalism. Islam does not condone chauvinist nationalism. This is assjabiah, which is haram according to Islam....' Bung Karno was right and his opinion was not contrary to Islamic teaching, this was the opinion of the Permi, as expressed by its spokesman, the late Muchtar Lutfi."

Sukarno, *Negara Nasional dan Tjita-Tjita Islam* (Djakarta: Pustaka Endang, 1954), pp. 19-20.
19 *Indisch Verslag*, 1933, p. 15.

obliged every Minangkabau to defend the honor of his world (alam). The obligation was imperative not only because it was morally right but also because it was a religious duty (ibadah).

> Allah has given us legs, hands and minds to enable us to endeavor and to work for our lives, our security and our prosperity, and for the benefit of our religion, our nation and our tanah air. All these [obligations] cannot be carried out without bravery and without willingness to sacrifice wealth and to maximize one's efforts.[20]

The traditional sense of shame and the code of bravery were also diligently cultivated by the PSII, a small radical Islamic party. The competition between Permi and PSII contributed much to snowballing political radicalism in Minangkabau and to the creation of a social climate in which bold speakers were idolized. In spite of their competition and disagreements about Islam and nationalism, Permi and the PSII shared the view that active engagement in politics was the most effective way to achieve the greatness of Islam and the independence of Indonesia. Muchtar Lutfi attacked Muhammadijah for becoming increasingly anti-political, saying:

> One should not forget the teachings of religion that Islam not only recognizes politics but considers it as an obligation [for Muslims]. The first step by the Prophet was to take political power into his hands.[21]

The Muhammadijah attitude of standing aloof from politics, he said, demonstrated their misunderstanding of the character of Islamic doctrine as well as a lack of persistence in belief and in the determination to fulfill religious obligations.

Muhammadijah leaders realized that this interpretation was designed to make the question of politicizing Islam a purely religious issue. It was

---

20 "Keberanian dalam Barisan Kebangsaan," *Medan Rakjat*, 1, No. 10 (June 15, 1931).
21 From speeches given at the July conference. Politieke Politioneel Overzicht, July 1932, *Mailrapport* 952x/'32. See also, "Critiek dan Komentar: Kepada PSII, Pembela Islam, Moehammadijah dan JIB," *Pembela Islam*, 46 (1932), pp. 30-34.

no longer simply a matter of the proper strategy to achieve the common goal, that is, the realization of Islamic ideals. Although in principle the Muhammadijah did not object to participation by its members in politics, as an organization it was determined to maintain a purely educational and religious character. Muhammadijah leaders believed that their activities could eliminate the present social ills and backwardness and create a religiously based society. Its leaders, such as Sutan Mansjur, thought that, as social and religious reformers, their main concerns were not in the political field but rather in the area of moral reconstruction. They therefore rejected political activities as being an inappropriate method for dealing with these problems.[22] Muhammadijah would not give priority to the political solution, that is, independence.

In one of his speeches, Saalah Sutan Mangkuto stated:

The Muhammadijah wants to bring Muslims to the true teachings of Islam and to deepen the Islamic soul among them. The Muhammadijah walks on a straight path. It will never be diverted to the right or to the left, as is the case with other organizations, such as Permi, PSII and others.[23]

The "straight path" meant the continuing effort to create an ideal society, beginning with the "conquest of one's self." The irreligious social environment and immoral behavior, according to this view, originated from the state of man's inner self, rather than foreign political domination. "Our fate now," a local Muhammadijah leader said, "can be compared with a tree which is being attacked by parasites." The parasites are uncontrolled hawa nafsu (human desires) which weaken the ability of akal (intelligence) to perceive the right path. The major objective of the Muhammadijah is "to eliminate these parasites."[24] "Individual purification," then, was the immediate goal of the Muhammadijah. Compared with this goal, the struggle to overcome foreign domination, as advocated by the political parties, was relatively easy because it meant fighting the enemy one

---

22 Al [pseud.], "Pentingnja Politiek bagi Pergerakan," *Pembela Islam*, 42 (1932), pp. 6-8.
23 Politieke Politioneel Overzicht, July 1932, *Mailrapport* 952x/'32.
24 Politieke Politioneel Overzicht, May and June 1932, *Mailrapport* 774x/'32, 794x/'32.

already hated. One simply channeled one's hawa nafsu against a readily available object. But the Muhammadijah wanted to lead man to the only real and true victory, that over his own self and his own weakness.

In an angry attack on Permi, during the Regional Conference of Muhammadijah in March 1932, Sutan Mansjur said:

> Now everybody is demanding freedom. Everybody is saying "Indonesia Raja." They are all avowing that they believe in God. These [statements] are all frauds, lies. Father is blind, mother is blind and children cursed. These are now the inhabitants of Indonesia. How easy and how nice to demand freedom and to say that "Islam is great," "Islam is pure." These are all complete lies.[25]

How, he asked, could Islamic leaders demand political independence while they were neglecting their more essential roles as social and religious reformers? How could they say "Islam is great," when in fact they did not work for the creation of a true Islamic society? Prevailing social ills and moral degradation could be eradicated only by an intensification of religious conviction leading to the creation of a right-guided society. The Muhammadijah leader argued that through a complete affirmation of the Faith (*aqidah*), any ideal could be realized. Man was not guided merely by his akal or motivated by his nafsu; he was also directed by God. In line with this concept, the independence of Indonesia should not be seen as the way toward social reformation but rather a consequence of the realization of aqidah.[26] Given the creation of a right-guided society, Permi ideals, such as Islamic greatness or a prosperous Indonesia, could easily be realized.

For the sake of the Islamic ummat and the realization of aqidah, the Muhammadijah leaders stressed the importance of social harmony. In practice, they believed, social harmony required personal subjection to religion, adat and governmental laws. The study of leaders was to avoid potential clashes among these three valid laws.[27]

---

25 Politieke Politioneel Overzicht, March 1932, *Mailrapport* 492x/'32.
26 Interview with A. R. Sutan Mansjur, Djakarta, September 1968; Politieke Politioneel Overzicht, April and July 1932, *Mailrapport* 659x/'32, 952x/'32.
27 A local Muhammadijah leader said in a speech: "We should be loyal to the three valid systems of

Permi and PSII leaders argued that the realization of aqidah was impossible while the country was dominated by a colonial power and subjected to kafir laws. They saw the problem in a different perspective and used different logic. Consequently, they believed that social ills and moral decadence did not exist in a vacuum but were the direct results of an unhealthy political and economic environment. In a colonial society, they argued, there was no freedom to practice and develop religious morality. In a colonized country, religious leaders and scholars were forced to become "the instruments of the colonizers" and abandon their roles as the guides of the people. Colonial domination and suppression resulted in the weakening of people's "minds and bodies." Moral solutions, therefore, were far from sufficient, because there was no guarantee that the Muhammadijah plan of creating an ideal society through the "conquest of one's self" could in fact be carried out. As a result, political independence was "the only remedy for a country which cannot raise its voice to the sky."[28] Muchtar Lutfi argued:

> Islam is truly a religion of independence. Therefore, we, the Muslims, should not remain passive while Islam is under the control of hypocrites [*kaum munafik*].[29]

The controversies between the leaders of Muhammadijah and Permi became so heated that each even accused the other of being kafir. In 1932, Hadji A. Malik Karim Amrullah, a son of Hadji Rasul, returned from the National Congress of Muhammadijah in Makasar and condemned the political activities of Permi and the PSII as deviations from the correct religious path. He said the Permi practice of singing the national anthem "Indonesia Raja" after the Quranic recitation at the opening of its public meetings was bid'ah.[30]

---

law, namely, religion, adat and government. In ordinary life, these three cannot and should not be separated." Politieke Politioneel Over-zicht, 3de kwartaal, 1931, *Mailrapport* 1200x/'31. On the role of this concept in Minangkabau social relationships, see Nancy Tanner, "Disputing and Dispute Settlement among the Minangkabau of Indonesia," *Indonesia*, 8 (October 1969), pp. 21-67.

28 "Ke Indonesia Merdeka: Kewadjiban Bangsa dan Tanah Air," *Medan Rakjat*, 1, No. 13 (August 1931). In 1933, after its top leaders had been arrested, Permi said that the immediate objective for it and other radical parties was "national reconstruction," which could be carried out through political independence. *Medan Rakjat*, 3, No. 28 (October 1, 1933).

29 Politieke Politioneel Overzicht, May 1934, *Mailrapport* 774x/'34.

30 Ibid., June 1932, *Mailrapport* 794x/'32. Hamka's views about Islam and nationalism changed in

Although the Kaum Muda ulama supported Muhammadijah's position, they denounced in general the way the younger generation of Islamic leaders conducted their controversies. In late 1932, Hadji Rasul, who had been highly critical of the Permi idea of "Islam and kebangsaan," and Sjech Daud Rasjidi, whose son and nephews were leaders of Permi, held a meeting with Sutan Mansjur and Saalah Sutan Mangkuto (from Muhammadijah) and Muchtar Lutfi, Hadji Djalaluddin Thaib and Mansur Daud (from Permi). Speaking for the Kaum Muda ulama, they reproved the young leaders for "their childish behavior." This reprimand curbed the intensity of conflict and brought changes in the way the leaders conducted their arguments. Nevertheless, dissension among the Kaum Muda educated group was not completely healed until the early 1940's.[31]

Despite extensive divisions among the Kaum Muda educated intellectuals, they did share certain basic ideological princi-ples. They were all profoundly concerned with the present and the future course of Islam. They saw themselves as leaders, teachers and reformers of their society. Basing their social philosophy on Islam, the young Islamic modernist leaders wanted to eradicate social ills and establish social justice. The Muhammadijah, for example, not only founded schools but also organized the "Helpers of Public Suffering" which ran clinics and orphanages. Permi leaders pictured their party as "the champion of the common people," working "to attain a prosperous Indonesia."[32] Calling for "Islamic socialism," the PSII wanted to apply religious laws to economic activities, thus making capitalist exploitation impossible and furthering development of the national economy.

Ideas of socialism and social justice, whether based on Islam, Marxism, or the conception of the indigenous Indonesian village, were common

---

the late 1930's. He said that if nationalism were not taken as exclusivism and chauvinism, then it was not contradictory with Islam. As a result of this new view, Hamka came under attack from A. Hassan, leader of Persatuan Islam. At the time, Hamka was the editor of an influential Islamic journal, the *Pedoman Masjarakat*, published in Medan.

31 Interview with Mansur Daud Dt. Palimo Kajo, Bukittinggi, July 1968. Mansur Daud is the son of Sjech Daud. Both Hadji Djalaluddin and Muchtar Lutfi were nephews of Sjech Daud. All were students of Hadji Rasul, father-in-law of Sutan Mansjur. Duski Samad, outspoken Permi leader, was a younger brother of Sutan Mansjur. One could then see the conflict between the Muhammadijah and the Permi leadership as a "family tragedy."

32 "Indonesia Sentosa dengan Djalan Indonesia Merdeka," *Medan Rakjat*, 3, No. 28 (October 1933).

denominators in the independence movement. But divergent sources of inspiration and quarrels on the sub-stance of socialism and social justice created controversies in the nationalist movement. In the 1920's, these issues had led to a split in the SI and to a polarization within the Kaum Muda educated group in Minangkabau which prepared the way for an emergent communist movement. In the early 1930's, these issues re-emerged when Mohammad Hatta introduced the Pendidikan Nasional Indonesia (Indonesian National Education), known as the PNI Baru (New PNI). The spread of this secular nationalist party in Minangkabau posed a challenge to Permi and extended into West Sumatra the conflict between the Hatta-Sjahrir PNI Baru and Sukarno's Partindo, with which Permi had a very close relationship.

In late 1932, Hatta, who had just returned from Holland, came to West Sumatra to visit his relatives. He used this occasion to promote his party. In the course of this he introduced a new element into local political controversies. As part of his fiery revolutionary speeches and writings, Hatta stressed the urgent need for mature mental and organizational preparations. He said in one speech:

> Freedom is sure to come, although we do not know when. But our goal for freedom cannot be attained simply by using our knives in the face of [Dutch] rifles and guns.[33]

He appealed for a change in the style of social mobilization from mass rallies to intensified cadre formation. Because he had a reputation as a militant nationalist, this call had a profound impact on the Minangkabau popular movement. It was especially attractive for Muhammadijah leaders who saw the PNI Baru as a new and more acceptable forum for challenging Permi. Older leaders of the PMDS youth organization and even some former leaders of the Permi itself were attracted by Hatta's ideas. They became promoters of the PNI Baru. Hatta, himself the son of a prominent ulama, the sjech of Batu Hampar, recruited his followers from among the Kaum Muda educated group.

Hatta was expelled from the West Coast of Sumatra in November

---

33 Politieke Politioneel Overzicht, November 1932, *Mailrapport* 115x/'33.

1932,[34] but the PNI Baru remained and posed a new challenge to Permi. In the ideological realm, the PNI Baru represented a logical extension of the increasingly secular activities of Permi. The PNI Baru had been introduced by Hatta, whose religious devotion was well-known, and it emphasized complete religious freedom. Though party policy remained neutral toward religion, the leaders of the PNI Baru pointed out that individual members of the party were not therefore unconcerned about religion. But the obvious distinction between party policy and its members' views on religious matters became a major target for Permi criticism. Permi was quick to attack for it had been accused by others of having compromised its own religious beliefs for the sake of political expediency. On the question of nationalism or kebangsaan, Permi attacks on the PNI Baru only echoed the arguments of other Islamic parties. Concerning the PNI Baru's concept of democracy, Permi argued that such a state system might eventually precipitate a clash between Islamic and state law. A more basic ideological objection to the PNI Baru centered on its concept of collectivism." In the traditional Indonesian "collective" system, there was a division between property and labor. The PNI Baru, however, wanted to establish a new society where property and labor belonged to the community. Unlike the traditional system, the new one was based on the assumption that, in order to achieve the highest degree of productivity and social justice, communal property should not be divided among individuals. It should be exploited communally "under the leadership of consensus (mufakat)."[35] Collectivism would eliminate capitalism and imperialism and put the means of production into the hands of the state.

Collectivism as promoted by the PNI Baru was attacked by Permi for several reasons. It was called an affront against adat law and a repudiation of Islamic law, which recognized a clear division between communal and individual property.[36] Collectivism was hardly an attractive social program for Minang-kabau traders who believed in the virtue of individual enterprise. More than anything else, the issue of collectivism

---

34 Ibid.
35 Mohammad Hatta, "Collectivisme Tua dan Baru," *Kumpulan Karangan* (Djakarta: Balai Ilmu, 1953), I, pp. 90-96.
36 On the debates, see *Berita*, April 25, 1932, and *Seng Po*, April 11, 1932.

became the main ideological block preventing the spread of the PNI Baru in Minangkabau.[37]

Another aspect of the conflict between the PNI Baru and Permi was an extension to Sumatra of the debate between Hatta and Sjahrir on the one hand, and Sukarno, on the other. This debate centered particularly around questions of the tactics needed to achieve success of specific social and political strategies. Though agreeing on the strategic importance of mass action, mass parties and non-cooperation, Hatta and Sjahrir saw a more urgent need for social education and cadre formation. They believed that without a sufficient number of cadres and given a lack of political consciousness by the masses, the independence movement would have to depend upon only a few leaders. In this situation, they argued, how could the spirit of modern democracy be effectively introduced to the people?[38]

As part of an indirect attack on the PNI Baru, Permi emphasized its own democratic and revolutionary platform. Permi called itself a "revolutionary party" not because it wanted to "conduct illegal actions" but because "it wanted to see Indonesian independence as soon as possible." Permi based its struggle on the principles of "self-confidence" and "self-help" because it believed that "*machtsvorming*" (formation of power) and mass action were of prime importance. Since "mass action" could be formed only with the support of the people's spirit and the people's confidence, a major function of a political party should be to magnify and to direct the "people's deter-mination."[39] The Permi organ, *Medan Rakjat*, stated:

> The emergence of the [independence] movement was not the result of the leaders' instigation, it originated in the hearts of the people. In the beginning it was only an evolution of mind, finally it became a tremendous movement...

---

37 Bouman, *Enige Beschouwingen*, pp. 86-87.
38 On the controversies, see Bernhard Dahm, *Sukarno and the Struggle for Indonesian Independence*, trans. by Mary Somers Heidhues (Ithaca: Cornell University Press, 1969), pp. 127-173; and Sutan Sjahrir, *Pikiran dan Perdjoeangan* (Djakarta: Poestaka Rakjat, 1947), pp. 5-78.
39 "Tjoekoep Tiga Tahoen Berdjoeang," *Medan Rakjat*, 3, No. 16 (June 1933).

In this situation, the function of political leaders was only "to direct the flow of emotions and sentiments" and "to design the best and the shortest ways toward the realization of the ideals." Referring to government oppression, Permi pointed out that a movement which was organized by and from the people could never die—especially if it based its struggle upon a strong belief in God.[40]

This was the last political appeal made by Permi, for the same month, October 1933, its leaders were arrested. Shortly after publication of this issue, *Medan Rakjat* was confiscated and its operations suspended. Ideological controversies among political leaders of the various parties and organizations and their attempts to implement political strategies were temporarily ended by government suppression.

Concluding Thoughts

The ideological controversies occurred during a period of intense political activity, the expansion of private schools and the modernization of religious schools. The visit and the return of perantau intellectuals from Java, Holland and Cairo, started a more intensive search for a suitable ideology among the Islamic modernists. This search was intensified by the desire of the Cairo returnees to play an important role in the national politics of independence and by the increasing flow of political ideas brought by the perantau intellectuals from Java. The two currents of ideas increased anti-government political activities and at the same time deepened dissension among the leaders of the Kaum Muda educated group.

Permi's Islamic nationalism, symbolized by the slogan "Islam and kebangsaan," and the notion of political activism, conceived as the way toward the attainment of Indonesian independence, were the most crucial issues in the political debates. Although the philosophical foundation of Permi's Islamic nationalism did not markedly differ from the ideas advanced by the PSII or other Islamic organizations, Permi openly acknowledged the importance of nationalist aspirations. In doing so, it completely rejected the feasibility and even the legitimacy of

---

40 "Revoloesi dan Gerakan Revoloetioner," *Medan Rakjat*, 3, No. 28 (October 1933).

Pan-Islamism, an ideal still cherished by orthodox Muslim leaders. The opposition to Permi was partly a reaction against its readiness to deal directly with political reality and abandon the notions of a Utopian society which had characterized the early Islamic modernists. In Minangkabau itself, however, the appeal for kebangsaan combined with Islam found followers among the politically oriented Kaum Muda educated group. The appeal for Indonesian unity in Minangkabau, which traditionally con-ceived itself as an open yet clearly defined world, suggested not only awareness of a common fate and destiny with other ethnic groups but also of the threat posed by the centripetal character of the traditional alam. It was on the latter problem that the Minangkabau character of the Permi can be clearly seen. Permi leaders, and other political leaders as well, urged the absorption of Minangkabau into Indonesia, but at the same time they tried to demonstrate the central position of the alam Minangkabau in this new and enlarged world. Permi ideology tried to find a compromise with contesting ideas and to harmonize a modern political appeal with the traditional conception of the Minangkabau world. This was partly responsible for its failure to attract orthodox Muslim leaders and to become a "national catalyst." But, on the other hand, these two factors were responsible for Permi's success in becoming the largest party in Sumatra. The weaknesses in its ideological formulation proved to be assets instead of obstacles in the party's development .

Controversy between Islamic political parties, such as the Permi and the PSII, on the one hand, and the Muhammadijah, on the other, were part of the more general tensions in Islamic thought "between ideal and actuality, the spiritual and the temporal, virtue and power."[41] The Muhammadij ah leaders and the Kaum Muda ulama were more concerned with the creation of an ideal religiously based society. Instead of dealing with the question of immediate power, they worried about conceptualizing Ultimate Power. Although Permi and the PSII leaders also believed that their struggles could not be separated from their religious duties, they preferred to face the actuality instead of the ideal, that is, power instead of virtue. In spite of the commonly acknowledged idea that ultimate power resided in the hands of God the Creator, the main

---

41 Kerr, *Islamic Reform*, p. 1.

concern of these political leaders was to confront the immediate holder of power, the colonial government. Tension between political (or temporal) and moral solutions was also evident in the career and teaching of the early protagonists of Islamic modernism. The Kaum Muda intellectuals brought to the surface the inner tension of Islamic modernist ideas.

In a time of crisis, this inherent ideological tension could become an impressive force, in which Utopian aspirations and immediate political concerns found a common front. The consequences of the inner tension became obvious when the crisis had passed and Islamic leaders were forced to deal with the problem of reconciling this dualism. But in the 1930's and throughout the colonial period generally, anti-government actions could still serve as the means of escape from the difficult task of solving such problems.

CHAPTER EIGHT
THE POLITICS OF RADICALISM

The period from early 1931 until the middle of 1933 formed the high watermark in the Indonesian independence movement. Radical political parties dominated the popular movements, and they influenced not only the non-cooperative but also the cooperative parties. Disillusionment with the government began to appear in those circles which had once maintained a "good faith in the colonial government."[1] Indonesian members in the Volks-raad became increasingly critical about the government's handling of the nationalist political parties.[2]

Anti-government activities intensified at the end of 1932 and in early 1933, as the divergent Indonesian political and educational organizations mounted their opposition to the "Wild Schools Ordinance," considered a direct assault on nationalist educational development. The climax of anti-government action was a mutiny by the Indonesian crew of the Dutch warship *Zeven Provinciën*. The government retaliated by sinking the ship. This senseless punitive action exacerbated political tension in Indonesia as well as in Holland, and the government was forced to re-examine the ethical basis of its colonial policy. "It has proved," said the leader of the nationalist group in the Volksraad, "that the Christian government is godless."[3]

---

1 Hatta, "Tudjuan dan Politik Pergerakan Kebangsaan di Indonesia (1930)," *Kumpulan Karangan*, I, pp. 26-57.
2 B. J. Brouwer, *De Houding van Idenburg en Colijn Tegenover de Indonesische Beweging* (Kampen: J. H. Kok, 1958), pp. 172-173.
3 *Handelingen van den Volksraad* (Batavia: n.p., 1932-1933), p. 2775. A leftist account of the mutiny is contained in, M. Sapija, *Sedjarah Pemberontakan di Kapal Tudjuh (Zeven Provinciën)* (Djakarta: n.p., 1960). The government account is contained in, S. L. van der Wal (ed.), *Herinneringen van Jhr. Mr. B. C. de Jonge: Met Brieven uit Zijn Nalatenschap* (Groningen: Wolters-Noordhoff, 1968), pp. 16-170.

The worsening of relations between the government and the nationalists was aggravated by the economic depression and the growing influence of reactionary elements within the Dutch administration. In September 1931, de Graeff, a liberal and paternalistic Governor-General, was succeeded by de Jonge, formerly director of a Dutch oil company. Although unfamiliar with Indonesian affairs, he was determined to use "practical politics" in dealing with economic and political problems. "Political make-believe," he stated in his inaugural speech, "which can be applied in a time of prosperity, is useless now; it is not what is desirable but rather what is possible that must now prevail."[4] True to his words, the new Governor-General instituted a retrenchment policy and liberally used his extraordinary powers to prosecute nationalist leaders. His motto was: "Live first, politics later."[5] De Jonge was a good choice to work under Colijn, then Minister of Colonies and a man who believed that Dutch power in the Netherlands Indies was as "firmly rooted as Mont Blanc in the Alps."[6] And he was determined to prove it. Before coming to power, Colijn had suggested that educational programs should be reduced because they had dangerous results. During his tenure of office, an important aspect of the retrenchment policy was a reduction in the program of government and subsidized school networks.

One of the most significant results of the change in Governors-General was a decline in the influence exercized by the Office for Native Affairs. The Attorney-General now had the decisive voice, which gave local authorities a freer hand in dealing with political problems. Central government sanctions against the use of an "iron hand" policy were removed. The Attorney-General, according to a former controleur, was always "in agreement with the Resident."[7] Under such circumstances, relations between the local administration and the popular movement in West Sumatra became increasingly difficult and strained.

Minangkabau continued as one of the most politicized regions in Indonesia. Led by Kaum Muda educated intellectuals, the political

---

4 van der Wal, *Herinneringen*, p. 91.
5 Cited in Brouwer, *Houding van Idenburg*, p. 172.
6 H. Colijn, *Koloniale Vraagstukken van Heden en Morgen* (Amsterdam: Drukkerij de Standard, 1928), p.39.
7 van der Meulen, *Ik Stond er Bij*, p. 111.

parties and social-educational organizations intensified their activities. They fostered people's industries, expanded private schools, both religious and secular, and modernized existing religious schools. It was characteristic of the early 1930's that religio-political publications, such as newspapers, journals and booklets, sprang up all over, public gatherings were held everywhere, and youth organizations proliferated. The spirit of independence was gaining momentum, and Minangkabau political parties, particularly Permi, began trying to influence the direction of popular movements throughout Indonesia. This was the final stage in the process. In the 1920's, the Communist Party in West Sumatra acted on the instruction of its central board in Java. Next came the Muhammadijah whose leaders had promoted their organization, which came from Java, by claiming it had the *tjap Minangkabau*, "Minangkabau style." Now Permi wanted to introduce its own version of the "Minangka-bau style" into Java itself as well as other parts of Sumatra. It hoped to solve the conflict between the Islamic and the kebangsaan group everywhere.

During this period, however, the Kaum Muda educated group also experienced its worst internal split since the earlier communist crisis. Political activities and questions of Islam and nationalism alienated the Kaum Muda ulama from their former students, who saw themselves as social reformers. But the same issues also caused a split between the Kaum Tua ulama and their younger assistants and students, whose training had stressed obedience to established religious authorities in general and one's teachers in particular.

During the economic depression, the numerous political and educational organizations sought new ways to finance their activities. Permi and the Muhammadijah ran small enterprises, producing cigarettes, cooking oil and soap, as well as consumer cooperatives. Both organizations strongly encouraged their affiliated organizations to develop their own cooperatives and schools.[8] A new method of collecting money was through sponsorship of soccer matches. Several private schools in Pajakumbuh and Padang, for example, were partially financed this way.[9]

---

8 *Berita*, September 3, 1932; Politieke Politioneel Overzicht, 3de kwartaal, 1931, *Mailrapport* 1200x/'31; *ibid.*, August 1932, *Mailrapport* 1017x/'32.
9 *Ibid.*, 4de kwartaal, 1930, *Mailrapport* 228x/'31.

During the period from January 1931 to July 1932 Permi changed rapidly from a politically oriented educational and economic organization to a radical nationalist political party. After the so-called "political education" phase, from November 1931 until July 1932, Permi proclaimed itself a "radical and non-cooperative" party. Prior to July, Permi had been actively engaged in realizing the educational programs of the former Sumatra Thawalib Union, such as establishing a standard school curriculum and improving the religious schools. As part of its extra-curricular activities, Permi had quickly developed its boy scout organization, El-Hilaal, into the largest in West Sumatra. After the official transformation of Permi into a political party, the boy scouts became an independent organization. From July 1932 to April 1933, Permi expanded into the largest and the most radical political party in Sumatra. It began preparations for expansion to Java after it already had branches scattered throughout Minangkabau and other parts of Sumatra. The extent of its influence was demonstrated in November 1932, when the organization of Kaum Tua schools, the PTI, changed its name to Pendidikan Islam Indonesia (Islamic Indonesian Education) and adopted Permi's slogan "Islam and kebangsaan" as its ideological foundation.

After the release of Datuk Singo Mangkuto from prison in April 1931, the PSII staged a robust comeback. At first, until November 1931, it attempted unsuccessfully to establish a kind of federation with Permi, after which the two parties became strong competitors. The PSII was particularly successful in rural areas in the districts of Manindjau, Agam Tua and Suliki. Manindjau was the site of its earliest branch and acted as the center of activities of the party's most important leaders, Datuk Singo Mangkuto, Hadji Uddin Rahmany and Sabilal Rasad. In Agam Tua, the party had been organized by perantau traders from Java. The PSII emerged as the first radical party in Kamang, a nagari which had been consistently and strongly anti-government since the anti-tax rebellion of 1908. In the district of Suliki, one of the strongest bases of the communist movement in the mid-1920's, the PSII branch was founded by local graduates of Sumatra Thawalib at Padang Pandjang. In November 1932, Minangkabau political life became even more complicated when the PNI Baru established branches in several towns, among them, Padang, Padang Pandjang, Bukittinggi and Pajakumbuh. In June 1933, branches of Sukarno's Partindo were formed with indirect

Permi support. By this time, however, the central government and the local administration were increasing their repressive attitude toward local organizations.

By the end of 1933, several important leaders had already suffered from the "extraordinary powers" of the Governor-General. A large number of the second echelon leaders were punished under the terms of highly flexible provisions concerning seditious speech or writing.

Participation in National Politics

In January 1931, Hadji Djalaluddin Thaib became first vice-chairman of the newly-established Permi. An experienced teacher, productive writer and owner of a small printing house, Hadji Djalaluddin proved the best organizer Permi ever had. In March, the organizational hierarchy was improved further by the formation of a Daily Executive Board to direct and coordinate its day-to-day activities. The leadership of this body consisted of Hadji Abdul Madjid, Djalaluddin Thaib, Iljas Jacub, Mansur Daud and H. Sjuib el-Jutusi,[10] and, under their direction, Permi was soon on its way toward becoming a radical party. Except for Hadji Abdul Madjid, a moderate Kaum Tua ulama and political leader, the members of the executive body were strongly inclined toward political activism. Muchtar Lutfi returned from Cairo in May, and after a time, he joined his cousins, Mansur Daud and Djalaluddin, and his friend, Iljas Jacub, in the leadership of Permi. By the middle of 1931, the so-called "political trio" of Djalaluddin the organizer, Iljas the ideologue and Muchtar the orator was complete.[11] But, by this time, the relationship between Permi and the Kaum Muda ulama had been severed. Sjech Ibrahim Musa of Parabek prohibited his students and assistants from joining Permi, and Sjech Abbas of Padang Pandjang renamed his school the Darulfunun Abbasiah in order to emphasize his distaste for the now "corrupted" Sumatra Thawalib.[12]

---

10 H. Sjuib el-Jutusi was a leader of the Padang Pandjang Thawalib. Already in 1922, he had strongly urged direct participation by his students in anti-government political action.
11 After January 1932, Hadji Abdul Madjid, the chairman, gradually lost his influence among the younger Permi leaders. Although he continued as chairman, in practice Hadji Djalaluddin Thaib functioned as the real director. Gonggrijp, "Memorie van Overgave," p. 61.
12 Politieke Politioneel Overzicht, 2de kwartaal, 1931, *Mailrapport* 808x/'31.

Permi began the new year with a determination to circulate its ideas about Islam and nationalism more extensively. It also clearly displayed its anti-colonial attitudes in several minor incidents. For example, Permi refused to hoist the Dutch flag during a religious celebration, and on another occasion ignored a government regulation to close its schools in honor of the Dutch Queen's birthday. It expressed an economic nationalism by a fairly successful effort to mobilize a boycott among Padang merchants against Italian imports after Mussolini's invasion of Libya.[13]

Of more immediate concern for Permi, and other organizations as well, was the depression, especially given the number of petty traders in the party. The issue was the main item on the agendy of the Second Permi Congress. Its goals were outlined as: "to save society from the effects of the depression and to seek ways for progress and welfare."[14] The congress was held in Padang from October 24 to November 1, 1931, and attended by representatives of the 50 Permi groups. It was extremely nationalist in character. The meeting hall was decorated with pictures of Indonesian and other Asian nationalist leaders. Refreshments were advertised as "Made in Indonesia." The congress participants wore national costume. The main theme of the speeches was the appeal for the application in Indonesia of the Gandhian *swadeshi*.[15] The most important results of the congress were a plan to expand Permi outside West Sumatra and a decision to encourage "political education." Permi was still officially an educational and economic organization.[16] At the suggestion of Muchtar Lutfi, the congress tabled the question of a possible fusion with the PSII.[17]

In January 1932, Permi took its first step toward involvement in the national independence movement; it sent a delegation to the Indonesia

---

13 *Moestika*, October 1931; *Pompai*, August 1931.
14 *Pompai*, October 15, 1931.
15 Gonggrijp, "Memorie van Overgave," pp. 60-61.
16 Debate on the formal transformation to a purely political party caused a heated exchange between the "moderates" and the "radicals." The proposal was defeated 50 to 20, but the radicals managed to achieve a compromise whereby the congress appointed a committee to study the politicization of Permi. Muchtar Lutfi and Iljas Jacub were members. In the end, the committee proposed that Permi avoid direct involvement but continue to observe and educate its members in politics. Gonggrijp, "Memorie van Overgave," p. 62.
17 Hadji Abdul Madjid was chairman of Permi and adviser of the PSII. He tried very hard to achieve a fusion of the two organizations, but his influence over Permi was waning. Report of the Provincial Bureau of Investigation, July 17, 1933, *Mailrapport* 934x/'33.

Raja Congress sponsored by PPPKI in Surabaja. The congress failed to achieve its main objectives—reunification of Partindo and the PNI Baru and reconciliation of Islamic and "secular" nationalist groups—but Permi delegates, Djala-luddin Thaib and Basa Bandaro, used the opportunity to establish cordial relations with Sukarno. They also managed to come to a better understanding with Dr. Sutomo, the chairman of the congress and the leader of the Nationalist Club of Surabaja, who had been on generally bad terms with the Islamic parties.[18] Although Permi did not join the federation, it used its participation in the Indonesia Raja Congress as a propaganda theme in West Sumatra. Permi wanted to resolve the conflict between the Islamic and the kebangsaan parties and feared that by joining the PPPKI it would become suspect in the eyes of both the Islamic parties and the radical secular parties.[19] During the congress, however, Permi delegates apparently reached an understanding with Partindo leaders whereby the former agreed not to block the expansion of the latter to West Sumatra.[20]

In February 1932, two Minangkabau Partindo leaders from Pekalongan came to West Sumatra to reinvigorate the party's effort to expand its influence in Minangkabau. It was the second such attempt. In October 1931, shortly before the Permi congress, several perantau from Java had tried to form Partindo branches but had failed because of effective Permi counter-propaganda.[21] Although Permi withheld its hand during the second attempt, the Partindo promoters failed again. By this time, the

---

[18] Noer, "Rise and Development," pp. 408-410. An attack by Sutomo on Hadji Agus Salim aroused some apprehension in non-Javanese secular nationalist circles, especially as it was supported by another Javanese leader. This and similar incidents provoked Dr. Abdul Rivai, an early nationalist leader, to announce: "There is no such thing as Indonesian nationalism,' for what is now being practiced is only 'Javanese nationalism.'" This statement from such a prominent figure created an uproar in the nationalist movement. Parada Harahap, *Riwajat Dr. A. Rivai* (Medan: n.p., 1939), pp. 144-157. An Islamic nationalist intellectual called Rivai's assessment "too frank." Is, "Indonesisch Nation-alisme," *Pembela Islam*, 36 (October 1931), pp. 14-17.
[19] On his return, Thaib wrote a booklet entitled *Peringatan Nasional* in which he said that the PPPKI would eventually succeed in achieving its objective, that is,unification of all nationalist parties. But he thought that Permi needed time to expand and develop itself first and to study the federation more closely. Cited in Politieke Politioneel Overzicht, January 1932, *Mailrapport* 335x/'32. Thaib's caution was understandable since as yet no Islamic organization had joined the federation. Moreover the PSI left it in December 1930. L. M. Sitorus, *Sedjarah Pergerakan Kebangsaan Indonesia* (Djakarta: Pustaka Rakjat, 1951), p. 56.
[20] Politieke Politioneel Overzicht, July 1932, *Mailrapport* 952x/'32.
[21] *Ibid.*, 4de kwartaal, 1931, *Mailrapport* 236x/'32.

urban political movement was already under the influence of Permi and the rural areas were caught up in the competition between Permi and the PSII. The secular character of the Partindo, moreover, proved a major stumbling block barring its expansion in Minangkabau.

After a month of fruitless campaigning, the Partindo promoters shifted their tactics and tried to attract Permi into a merger. On March 25, in a meeting with the members of the Permi executive board, the Partindo promoters pointed to ideological similarities between the two parties. But, they argued that, by using Islam as its ideological foundation, Permi excluded the non-Muslim minorities. The Partindo promoters asserted that religion was no longer a suitable ideology given the nature of modern politics; they invited Permi to merge with the Partindo.[22] Although the Permi leaders agreed to bring the problem before their congress, the Partindo promoters realized that most of the Permi leaders strongly opposed the proposal. Anticipating an eventual rejection by Permi, the Partindo promoters offered another proposal. In view of the fact that Permi was active in social and educational fields as well as politics, they suggested the organization be divided into two parts. The first part could be a purely Islamic educational organization and the second a secular nationalist political party which could either merge or federate with Partindo. The Islamic part might then join the Muhammadijah or the PSII if it too wanted to participate in politics.[23] This proposal in effect meant nothing less than the elimination of Permi, and it seriously threatened relations between Permi and Partindo. Muchtar Lutfi and other leaders felt that the Partindo people were purposely ridiculing the ideas propagated by Permi and its intention to act as a "national catalyst." They considered the Partindo proposal clear proof that the Java-based party had a low opinion of Permi. As a reaction to the incident, Permi intensified its campaign emphasizing the vital importance of religion in the nationalist movement.

In an effort to end the friction, Permi adviser Basa Bandaro decided to go to Java and meet with the Partindo central executive board. He managed to convince Partindo leaders to come to West Sumatra and

---

22 *Ibid.*, July 1932, *Mailrapport* 952x/'32.
23 *Ibid.*, August 1932, *Mailrapport* 659x/'32.

campaign for Permi. Both sides agreed that each party would refrain from campaigns in the other's sphere of influence—Permi would not form branches in Java and the Partindo would not open more branches in Sumatra.[24] The agreement was reaffirmed by two Partindo leaders at a special Permi conference in July 1932. The agreement remained in effect until June 1933, when three small branches of the Partindo were organized with the approval of Djalaluddin Thaib after discussions with Sukarno.[25] Permi by then had begun preparations for its own expansion to Java.

Shortly after the July 1932 conference, Permi organized branches in several areas of Sumatra. In August, Duski Samad, a member of the central board, assisted by local Minangkabau traders, formed branches in Benkulen[26] and in South Sumatra.[27] In the same month, Mansur Daud and H. Sjuib el-Jutusi organized Permi branches in Atjeh and in East Sumatra. Several branches were also begun in South Tapanuli.

In order to strengthen its relationship with the nationalist movement in Java, particularly with the PPPKI and the Partindo (now led by Sukarno), Permi sent Muchtar Lutfi to Java in September. For about a month, he was a guest of Partindo and participated in various of its public meetings. His activities and speeches on Islam and kebangsaan, though harshly attacked by the Persatuan Islam and other Muslim organizations, made Permi widely known in nationalist political circles on Java.[28] In October, Permi appointed Abdul Gaffar Ismail as its representative in Java and authorized him to participate in political activities and establish contact with other nationalist parties.

In its competition locally with the PSII and the Muhammadi-jah, Permi had an advantage because its central board was in West Sumatra rather than Java. It could show the Minangkabau people that it had the potential to make Minangkabau a leader in the nationalist movement. The question of the role of Minangkabau in the national sphere continued

---

24 van Heuven, "Memorie van Overgave," p. 24; Tamar Djaja, "Islam di Indonesia."
25 Hadji Djalaluddin Thaib had gone to Java to discuss joint opposition to the Wild Schools Ordinance. Politieke Poli-tioneel Overzicht, February 1933, *Mailrapport* 590x/'33.
26 Concerning the Permi in Bengkulen, see G. F. Pijper, *Fragmenta Islamica: Studien over het Islamisme in Neder-landsch-Indië* (Leiden: E. J. Brill, 1934), pp. 177-182.
27 Politieke Politioneel Overzicht, September 1932, *Mailrapport* 1159x/'32.
28 van Heuven, "Memorie van Overgave," p. 24; Report of the Provincial Bureau of Investigation, July 17, 1933, *Mailrapport* 934x/'33.

to be important. Muhammadijah successfully began its activities in Minangkabau before 1931 when it was still relatively free from the direct control of its Central Board in Java. It was protected by Central Board intervention on its behalf with the Office for Native Affairs, but its real appeal in Minangkabau stemmed from a claim that it was not a mere copy of some Javanese organization.

The radical PSII relied heavily on the fiery anti-colonial speeches of its leaders in its competition with Permi. But party leaders realized that they needed more freedom from the PSII central board because merely adopting a "Minangkabau style" proved inadequate. As long as the PSII in West Sumatra served only as a "regional representative" for the central board in Java, the party leaders felt the urban Minangkabau would consider it no more than a mouthpiece for Java. Shortly after the party's regional conference in April 1932, a move began to change this situation. Several local leaders urged the regional chairman, Datuk Singo Mangkuto, to seek approval from the central board for the transformation of the West Sumatra group into a semi-autonomous organization. They wanted to reorganize the local branches into a Perserikatan PSII Minangkabau (Union of Minangkabau PSII). By so doing, they thought the PSII in Minangkabau could design its own activities in accordance with the local environment and its specific problems. The central board, however, feared this would cause further dismemberment of the party and rejected the proposal, though Datuk Singo Mangkuto was reaffirmed as regional chairman.[29] As a result of this rejection, however, Datuk Singo Mangkuto began to lose ground in his competition for leadership with Hadji Uddin Rahmany and Sabilal Rasad.

The PNI Baru in West Sumatra experienced a similar development. Since the establishment of its branches in November 1932, the party had been under attack by Permi, the PSII and other Muslim organizations. Its concept of "collectivism" was denounced as being anti-Islamic and its neutral stand on religion was condemned as a threat to Islam. The local leaders of the PNI Baru, mostly from the Kaum Muda educated group, found themselves in ideological difficulty. They wanted to lessen the ideological control exercised by the central board in Java. In June

---

29 Politieke Politioneel Overzicht, December 1932, *Mailrapport* 227x/'33.

1933, at the preparatory meeting for a forthcoming national congress, the Minangkabau leaders decided to propose to the congress that, in matters of religion and adat, the regional board should be given complete authority. Furthermore, in accordance with the structure of other Minangkabau Islamic organizations, they would propose the formation of a women's section for the party.[30] The national congress was never held, however, because a few months later several party leaders, including Hatta and Sjahrir, were arrested.

After the campaign against the Wild Schools Ordinance, which reached its climax in December 1932, Permi began seeking an opportunity to transfer its own central board to Java to evade the increased pressure being exerted by the government in West Sumatra. In July 1933, the Permi representative in Java, A. Gaffar Ismail, and leaders of a new Islamic party, the Partai Islam Indonesia (Parii, Indonesian Islamic Party), discussed the possibility of a merger. The Parii was a splinter of the PSII and was led by a former PSII leader. Its program stressed the harmonious development and independence of Indonesia on the basis of Islam.[31] The First Parii Congress resolved to carry out the merger.[32] Some nationalist leaders hailed the move as the beginning of a "new climate inpolitical life in Indonesia."[33] The fusion of the two Islamic nationalist parties, it was hoped, might eventually lead to a federation with the Partindo, a close Permi associate. The prospect seemed bright for fulfilling Permi's objective of becoming a "national catalyst."

The dreams of a "new climate" in Indonesian political life were soon shattered by government action. In August the government cracked down on Permi and imposed severe restrictions on party activities. This was soon followed by the arrest of its top leaders. The Partindo experienced a similar fate with the arrest of Sukarno.

Education in Politics

In January 1933, about 11,000 Minangkabau, 30% of whom were women,

---

30 *Ibid.*, June 1933, *Mailrapport* 1011x/'33.
31 *Oetoesan Indonesia*, May 19, 1933 in *Overzicht van de Inlandsche Pers*, 1933, pp. 327-328.
32 Politieke Politioneel Overzicht, September 1932, *Mailrapport* 1369x/'33.
33 *Sikap*, July 8, 1933 in *Overzicht van de Inlandsche Pers*, 28/1933, p. 442.

were registered as active members of Permi, the PSII or the PNI Baru. These parties had branches or groups in over 20% of the 500 nagari and in every town. Permi alone had more than 160 groups. In the rural areas of Suliki, Manindjau and Agam Tua, Permi had to compete with the PSII, which, despite continuing internal dissension, had over 2,000 members.[34] When the government began to crack down on the activities of the political parties in August 1933, there were more than 13,000 registered active members in the various parties. Permi had expanded to over 200 groups in 180 nagari and claimed more than 10,000 members, 40% of whom were women. The party's major strongholds were the districts of Manindjau and Agam Tua where it had groups in almost every nagari.

Table 2
Permi Groups in Rural Areas

Sub-Regencies	Number of Nagari	Number of Groups
Padang	3	4
Pariaman	20	29
Batu Sangkar	9	11
Padang Pandjang	15	25
Agam Tua	19	38
Manindjau	14	14
Ophir	1	1
Pajakumbuh	11	14
Suliki (only in the sub-district of Guguk)	3	13
Bangkinang	1	1
Solok	4	4
Muara Labuh	1	1
Painan	11	21
Kerintji	4	5

Source: van Heuven, "Memorie," p. 28.

---

[34] van Heuven, "Memorie van Overgave"; Politieke Politioneel Overzicht, January 1933, *Mailrapport* 351x/'33.

In the same period, the PSII had about 2,800 registered members, of whom 600 were women. The PNI Baru and the Partindo, which were still in the early stages of their development, had about 250 and 100 respectively. Their branches were located only in the towns.

The extent of the influence which political parties exercised cannot be properly assessed through these figures. Most of the local party leaders were respected members of their communities. Large numbers of them had graduated from the Kaum Muda schools and were muballigh or teachers in local religious schools. Their superior education and respected positions strengthened the influence of these leaders so that it extended beyond the members of their respective parties. Furthermore, the figures do not include the youth movements which were to a large extent inseparable from the political parties. By January 1933, the Kaum Tua organization had also been politicized and the Kaum Muda Muhammadijah, despite its official strongly anti-political attitude, was being increasingly infiltrated by the radical elements.

The ability of political parties to create a social climate which idolized radical, anti-government leaders and idealized the notion of political independence contributed to a temporary withdrawal by the adat authorities. Moreover, some of the top leaders of the political parties were themselves penghulu. Hadji Djalaluddin Thaib and Mansur Daud, the chairman and secretary of Permi, were both penghulu of Balingka. Except for Hadji Uddin Rahmany and a woman leader, the wife of Datuk Singo Mang-kuto, all members of the PSII regional board were also penghulu. The parties, particularly Permi, encouraged members who had the right to become penghulu to retain their penghuluships. In several nagari, the majority of the penghulu joined political parties. By the end of 1932, for example, government reports indicated that 50 out of the 63 penghulu in Aur Perumahan (Agam Tua) were registered members or sympathizers of the PSII.[35] In Ampat Angkat, PSII outnumbered SAAM, the oldest adat party, not only in terms of the general populace but in the number of penghulu members. Adat parties had tended to decline generally. In the face of rising government repression in several nagari, such as Situdjuh and Batu Hampar (both in the Regency of Lima Puluh Kota), penghulu

---

35 *Ibid.*, August 1933, *Mailrapport* 1017x/'33.

who belonged to Permi began organizing new adat associations. These politically oriented penghulu wanted to extend party influence and also reduce the tension between the adat authorities and the political parties generally.

Although the extent of penghulu participation in the nationalist political parties greatly varied from nagari to nagari, it was a reflection of the continuing growth in the prestige of leaders of modern organizations at the expense of the penghulu's traditional position. It also showed the influence of political and economic changes on the attitudes of the rural adat chiefs. The involvement of the penghulu reflected their awareness of the people's needs, also shown in their active support of the various village educational and mutual help organizations. This explains why, in places such as Padang Djapang, the penghulu tried to organize forums where they could discuss the social and political problems they faced as the natural and traditional leaders of the people.[36] Such forums were intended to minimize the gulf between the people, who were increasingly influenced by the religious political parties, and the adat authorities, who were the traditional maintainers of social order and harmony.

The consequences of the penghulu's participation in the anti-government political movement became evident when the local administration began to mobilize adat authorities against the political parties. In some places a kind of "intra-elite" conflict broke out; in others hostility between the non-political penghulu in one nagari and the nationalist penghulu from other nagari was sharpened. The nationalist penghulu, however, helped maintain political moderation in Minangkabau. In the beginning of 1933, they established the Dewan Penghulu Minangkabau (Council of Penghulu of Minangkabau) in Padang Pandjang. The Council represented the first attempt since the communist rebellion to unite the penghulu. The top leaders of the Council were without exception already members of Permi, the PSII or Muhammadijah. The membership included penghulu from several districts. The Council had been organized by urbanized and politically oriented penghulu and became a temporary sanctuary for nationalist penghulu during the government repression.[37]

---

36 *Ibid.*, June 1932, *Mailrapport* 794x/'32.
37 Roesad, "Nota: Het Modernisme in Penghoeloe-Kringen," in van Heuven, "Memorie van Overgave," pp. 73-88.

As with the young, urbanized penghulu, the Kaum Tua group was also influenced by the nationalist Islamic modernists. The politicization of Minangkabau under the "Greater Indonesia" and Islamic appeals brought with it the demise of the Kaum Tua organization, the PTI. The PTI had been established with official encouragement in an effort to unite the Kaum Tua schools against the influence of the Kaum Muda organizations. Ironically, however, the PTI was captured by the Islamic nationalist movement under Permi. Permi infiltration began in Manindjau, the most radical district, with the Kaum Tua students' organization. Competition between the Permi and the PSII, and the great influence exercised by Hadji Rasul, had caused heightened anti-government feeling in the area. As a result, Permi ideas easily penetrated the Kaum Tua organization. Moreover, Hadji Abdul Madjid, the first chairman of Permi, was an influential Kaum Tua ulama from Manindjau. In March 1932, the PTI, under the leadership of its founder, Sjech Sulaiman Arrasuli, held a conference in Manindjau to make plans for the Second PTI Congress. The Manindjau PTI leaders wanted the conference to add the word "Indonesia" to the organization's name. The chairman of one local branch urged cooperation with the PSII because, according to him, there was no difference in the principles and the goals of the two organizations. A vice-chairman of another local branch began a speech with the Permi slogan "Islam and kebangsaan."[38]

In September 1932, the Persatuan Murid-Murid Tarbijah Islamijah (Union of Students of Tarbijah Islamijah Schools) celebrated its first anniversary. At the celebration the students decided that their organization should be based on four principles: "submission to Allah, love of tanah air, love of the people, and dedication to religion and the nation."[39] These four principles were in fact a revised version of the ideological foundation of a Permi-influenced Kaum Muda youth organization.

The incipient "revolt" within the PTI came to the surface at its second congress held in Pajakumbuh in November 1932. For the first time, the PTI opened the meeting by singing the national anthem, "Indonesia

---

38 Politieke Politioneel Overzicht, March 1932, *Mailrapport* 492x/'32. The Resident noted that the Kaum Tua organization in the Danau and Pajakumbuh districts, as well as some others, participated in the activities of Kaum Muda organizations. *Ibid.*, February 1932, *Mailrapport* 415x/'32.
39 *Ibid.*, September 1932, *Mailrapport* 1159x/'32.

Raja." Iljas Jacub of Permi was the guest speaker. During the meeting a young leader of the PTI announced support for Iljas Jacub's appeals by boldly stating:

> The PTI stands in the middle of the people. It is struggling toward the achievement of "the greatness of Islam," "Islam in Honor" and a "Prosperous Indonesia" on the basis of "Islam and kebangsaan."

In defiance of its founders, the Kaum Tua ulama, the PTI Congress, in an intensely nationalist mood, decided to alter the name of the organization to Pendidikan Islam Indonesia (PII, Islamic Indonesian Education) and to adopt Permi's "Islam and kebangsaan" as its official ideology. The congress elected a new central board consisting exclusively of young leaders. The Kaum Tua ulama were elected to the prestigious but powerless advisory board.[40] The young PTI leaders had avoided the fate which had befallen the Muhammadijah, whose older ulama with the cooperation of the Central Board had overpowered the young and politically oriented leaders. Under the influence of Permi, the younger PTI leadership, all of whom were teachers in Kaum Tua schools, managed to defeat their teachers, the PTI founders.

Success at the congress, however, did not guarantee that the membership would remain faithful to the new group. Prominent Kaum Tua ulama, embittered by the betrayal of their assistants and prodded by criticism from the Dutch local administration for their failure to maintain control,[41] refused to accept the changes or work for the new organization. The PII could not continue without the support of the Kaum Tua ulama, whose schools and personal influence formed the real base of the organization. As a result it gradually dissolved, and the Kaum Tua group was without an organization until 1936.

The politicization of Minangkabau and the success of political parties were facilitated by the nagari political tradition and the nature of Islamic doctrine. In the 1930's, the accumulation of anti-Dutch feeling was affected by the influence of Indonesian nationalism, the independence movement

---

40 *Ibid.*, November 1932, *Mailrapport* 115x/'33.
41 Interview with Rusli A. Wahid, Djakarta, November 1968.

and by the social effects of the economic depression. By the third quarter of 1931, no less than 60 perantau traders from Manindjau had come home as the result of the depression. Since most of them were also graduates of religious schools, they provided the sparsely populated district with more energetic religious propagators and political speakers.[42]

These factors, in different degrees, benefited all political parties. The success of Permi was due to the numerous Thawalib schools and graduates,combined with the compactness of its central board. Under the leadership of Djalaluddin Thaib, the Cairo returnees worked harmoniously with the Thawalib graduates. Under the supervision of Basa Bandaro, the commonly acknowledged "local political genius," the young radical leaders were able to maintain their comradeship. By July 1932, the Permi central board included women, such as Rasuna Said (whose arrest later made big news in Indonesian nationalist circles). In December 1932, in the midst of the mounting opposition to the Wild Schools Ordinance, Permi added five women leaders to the central board. This caused a further expansion of the party because it not only attracted more women followers but also shamed many still uninvolved Minangkabau men.[43]

The growth of the political parties magnified their problems with internal consolidation. Since membership in a particular party was motivated more by a sense of individual participation than by attachment to any one specific ideology, overlapping membership commonly occurred. There were cases where the local chairman of the Permi held the same position in the PSII, while serving as an active leader of the Muhammadijah.[44] Some local leaders, assuming that increasing the number of organizations would increase popular participation, helped establish new organizations.[45] By the first quarter of 1932, however, the trend reversed and the parties began to consolidate.

---

42 Politieke Politioneel Overzicht, 3de kwartaal, 1931, *Mailrapport* 1200x/'31.
43 Letter of the Attorney-General to the Governor-General, Medan, July 1933, secret, *Mailrapport* 920x/'33.
44 An example of the overlapping leadership is shown in the Kubang Permi, formed in January 1932. Its chairman was also the chairman of the PSII; its vice-chairman a Muhamma-dijah leader; its secretary a member of PSII and Muhammadijah, a teacher at the Dinijah school and former teacher at the Thawalib; its treasurer a member of Muhammadijah and former member of the communist Sarekat Rakjat. Politieke Politioneel Overzicht, January 1932, *Mailrapport* 335x/'32.
45 The head of Permi's Islamic Propaganda Department, Hadji Rasul Hamidy, established a PSII branch in Pajakumbuh in March 1932. *Mailrapport* 492x/'32.

By the middle of 1932, Permi and the PSII, both of which had consciously tried to make themselves mass parties, faced a problem of maintaining control over their various regional boards while continuing to expand. They also had problems maintaining the loyalty of their respective members. The parties had to guard themselves against infiltration by government informers, especially as it became apparent that many political arrests were made on the basis of speeches which had been delivered in closed sessions.

The drive toward internal consolidation was conducted under the slogan, "One man for one party." It started when the competition and ideological conflict among the various organizations became extreme. At its regional conference in March 1932, the Muhammadijah, which had a principle of open membership that allowed members to participate in other organizations, decided to dissuade its members from involvement in political parties.[46] Both Permi and the PSII began trying to impose "party discipline" in April. Such attempts could be successful only if the parties had strong centralized organizational structures, which was not the case with Permi and even less with the PSII. The application of party discipline was entirely dependent on the local situation and local party leaders. In Padang Pandjang and Ampat Angkat, where the triangular competition among the Muhammadijah, Permi, and PSII was very intense, internal consolidation efforts went smoothly. In Manindjau, where the leaders of the organizations maintained a relatively cordial relationship, party discipline did not work very well. More to the point, neither Permi nor the PSII took the need for internal consolidation very seriously. They were still too much wedded to the desire to become big, mass parties.

An issue of great urgency to both Permi and the PSII, and later also to the PNI Baru,was the preservation of their members' loyalty. The criteria for judging loyalty ranged from regular payment of dues to correct political attitudes. In September 1932, for example, the central board of Permi temporarily suspended 530 of the 700 members of its Pariaman branch for failure to pay regular party contributions. In Painan and Lubuk Baga-lung, many members were purged because the central

---

46 Politieke Politioneel Overzicht, March 1932, *Mailrapport* 492x/!32.

board suspected their political loyalties.⁴⁷ In early 1933, the problem of government informers, locally known as *tjoro* ("creeps"), and that of increased government pressure caused Iljas Jacub to draw up a plan for drastic organizational changes in Permi. He proposed that full members of the party should pass a discipline test and also demonstrate their intellectual ability. Likewise a new group could be approved only after it passed a group discipline test and proved its loyalty to the central board. In short, Iljas wanted to make Permi into a centralized and highly disciplined party. His proposal, however, was rejected by the majority of the central board's members. They feared such structural changes might weaken the mass and revolutionary character of the party, making it a pale imitation of the PNI Baru.

In early 1931, political leaders began working to strengthen the ideological consciousness of the membership and also to form party cadres among the youth. The most obvious medium for such programs consisted of politically-oriented educational and religious journals and booklets. In addition to the official party organ, published by the central or regional boards, some local branches began their own publications. Permi, the PSII and the PNI Baru strongly encouraged their respective branches to establish their own libraries, where members would regularly obtain political literature and nationalist newspapers.⁴⁸ Regular party political courses became important in 1932. In September, in order to intensify its program of political courses, Permi instituted special departments for external propaganda and party political courses. Under the leadership of Iljas Jacub and Hadji Djalaluddin Thaib, the department of political courses expanded its operation "in order to enliven the national independence spirit."⁴⁹ The PNI Baru adopted a "social-peda gogic" strategy which used the party courses as a requirement for acceptance as a full member. In the middle of 1933, after the government began restricting public activities, the parties intensified these political courses. Both Permi and the PSII, which had gained prominence through their ability to recruit followers at mass rallies, had to shift their activities to various types of political courses. These courses, known as "the five minute individual course,"

---

47 *Ibid.*, September 1932, *Mailrapport* 1227x/'32, and October 1932, *Mailrapport* 1159x/'32.
48 *Berita*, September 12, 1932.
49 Politieke Politioneel Overzicht, October 1932, *Mailrapport* 1227x/'32.

"the peripatetic course" and "the course in the rice-field," enabled them to survive as radical parties until the middle of 1934.

In April 1932, a representative of the PSII Central Board, a Minangkabau perantau leader, took three young men back with him to Java to train at party headquarters as future PSII leaders for their respective home districts. A general awareness of the importance of cadre-formation caused the various political and social organizations to pay more attention to youth. Some of them, such as the PSII and the Muhammadijah, had their own youth and boy scout subsidiaries, Pemuda Muslimin Indonesia (PMI, Indonesian Muslim Youth) and Pemuda Muhammadijah respectively. These organizations were used to expand the influence of their respective mother-organizations and to serve as a training ground for future leaders. The Muhammadijah and the Association of the Dinijah Schools had formed youth and boy scout organizations as a means for directing extra-curricular activities of their pupils. The members of the Persatuan Murid Dinijah School (PMDS, Association of the Students of Dinijah Schools), the largest youth organization, and its affiliate, the Kepanduan Indonesia Muslim (KIM, Indonesian Muslim Boy Scouts), were exclusively students or former students of the Dinijah schools. Permi had cut its organizational ties with El-Hilaal, the second largest boy scout organization, and had never formed its own youth organization, but the party was ideologically very influential among the Kaum Muda youth. The Himpunan Pemuda Islam Indonesia (HPII, Association of Indonesian Muslim Youth), established by Permi in July 1931, was more a youth section of the party than an independent youth organization. It recruited members particularly from among the students of the Sumatra Thawalib schools and the newly established Permi schools, and, in a relatively short time, it rivaled the PMDS in the number of its members and groups. The HPII also contributed to the further expansion of Permi.

Given the intensely nationalist and anti-colonial activities and ideological controversies among the political leaders, it is not surprising that the youth organizations also became involved in the politics of the independence movement. In spite of a government law which forbade youths under eighteen to attend political meetings or discuss political problems, the meetings of the HPII were full of anti-colonialist speeches. As a result of this political character, which the government said had been revealed during the first HPII congress in July 1932, the Attorney-

General officially changed the legal status of the youth organization to that of a "political party."⁵⁰ In fact, one of the earliest victims of the Islamic-nationalist movement was a leader of HPII, convicted in early 1932.⁵¹

By the middle of 1932, the youth movements began to graduate mature leaders for the political parties. The HPII provided Permi with several local leaders, some of whom became members of the central board. After the middle of 1933, they and some women leaders were the only active leaders of the party. A former chairman of the HPII later became the last chairman of the Permi. The PMDS, although it denied that it had any outside influence and insisted on maintaining its Islamic educational character, nonetheless contributed its share of leaders to the political parties. In the second part of 1932, several members of the PMDS central board became local leaders of the PSII. In the beginning of 1933, these young leaders challenged the position of the older leaders of the party. Not unlike the former leaders of the HPII, the young leaders of the PSII by the mid-1930's had taken over the party from the older generation. In November 1932, shortly after Hatta's visit, PMDS adviser Chatib Suleiman and chairman Leon Salim became the promoters of the PNI Baru.

Youth organizations had always been inseparable parts of the popular movement. Almost all Minangkabau political leaders were themselves former members of youth organizations. These younger leaders tended to idealize bravery in the pursuit of independence and to make sacrifices for the benefit of the people. They appealed for the participation of youth in reforming the ummat. This attracted young men and women and helped them to define their responsibilities and roles. A "*pemuda* [young man]," according to the definition of the HPII, "is a person with an independent spirit." The pemuda movement, therefore, should mean "a movement toward independence...It should stand in the middle of the arena of the people's movement."⁵² It is understandable therefore that the youth organizations did not always follow the leadership of the political

---

50 Office of the Attorney-General, July 12, 1932, no. 3270/AP/ secret. "Every meeting of the Congress was dispersed by the police because the speakers discussed politics." *Indisch Verslag*, 1933, p. 19.
51 The youth leader, A. F. Hadjat, had written a nationalist poem in the Permi paper, *Medan Rakjat* He was sentenced to three years in prison. Politieke Politioneel Overzicht, May 1932, *Mailrapport* 772x/'32.
52 "Toedjoean Pergerakan Pemoeda," *Pahlawan Moeda*, 1, Nos. 2, 3 (August and September 1933), pp. 25, 45.

parties. The Dutch records show that the PSII, not infrequently, failed to control the activities of its youth section. The Muhammadijah had always encountered difficulty in restraining its Hizbul Wathan, whose members pictured themselves as the "soldiers of Muhammadijah." The actions taken by leaders of the PMDS clearly demonstrate the continuing search by young men to find their own proper places and ideologies in the independence movement. Despite their competition, the Islamic youth movements shared some basic ideological similarities. These were best expressed by the preamble to the statutes of the HPII:

We work for the nation but because of Allah. We work for the benefit of the people but because of God.[53]

This formulation explains the idealism of the Islamic youth movement, with its belief in social reformation guided by religious devotion and nationalist feeling.

The Kaum Muda schools also contributed to the political education of the youth. The most obvious example was the Sumatra Thawalib of Padang Pandjang, which from its early history had been an intellectual center of the anti-colonial political movement. This school and other Kaum Muda schools, such as Darulfunun Abbasiah in Padang Djapang and Permi's Tsanawijah and teachers' training school for girls in Bukittinggi, trained future political teachers as well as future politicians. Stu-dents in the lower grades belonged to the various boy scout and youth organizations, but the upper classmen joined the political parties. Some 150 of the 450 students in the two highest grades of the Sumatra Thawalib in Padang Pandjang were members of political parties—70% belonged to Permi, the rest to the PSII or PNI Baru. Over 90% of the students at the teachers' training school for girls joined political parties or politically oriented youth organizations.[54] Two of the most important women leaders of Permi, Rasuna Said and Rasimah Ismail, later famous as "the heroines" of the Indonesian independence movement, were graduates of this school. The school was directed by Muchtar Lutfi. Members of Permi's central

---

53 *Pahlawan Moeda*, 2, Nos. 5, 6 (September 1935).
54 Roesad, "Rapport," *Mailrapport* 1518x/'33.

board, such as Iljas Jacub, Ali Emran Djamil and other Cairo returnees, often taught at Permi schools.

Although the teachers' personal influence was an important factor,[55] the character of the Kaum Muda school itself led to political action. Kaum Muda Islamic modernism taught the need for reform and for the rediscovery of the true religious ethic. These appeals induced not only a profound awareness of the inherent antagonism between the kafir and the Muslim but also that between the ruler and the ruled. In short, the religious education provided by Kaum Muda teachers, consciously or unconsciously, created an interest in politics among the students. Several subjects, such as Islamic history (*tarich*), Quranic exegesis, sociology and the study of the love of fatherland (*tarbijah wathaniah*), were easily turned to political purposes. Even Arabic language studies, through the use of nationalist poems and compositions, could introduce the students to a kind of romantic nationalism and patriotism. The extent of these political influences was not the same in all Kaum Muda schools, but it was sufficient to guarantee continuity of leadership by the Kaum Muda educated group until the early 1950's. In spite of ideological controversy, competition and political activities, expansion and modernization of religious schools remained important parts of the Islamic modernists' programs.

The extensive politicization of Minangkabau made it one of the most dangerous regions in the eyes of the government. The government vigorously applied the repressive measures which characterized the policy of *rust en orde*. Minangkabau became the test case for the government's hard-line policies. "From the West Coast [of Sumatra]," according to a famous colonial theoretician, de Kat Angelino, "the victory begins."[56]

Action and Reaction

July 1932 was a month of mounting political activity. In the middle of the month, Permi held its biggest conference ever in Bukittinggi. Attended by Muhammad Yamin and Gatot Mangku-pradja, Partindo

---

55 The local Permi leaders were teachers at the Padang Pandjang Thawalib. *Mailrapport* 1518x/'33.
56 The remark was made during de Kat Angelino's visit to the area and is cited by van Heuven, "Memorie van Overgave," p. 14.

leaders from Java, the conference voted to declare Permi "a radical and non-cooperative political party." The mood of the conference can be measured by the police action used by the government to disperse the mass rallies and open meetings. Muchtar Lutfi was interrupted in the middle of his speech and forbidden by the local government to address any more public meetings in Minangkabau. Muhammad Yamin, a perantau leader, experienced a similar fate after he said, "Minangkabau, the land of the three luhak, has been pledged and sold." He and Gatot soon were forced to leave Minangkabau. During the conference, the police found wall posters in several areas of Padang which declared: "Indonesia should be freed from the Netherlands."[57] "It seemed," as a participant of the conference reminisced, "that Indonesia would be free tomorrow morning."[58]

In the same month, the youth organization HPII held its congress in Padang Pandjang. But, according to a government report, "all public meetings had to be closed by the police, because the speeches had a political character which cannot be tolerated in a youth movement."[59] Not to be outdone by the HPII, the organizations of the Dinijah schools' students, PMDS and the KIM, held their own first congress the same month. Although the young leaders of the PMDS rejected what they termed the "Sukarnoism" followed by the HPII, they discussed the advisability of studying politics.[60]

At the same time that Permi was holding its special conference, the PSII was using the occasion of the Prophet's Birthday to conduct public meetings and religious gatherings. PSII regional leaders traveled throughout the districts where the party had followers in order to direct these activities, which they referred to as "general actions." The main purpose of holding the simultaneous public meetings was to intensify the idea of independence based on Islam and to repudiate so-called "Madjapahitism," the notion of a re-emergence of pre-Islamic cultural imperialism.[61] By stressing anti-"Madjapahitism," the PSII followed the

---

57 *Sinar Soematra*, July 21, 1932 in *Overzicht van de Inlandsche Pers* 30/1932, p. 71; Politieke Politioneel Overzicht, July 1932, *Mailrapport* 952x/'32.
58 Tamar Djaja, "Islam di Indonesia."
59 *Indisch Verslag*, 1933, p. 19.
60 Politieke Politioneel Overzicht, July 1932, *Mailrapport* 952x/'32.
61 *Sinar Soematra*, July 14, 1933 in *Overzicht van de Inlandsche Pers*, 30/1932.

direction of its central board in Java, which was engaged in an ideological controversy with the secular nationalist parties. At the same time it attacked Permi's kebangsaan slogan, at least indirectly.

An important decision taken by the Permi July conference was to exclude Muchtar Lutfi from the central board, because he had been under police surveillance for some time. He was replaced by two of his students, Rasuna Said and Chasijah, both women.[62] It was hoped that the changes would extend Permi's influence among Minangkabau women and at the same time remove Muchtar from direct involvement in the party's expansion drive. At the end of 1932, Rasuna Said, who usually began her speech with a salute to her "humiliated and oppressed brothers and sisters," was convicted for sedition, thus becoming the first woman "martyr" of the Indonesian nationalists.[63] In December, another woman leader, Rasimah Ismail, was also arrested.

In a letter to the Permi central board, nineteen-year-old Rasimah dissuaded her party from providing a counsel for her defense.

> I am convinced that the struggle of the people, who are aware of their dignity, will be victorious.. .. [The cost of] struggle to achieve perity is, indeed, very high.[64]

Rasimah, like Rasuna Said, was accused of planting seeds of hatred and hostility toward the government. Her trial brought out the nationalist

---

[62] The new Permi central board consisted of:
Chairman:	Hadji Djalaluddin Thaib
Vice-Chairman:	Hadji Abdu+l Madjid
Secretary:	Mansur Daud Dt. Palimo Kajo
Treasurer:	Asah Djaminuddin (a merchant)
Commissioners:	Iljas Jacub
	Duski Samad
	Tondeh Sutan Mangkuto Alam (a merchant)
Department of Education:	Iljas Jacub
Department of Enterprise:	Ali Emran Djamil
Department of Islamic Propaganda and Publication:	Hadji Rasul Hamidy
Department of Finance:	Tondeh Sutan Mangkuto Alam

[63] On the reactions in the press to this arrest see, *Overzicht van de Inlandsche Pers*, 51/1932, pp. 390-391. A Javanese nationalist in Surabaja called Rasuna Said the true "Srikandi" of the independence movement. *Soeara Oemoem*, in *ibid.*, 7/1933, p. 95. In Tapanuli, a book was published in her honor. *Sinar Soematra*, February 9, 1933.

[64] *Tjaja Soematra*, February 10, 1932; *Sinar Soematra*, February 9, 1932.

mood prevailing among the younger generation of the Kaum Muda educated group. It was attended by some 2,000 spectators. The judge questioned Rasimah about her statement that the Islamic nations were no longer equal with other nations.

> Rasimah: The Indonesian nation and the Islamic nations in general are looked upon as inferior by other nations.
> Judge: What is the meaning of *merdeka* [independence]?
> Rasimah: Merdeka means to be free from foreign rule and that the Dutch government should go home [to Holland].
> Judge: What do you mean by saying that the fate of a nation depends on the nation itself?
> Rasimah: It is true that every nation should be developed by itself. It has never occurred in history that a nation was developed by other nations.
> Judge: What do you mean that the Indonesian people have been butchered by foreign imperialism?
> Rasimah: Imperialism is a foreign word which means greed, avarice and acquisitiveness. The presence of imperialism has resulted in the sufferings of the Indonesian people.[65]

This exchange explains the actions of the youth movement. It is in this mood of self-confidence that the motivating force behind the independence movement can be found.

In his comments on the mounting political activities and the prevailing anti-government feeling in Minangkabau, Resident van Heuven stated:

---

65 *Tjaja Soematra*, February 16, 1933.

The susceptibility of these people [the Minangkabau] to fanaticism and militancy is far greater than their political knowledge. They are, therefore, not fully aware of political realities.[66]

"Political realities" meant the strength of Dutch power and the government's determination to maintain rust en orde. Public meetings featuring fiery nationalist speeches and publications containing anti-colonial articles were regarded as leading to the disruption of "public order," the maintenance of which, according to Colijn, was one of the government's "moral responsibilities" (zedelijk verplichtingen). It is understandable that Zentgraff, the editor of *Java Bode*, concluded a report on the West Coast of Sumatra with the proposal that "all meetings in Minangkabau should be dispersed."[67] But a liberal Dutch member of the Volksraad argued that the difference between the political movement in Java and on the West Coast of Sumatra was that in the latter region the police was more oppressive.[68] In such a situation, where the government considered any nationalist agitation as "destructive activity" and the nationalist parties distrusted the government, antagonism between them mounted steadily.

The period between early 1932 and the third quarter of 1933 saw a growing radicalism in political developments. Each government action resulted in an intensification of nationalist activities. In the antagonistic climate, political parties moved to minimize the consequences of government pressure on their respective members. In April 1932, the PSII formed a "victims' fund" (*korban fonds*) to help those of its members who had been arrested. In January 1933, after the arrest of Rasuna Said, a nationalist lawyer formed a committee to help political detainees with legal procedures.[69] Legal efforts, however, proved fruitless. In dealing with the nationalist movement, the government preferred to use its extraordinary powers, which could not be contested in the courts. The

---

66 Politieke Politioneel Overzicht, February 1932, *Mailrapport* 41x/'32.
67 Quoted by Husni Thamrin in his protest against the government's suppressive policies. *Handelingen van den Volksraad*, 1933-1934, pp. 2015-2016. "The intensification of [government] action, indeed, occurred; it was necessary because agitation could not be tolerated in such a period of precarious economic conditions." Governor-General de Jonge in van der Wal, *Herinneringen*, p. 182.
68 *Handelingen van den Volksraad*, 1933, p. 2009.
69 *Berita*, January 31, 1933; Politieke Politioneel Overzicht, January 1933, *Mailrapport* 357x/'33.

most common government weapon was a severe restriction on freedom of speech. In April 1932, the Attorney-General, replying to an inquiry from the Resident on how to handle mounting political activities, urged an effective use of police power. The police, he said, should interrupt speakers and, if necessary, disperse public meetings.[70] A few days before the Permi conference in July 1932, the Resident summoned Djalaluddin Thaib, Iljas Jacub and Muchtar Lutfi and warned them that anti-government speeches would not be tolerated. He advised that the party's guests, the Partindo leaders, should be careful in their speeches.[71] Muchtar Lutfi chose to ignore the warning, and, as a result, this conference proved to be the occasion of his last public address.

Another measure used to curb political activity was the application of *reisregelingen*, travel restrictions, on allegedly "dangerous" leaders. This measure required them to obtain special permission before leaving their respective districts or visiting certain regions. Until 1932 travel restrictions were usually only imposed on newcomers from rantau regions, especially from Cairo and Java. In 1933, after Permi and the PSII had expanded to other parts of Sumatra, some of their leaders were also subjected to restrictions.

The government's use of an extensive informer network and its attempt to mobilize the adat authorities had a more demoralizing effect on the political parties. The informer network was employed not only to get information about the internal activities of the parties but, more important, to create mutual suspicion within the nationalist ranks. Political courses and closed meetings often had to be cancelled because local leaders could not trust their own colleagues. From March to May 1933, the Dutch authorities reported that political activities in Minangkabau seemed to have reached a standstill because the parties could not cope with the suspected existence of informers in their midst and because hostility by the adat authorities had increased.

The attraction of penghulu in some nagari and in the towns to the nationalist parties had aroused considerable concern in the government. As in the past, the government turned to the adat authorities, such as

---

70 Office of the Attorney-General, April 12, 1932, 1713/AP, *Mailrapport* 1202x/'32.
71 *Tjaja Soematra*, July 14, 1932.

the nagari council and the nagari head, to combat both the defecting penghulu and the political parties. In addition to the conventional policy of urging the adat authorities to take preventive action against political parties, the local government played on the fears of rural peng-hulu by warning them that the tragic events of 1927 might be repeated. In early 1933, Permi faced strong opposition in Rao-Rao, a nagari in the district of Batu Sangkar which had been a "financial power" of the communist movement.[72] The penghulu, who continued to blame themselves for their failure to "protect" their people from the communist party, were extremely sensitive to the potentially negative effects resulting from the presence of a political party in the nagari. The communist movement had cost the nagari a large number of its religious teachers and traders; they had been exiled to Digul.

In order to strengthen the adat authorities in combating radical political parties, the local government tried to prevent any clash between adat and government laws; in the past these had benefited the Muhammadijah. On many occasions, the local administration tried to coordinate its actions with those of the adat authorities, and it lent political and legal support to actions taken by them. In late 1932, six local leaders of the Permi in Sungai Penuh were convicted by the nagari council on the grounds that in promoting their party's cause they disrupted peace in the nagari and undermined the authority of the penghulu. The nagari council decided that the defendants should choose between paying an adat fine or entering the government prison for several weeks. Ironically,the nagari council had been presided over by the controleur. This use of adat power in combating political parties, according to the leader of the Nationalist Fraction in the Volksraad, M. Husni Thamrin, resulted in the arbitrary infringement of the people's rights. In early 1933, Permi and the PSII had to abandon their activities in many nagari because of the cooperation between the district administration and the adat authorities.[73]

In the face of this harassment, political parties had to design new

---

72 Politieke Politioneel Overzicht, 1927, *Mailrapport* 741x/'28.
73 *Handelingen van den Volksraad*, 1933-1934, pp. 153-154; Politieke Politioneel Overzicht, January 1933, *Mailrapport* 351x/'33; *ibid.*, February 1933, *Mailrapport* 590x/'33; ibid., March 1933, *Mailrapport* 669x/'33.

tactics for survival. In the beginning of 1933, a representative of the PSII central board from Java advised branches in Minangkabau to refrain from "irritating" the government. In February 1932, Datuk Singo Mangkuto, chairman of the PSII regional board, tried to revive his old adat-party, the Persatuan Adat, for use as camouflage for his political activities; the attempt failed. A considerable number of the penghulu in Mangkuto's nagari, Sungai Batang, had joined Permi or Muhammadijah. The small secular party PNI Baru instructed its members to avoid religious and adat discussions and to moderate their anti-colonial speeches and writings. The party's platform emphasized the need for education in politics through courses and individual propaganda.[74]

Determined to continue its expansion drive in spite of the government's hostility, Permi held an emergency conference on December 15, 1932. At the conference the party designed a "struggle program" (*strijdprogram*) which stressed opposition to the Wild Schools Ordinance and maintenance of continuity in the party leadership. It was decided to enlarge the party's central board. Five male second echelon leaders and five young women were added to the nine members of the central board as part of an effort to train new leaders. They could become replacements for those who had been arrested. In January, one of the new members was appointed as the reserve chairman. Several branches, for example, Bukittinggi, Batu Sangkar and Painan, instituted reserve local boards.[75]

In January and April, Permi issued guidelines for its local leaders. They were instructed among other things to examine carefully all those who attended the closed meetings and to limit their activities outside the party. They were urged to watch the activities of the members as well as those of their colleagues on the boards. In order to avoid the trap of "sedition," local leaders were advised to prepare written drafts of their speeches and to obtain proper translations of their quotations from the

---

74 *Ibid.*, May 1933, *Mailrapport* 848x/'33.
75 Statements given by H. Djalaluddin Thaib and Iljas Jacub in *Mailrapport* 861x/'34. The government's suspicion is documented by Tamar Djaja in his "Islam di Indonesia." The newly elected members of the central board were Darwis Taram (an Al-Azhar graduate), Hadji Sjuib el-Jutusi (a former member of the central board), Hadji Rasul Hamidy, Achmad Nakib (a local leader from Manindjau), Tjut Saiman (a leader in Atjeh), Chasijah (a teacher of the Dinijah Putri), Ratna Sari (a student of the Islamic College), Fatimah Hatta (a graduate of the Dinijah School), Tinur M. Nur (a graduate of the Dinijah school), and Rasimah Ismail (a graduate of the Dinijah Putri). *Tjaja Soematra*, December 19, 1932.

Quran and the Hadith. Finally they were instructed to intensify their political courses.[76]

Permi's determination to continue its activities even to the extent of creating a kind of "counterespionage" network within the party made collision between the party and the government unavoidable. After a three-month stalemate, from March to May, Permi renewed its activities. Its paper *Medan Rakjat* praised this renewed vigor with a quote from an Indian nationalist leader, which stated that, although repression was on the increase, "our answer to it should be a greater intensification of our movement for freedom."[77] Permi began preparations for its national congress, which was planned to promote the party's consolidation program and to further its *élan*. But the government had decided to use its extraordinary powers and, in July, the Resident imposed travel restrictions on several Permi and HPII leaders, including Hadji Djalaluddin Thaib, Muchtar Lutfi and Iljas Jacub. They were forbidden to enter the Residency of Tapanuli, an area where Permi had been rapidly gaining ground.

Travel restriction was the first important step in the government's campaign to paralyze Permi. The local government had determined to settle the political problem in Minangkabau as soon as possible. On April 1933, the Resident proposed that the Attorney-General invoke the provision for limited prohibitions on public meetings (*beperkt vergaderverbod*) against Permi and the PSII.[78] Under this clause, the parties could no longer hold open public meetings and would need special permission to hold closed sessions. The Resident thought this action would demonstrate that, in the eyes of the government, Permi and the PSII were legally discredited and politically disgraced. It would in effect force the parties' followers to renounce their membership. In pursuit of this proposal, the central government sent a special commission, consisting of Prof. Schrieke, Director of Education and an acknowledged expert on Minangkabau affairs, and Dr. de Kat Angelino, former Director

---

76 Politieke Politioneel Overzicht, January 1933, *Mailrapport* 351x/'33; *ibid.*, April 1933, *Mailrapport* 813x/'33.
77 "Tegoehkan Barisan Kemerdekaan," *Medan Rakjat*, 3, No. 17 (June 18, 1933).
78 Resident's letter, April 1, 1933, no. 943/P/33, an appendix in the Politieke Politioneel Overzicht of March 1933, *Mailrapport* 669x/'33.

of Administrative Affairs, to West Sumatra to investigate the political situation. The special commission was accompanied by the Attorney-General. In his report to these high officials, the Resident cited the increased political activities and the sharper criticism of the government on the part of the political leaders. He reaffirmed his determination to curb the activities of the existing political parties.[79] His proposal came at the right moment, for the Minangkabau political leaders had already lost their composure as the result of continued harassment by the local administration. The central government moreover had already decreed that Partindo and the PNI Baru were forbidden parties for government employees.

Muchtar Lutfi, who had not addressed a public meeting since July 1932, was enraged by the travel restriction and made a bold speech to a closed meeting of party cadres on July 8. After elaborating the difference between the evolutionary "cultural nationalists," "who want to achieve independence as politely as possible," and the revolutionaries, Muchtar claimed that the immediate goal of Permi was to create a new Indonesia, "to be ruled by the *Dang Tuanku*, as the President of the Republic of Indonesia." This reference to the legendary just and wise ruler of Minangkabau made his statement the most quoted political speech in Minangkabau. But in the opinion of the Attorney-General, this statement was "intolerable."[80] On July 13, the Attorney-General ordered Muchtar Lutfi's arrest. In spite of an appeal by the penghulu and religious teachers of Balingka, who guaranteed that Muchtar would abandon politics, his fate was already decided and on March 1934 he was exiled to Digul.[81]

On the basis of his observations on the West Coast of Sumatra and in Tapanuli, the Attorney-General recommended to the Governor-General that Permi, the PSII and the smaller parties, the PNI Baru and the

---

79 Resident's letter, Padang, July 7, 1933, *Mailrapport* 920x/'33.
80 Telegram of the Attorney-General to the Governor-General, July 17, 1933, *Mailrapport* 849x/'33. Excerpts from Muchtar Lutfi's speech are attached to the Resident's report to the Governor-General, July 25, 1933, no. 1050/C/secret and August 17, 1933, no. 1598/secret/"Eigenhandig," *Mailrapport* 938x/'33. Dang Tuanku is a major figure in the Minangkabau epic *Kaba Tjindua Mato*. Taufik Abdullah, "Some Notes on the *Kaba Tjindua Mato*: An Example of Minangkabau Traditional Literature," *Indonesia*, 9 (April 1970), pp. 1-23.
81 Correspondence on the Muchtar Lutfi case is contained in *Mailrapport* 934x/'33, 1451x/'33, 327x/'34.

Partindo,be curbed. Although the two smaller parties were not obviously anti-government, he believed that: "Their activities will become more successful if the others [Permi and the PSII] are paralyzed."[82] Shortly after his arrival in Batavia, the Attorney-General proposed that the Governor-General proclaim Permi and the PSII forbidden parties for government officials throughout Indonesia and that he impose the "limited prohibition" against their holding public meetings in West Sumatra and Tapanuli. Without further deliberation, on August 4, the Governor-General decided to follow the recommendations of the Attorney-General.[83] On August 5, the Governor-General further instructed the two Residents that, if the new decree failed to curb political activities, the next step would have to be "the elimination of the important leaders."[84]

The repressive mood of the Governor-General, who had just imposed the vergaderverbod on the PNI Baru and the Partindo throughout Indonesia, is shown by his hasty decision concerning the PSII. Although the party was strongly anti-government in West Sumatra and Tapanuli, that was not the case in Java, In spite of its consistent non-cooperative policy, the Java portion of the party was at that time far more moderate than its Minangkabau branches. The decision concerning the PSII was soon amended by the Council of the Netherlands Indies, and the legal position of the PSII outside West Sumatra and Tapanuli remained unchanged.[85]

Legal obstacles to public meetings forced Permi and the PSII to shift their activities to written political courses. On September 5, 1933, Permi issued its first series of brochures on popular political knowledge, mostly written by the director of Permi's Islamic College. Before it reached a wide audience, however, it was confiscated by the police. On the pretext that a one-page article (and its continuation which was still in manuscript form) written by Iljas Jacub was "disparaging and incited the people against Dutch authority in all its historical phases,"[86] the

---

[82] Attorney-General's Report on the Political Situation in West Sumatra, Medan, July 23, 1933, secret, *Mailrapport* 920x/'33.
[83] Office of the Attorney-General, Weltevreden, August 3, 1933, no. 3823/AP and Extract from the Decision of the Governor-General, August 4, 1933, no. lz, *Verbaal* January 9, 1933, no. 6.
[84] Telegram of the Governor-General, August 1933, no. 653, *Verbaal* January 9, 1933, no. 6.
[85] Decision of the Raad van Nederlandsch-Indië, August 4, 1933, no. 1, *Mailrapport* 934x/'33.
[86] Resident van Heuven's letter, September 26, 1933, no. 2055/ secret, *Mailrapport* 861x/'34.

writer and the publisher of the ill-fated series were arrested. Through the arrests of Iljas Jacub and Djala-luddin Thaib the Dutch government with one stroke had deprived Permi of its most important leaders. Permi was left under the leadership of Mansur Daud and his colleagues, who could not match the arrested leaders in either organizational skill or leadership.

In the same month a similar fate befell the PSII when Hadji Uddin Rahmany and Sabilal Rasad were arrested. Datuk Singo Mangkuto, who was in Java at the time, could not return to Minangkabau because he was next on the list of persons to be arrested. The local authorities were determined to suppress the radical parties following central government guidelines. Although the arrests of Permi and PSII leaders were made without the approval of the central government, the Resident's action was, nevertheless, hailed by the Attorney-General.[87] In October, in order to sever relations between the remnants of Permi's top leadership and its followers, the central government approved the Resident's proposal for the confiscation and suspension of the party newspaper *Medan Rakjat*.[88] In early November, Datuk Singo Radjo, a penghulu and a leader of the PSII in Manindjau, was arrested after he tried to expel a penghulu-informer from the nagari council of Sungai Batang. In early 1934 Permi leaders Muchtar Lutfi, Iljas Jacub and Djalaluddin Thaib and PSII leaders Hadji Uddin Rahmany, Sabilal Rasad and Datuk Singo Radjo were sent to Digul.

From November 1932 until September 1933, Permi had lost no less than 55 of its leaders (including ten women) in the struggle to achieve "Islam in Honor" and a "Prosperous Indonesia." Although not actually a rebellious party, Permi had paid a high price for being a radical party. The arrests continued until the middle of 1934 with the temporary detention of Mansur Daud and other members of the central board. Imposition of the vergaderverbod and liberal use of the "extraordinary powers" paralyzed nationalist movements in Minangkabau and in other parts of Indonesia.

---

87 Office of the Attorney-General, September 12, 1933, no. 4643/AP, *Mailrapport* 1108x/'33 (Luchtpost 20/9, 1933).
88 Office of the Attorney-General, October 27, 1933, no. 5791/AP. The Resident made his proposal on October 13, and, in accordance with the recommendation of the Raad van Nederlandsch-Indië, the Governor-General prohibited publication of *Medan Rakjat*. Decision no. 18, November 22, 1933, *Mailrapport* 1400x/'33.

According to the memoirs of former con-troleur (Pajakumbuh) van der Meulen, under Governor-General de Jonge, the Dutch Indies government "became a police state." The politics of suppression, he believed, caused the Dutch great loss: "We missed a chance, a chance which we can never have again."[89]

---

[89] van der Meulen, *Ik Stond er Bij*, pp. 110-111.

CHAPTER NINE
PRIVATE SCHOOLS AND POLITICS

In early 1933, an editor of *Pewarta Deli*, a nationalist newspaper published in Medan, concluded his report on a visit to the West Coast of Sumatra with the following words:

> It is very difficult to understand the political situation on the West Coast from the outside. This situation can be properly assessed only by listening to people's opinions in the villages. Basically it is the morale of these little people, not that of the [Western educated] intellectuals, that must be carefully watched. It can be said that the *kaum intelek*, the Western and highly educated intellectuals, have no influence on the people's hearts. The upper class persons do not understand what has entered the people's minds…[In this situation], the government distrusts the popular movement, while the radicals are suspicious of the government and officials. The kaum intelek do not understand the Eastern or Islamic educated people. In short what we find on the West Coast is a kind of nervous strain (*nerveus spanning*) among some social groups.[1]

Despite the political anxiety, private schools continued to expand and religious schools continued to modernize their teaching methods and curriculum. In spite of the almost complete isolation of the kaum intelek from the mainstream of the political movement in West Sumatra, they contributed much to the progress of educational development.

The expansion of private schools and the modernization of religious

---

1 Reprinted in *Berita*, April 22, 1933.

schools were direct consequences of the Kaum Muda movement. The Islamic modernist group resulted from the changes in the religious schools, and they were trained to continue improving the new madrasah system. In spite of growing involvement in the politics of national independence and in economic enterprises, religious schools remained the common focus of the Kaum Muda educated intellectuals. Schools not only provided them a base for influence but also a channel through which the Kaum Muda educated intellectuals could carry out their social and religious reforms. As in the past, schools remained the institutions through which the reformers endeavored to change their social and religious environment and formulate new conceptions of the Minangkabau world. Changes and reforms in the religious schools helped spread the ideology of particular Kaum Muda organizations and, more importantly, were an effective way to introduce "modern" ideas into the nagari. Using Islam, which along with adat formed an inseparable part of the alam Minangkabau, the Kaum Muda schools spread the idea of modernization and its corollaries—nationalism and the awareness of the need for secular knowledge. The continuing expansion of private schools and the modernization of religious schools were the most permanent concerns of the Kaum Muda educated group as well as its most important achievements.

Several social and economic factors contributed to the expansion and dispersion of the private schools. The increased number of graduates from the Kaum Muda religious schools and competition among the various political and educational organizations contributed much to the emergence of new religious schools and to the establishment of the "combined" schools, in which religious education was given as part of a predominantly secular curriculum. The economic depression had caused a halt in the expansion of the government's educational program, but it precipitated the development of private schools. The economic depression produced unemployed Western educated persons, many of whom established private "secular" and "combined" schools or became teachers in the "modernized" religious schools. The depression also made it difficult for people to send their children to outside educational centers, which meant that the local communities had to form their own schools.[2] The estab motivated by disillusionment with the government school system (which was thought to have corrupted the younger generation) and by the desire for an ideologically more appropriate education. The nationalist Taman Siswa school network, founded by Ki Hadjar Dewantara in Jogjakarta, for example, was based on such motives. In 1933, the Taman Siswa began to set up branches in Minangkabau. Using a similar motive but different approach, Muhammad Sjafei founded the INS in Kaju Tanam. Motivated by the desire to train dynamic and independent Islamic intellectuals, Abdul Aziz established the Kweekschool Islamijah, which won praise from Kaum Muda political leaders as well as from Dutch officials. Permi founded its Islamic College in 1931 in order to train qualified teachers and nationalist political leaders. A government regulation (*Staatsblad* 1923, no. 136) provided legal protection for the ex-panding private schools. Although the government reserved the right to inspect all schools, the promoter or teacher of a new school only had to report his intentions to the district office. With this proviso any organization or any person could found a private school. The government would intervene only if the school began to follow what was considered an undesirable political direction.[3]

Improvements in the system of instruction (replacing the "circle" with the graded system) and changes in the character of learning (by repudiating the tradition of complete dependence on old textual authorities) freed the madrasah from its traditional past. These developments, which began in the 1910's, paved the way for further changes. The religious schools began working to make their programs more relevant to changing political and economic situations, especially after the mid-1920's when the economic slump had exposed the weaknesses of religious schools and the communist movement had created a profound crisis in the Kaum Muda movement. The second stage of religious reform, which gained

---

2 Roesad, "Rapport over het Onderwijs," *Mailrapport* 1518x/'33.
3 Wilminck, Inspector of Education, flatly stated that *Staatsblad* 1923,no. 136 was "an unjustified, unnecessary and ill-advised assault on the village's right of sanction," because it gave a legal right to anyone to establish a school without permission from the penghulu. Most such schools, he said, taught nothing but hatred against the government. Wilminck, Fort de Kock, January 4, 1927, *Mailrapport* 214x/ '27. Officials of the Office for Native Affairs refuted this viewpoint. January 27, 1927, no. I/51/secret, in *ibid*.

momentum in the early 1930's, was characterized by concern about improving instruction and also a desire to provide the graduates with more useful tools for their daily needs. The Kaum Muda educators were also concerned with the intellectual gulf between Islamic modernists and Western-educated persons. The main features of modernization were the inclusion of "secular" subjects in the curriculum of religious schools and the establishment of higher teachers' training schools, usually called "colleges." The colleges used Arabic and Indonesian as media of instruction. Their aim was to produce new Islamic intellectuals who were not only experts in religious knowledge but who were also familiar with secular subjects. These trends in the Kaum Muda religious schools contributed to the spread of the "combined" elementary school and precipitated a "secularization" tendency in the non-government school system.

During the period of expansion and modernization of private schools, the central government promulgated the so-called Wild Schools Ordinance which enabled it to halt the establishment of new private schools and to close down old ones. Opposition to this ordinance, which reached a climax in late 1932 and early 1933, sharpened the anti-government political campaign and provided a common forum for all political and educational organizations. The non-political Muhammadijah and the Kaum Muda ulama collaborated with the radical parties in opposition to the ordinance. More than the earlier Guru Ordinance issue, the campaign against the Wild Schools Ordinance reveals the close ties between private schools and politics. The already extensive private school network and the determination of nationalist organizations in Minangkabau and in Java resulted in a political defeat for the government.

Expansion of Private Schools

A major consequence of the government's retrenchment policy was the suspension of educational development. In 1931, the government stopped further expansion of its schools and raised the financial burden on local communities. Several schools were closed. In 1931, the government closed down the Bukittinggi MOSVIA, a training school for civil servants.⁴ In the same year, it refused to accept new students for the Sekolah Radja, the teachers' training school. In spite of the protest by the penghulu and other "loyal" groups, the central government announced in 1933 that the Sekolah Radja would be closed permanently.⁵ In order to ensure the success of its retrenchment policy, in 1932, the government issued new regulations which raised tuition at its secondary schools (MULO) and sharply reduced subsidies to qualified private schools. In early 1933, the central government announced that village communities would henceforth have to contribute a greater share to the upkeep of local volksschool.⁶

From 1931 until 1933, no new volksschool were opened in West Sumatra. In 1931 there were 669 volksschool with an enrollment of 65,950 pupils. In 1933 the number of schools remained the same but enrollment had increased to 75,839, about 46% of all Minangkabau school children. The stagnancy of government sponsored schools showed more obviously in the development of the vernacular schools (the second class schools and the vervolgschool) and the "Dutch-Native" schools (HIS and schakelschool). In 1931 there were 197 of these schools. In 1933 the total number had decreased to 189. Enrollment, on the other hand, had increased from 22,663 to 32,286, about 16% of the total number of school children. Private schools, religious or otherwise, accommodated the remaining 44%.

---

4 *Indisch Verslag*, 1932, p. 231.
5 *Ibid.*, 1934, p. 244.
6 *Ibid.*, p. 234.

Table 3

Government and Subsidized Schools

Type of Schools	1926		1931		1933	
	School	Students	Schools	Students	Schools	Students
HIS	8	2,148	13	3,152	13	3,435
Schakelschool	2	199	3	329	3	401
Second Class School (including vervolgschool)	124	14,974	171	25,417	163	26,866
Racially Mixed Schools						
Europeesche Lagere School	7	881	6	1,111	6	1,068
MULO	3	458	4	654	4	516

Source: Spits, "Memorie van Overgave."

The above schools were generally located in the district capitals; the isolated rural areas were served only by the volks-school or private schools. The expansion of private schools increased the school attendance to about 9% of the total population of West Sumatra.

In 1931, after many schools of the Kaum Muda ulama had severed their relationship with the Sumatra Thawalib, 30 Thawalib schools remained. By 1933 the number had already increased to 44. In the same year, there were 120 Dinijah schools. The Muhammadijah, in spite of its weakening influence over the increasingly radical popular movements, managed to expand its school network rapidly. At the end of 1930, the Muhammadijah had only nineteen schools. By 1933 it controlled 122 schools, including several "combined" schools. Many branches of the Muhammadijah and of other organizations also conducted adult literacy courses.[7] But the majority of private schools, particularly the secular and "combined" schools, were not affiliated with any major organizations. No less than 160 Kaum Muda and 95 Kaum Tua religious schools were not

---

7 In 1930, 30% of the literate Minangkabau had received their training outside the regular private or government schools.

affiliated with the big organizations.

Table 4

Private Schools and School Organizations in 1933

Organization/School Affiliation	Schools	Students
1. Muhammadijah	122	5,835
2. Permi	4	249
3. Dinijah	120	7,136
4. Thawalib	44	3,031
5. PII (Kaum Tua)	45	3,651
6. Non-affiliated schools	878	50,082

Source: *Mailrapport* 881x/'33.

In spite of this expansion in the private school network, the geographical distribution pattern of the schools did not change. The Padang and Pariaman sub-regencies on the coast and the Manindjau and Agam Tua sub-regencies in the interior remained the chief centers of private schools. In these sub-regencies there was one private school for every 5,000 inhabitants. In the Ophir sub-regency, on the other hand, for a population of 10,000 there was only one private school. In Manindjau, the most politicized sub-regency, private schools could accommodate 8% of the population. In Bangkinang, private schools accommodated less than 1.5% of the population.

A more important change was the "secularization" tendency within the Minangkabau educational system. Although the number of purely secular private schools was still very small, the num-ber of "combined" schools offering religious education as well as predominantly secular subjects rapidly increased. The secularization trend began with the inclusion of several secular subjects in the Kaum Muda schools. The Kaum Tua schools remained purely religious in the traditional sense until the 1940's, but by 1934 they were distinctly a minority, especially in terms of their student enrollment.

The above trend does not mean a decline in the absolute number of purely religious schools. The Kaum Tua school network was also expanding. In 1933 the PII had only 45 schools. In 1938, the organization, under a new name, controlled about 200 schools, most of them newly founded. Moreover, traditional sekolah and surau mengadji, Quranic recital schools, remained important.

Table 5
Types of Private Schools

Type of School	Schools	Students
1. Kaum Tua schools: purely religious education	589	9,285
2. Kaum Muda schools: religious schools with secular subjects	452	25,292
3. "Combined" schools: secular schools with religious education	132	44,577
4. Secular schools	35	824
Total	1,213	69,983

Source: *Mailrapport* 881x/'33.

Emergence of Islamic Colleges

In the mid-1920's, new attempts were made to stimulate the process of modernization in the religious schools. Hadji Abdullah Ahmad started preparations for a modern Normal Islam, and the Sumatra Thawalib schools began to draw up plans for a standardization of their school system and for the inclusion of secular subjects in the curriculum. In the meantime, Mahmud Junus, following up on his experience in Cairo, designed a plan for religious school reform and began writing new textbooks.

A turning point in the modernization of the religious schools came in 1931 when the Dinijah and Thawalib schools adopted Mahmud Junus' plan and Permi and the PGAI opened modern teachers' training schools. In late 1930, Mahmud Junus founded a school, Al-Djamiah Islamijah, in Sungajang, which was divided into elementary (*ibtidaijah*) and secondary (*tsanawijah*) levels. Each had a four year program. Students at the elementary level were graduates of the volksschool or the second class school. The secondary level only admitted students who had already attended the Thawalib or Dinijah schools. The class time was evenly divided among Arabic, religious and secular subjects. The elementary level was modeled on the government schakelschoo Secular subjects in the secondary level followed the program used in the government elementary teachers' training schools.[8]

The Djamiah closed in 1933 for lack of qualified teachers, but its system was adopted by the Dinijah and Thawalib schools. In late 1931, the Dinijah school for girls (Dinijah Putri) divided its seven-year program into a four-year ibtidaijah and a three year tsanawijah. The school gradually introduced secular subjects, such as geography, English, botany, and others. By 1933 the secular subjects formed 30 to 35% of the school's total teaching hours.[9] Although varying in the arrangement of the curricula, other Dinijah and Thawalib schools began to introduce the new system in 1932. These trends became more pronounced as graduates from the new teachers' training schools began to take positions in the schools.

The emergence of the new teachers' training schools was an important achievement for the Kaum Muda educators. These colleges recruited their students from the graduates of the Kaum Muda and the Kaum Tua religious schools and also from the HIS and schakelschool. The earliest college was the Normal Islam, which was financially supported by Minangkabau traders and a government sponsored lottery. On July 7, 1930, almost five years after he had begun his campaign, Hadji Abdullah Ahmad opened a modern teachers' training school, complete with a library and student dormitories. The Padang-based school began its program in early 1931 with Mahmud Junus as director. Since the students were mostly graduates of the Thawalib, Dinijah and the Kaum Tua Tarbijah schools, the four year program of the Normal Islam put more emphasis on secular subjects and Arabic. Mahmud held a degree in Arabic from the Darul Ulum in Cairo. The Normal Islam was the first Islamic school to use Arabic as its main medium of instruction, and some 20% of the teaching hours were spent on Arabic. In spite of its name, the school used only 15% of its

---

8 Junus, *Sedjarah Pendidikan*, pp. 89-90, 96-97.
9 L. de Vries, Report, September 5, 1928, *Mailrapport* 966x/ '28.

teaching hours for religious subjects, such as law, Quranic commentaries, Hadith and tauhid. Another 65% of class time was devoted to instruction in secular subjects, such as mathematics, geography, history, and Western languages, particularly English.

The establishment of the Islamic College on May 1, 1931 in Padang was a result of the disenchantment among Permi leaders with Hadji Abdullah Ahmad because of his relationship with the Dutch. Also Permi desired to have its own modern school. The new teachers' training school, called Al-Kulijat-ul Islamijah, was founded, according to its promoters, in order to create "perfect men with solid personalities." Trained in the spirit of "Islam and nationalism," the students were expected to be knowledgeable in both secular and religious subjects.[10] Permi's Islamic College, unlike the Normal Islam, was designed to train not only future teachers but future political leaders as well.

Preparations for the founding of the Islamic College began while Permi was still in the process of transferring its head-quarters to Padang in late 1930. The school's promoters, Iljas Jacub and Basa Bandaro, managed to gain support from several Western educated persons and traders in Padang. The "board of advisers" of the school, the men responsible for designing the school program and curriculum, consisted of Western educated intellectuals. Some of them were high government officials. The chairman of the board was Dr. Kusuma Atmadja, a Sundanese judge, called by Permi "the father of the Islamic College."[11] Chaired by Basa Bandaro, the permanent board of trustees consisted of Padang merchants, two of whom were coastal aristocrats and the other two penghulu from the interior. Djalaluddin Thaib and Iljas Jacub were the prominent members of the school board, which actually supervised the school. The school's promoters and Permi wanted to install Mahmud Junus, Iljas' opponent in Cairo, as the director of the college. They failed, however, because Mahmud had been committed to Hadji Abdullah Ahmad's organization, the PGAI, since 1929. Also he wanted to remain aloof from politics. Permi then tried to appoint Djanan Thaib, the director of Sekolah Indonesia in Mecca. In spite of his initial willingness to return to Minangkabau, Djanan

---

10 *Tjaja Soematra*, April 10, 1937.
11 *Medan Rakjat*, 1, No. 9 (June 1931); Politieke Politioneel Overzicht, 2de kwartaal, 1931, *Mailrapport* 808x/'31.

Thaib remained in Mecca, where he served as an inspector of education under the new Arab government. Until 1938, the Islamic College was under the directorship of Abdul Hakim, a lawyer. Teachers at the school were recruited from graduates of Al-Azhar and of the government AMS and HIK.

As far as curriculum was concerned, there was no major difference between the Normal Islam and the Islamic College. Both emphasized secular subjects and Arabic and both taught English, rather than Dutch, as their second foreign language. But, since the Islamic College also admitted the graduates of the HIS and the schakelschool, its first grade was divided into two programs. The graduates of the government secular schools had to take a special class in order to make up for their lack of religious training.

The Normal Islam and the Islamic College were the earliest successful colleges in Minangkabau. By 1934, the Muhammadijah and two other organizations also established their own colleges. These colleges not only provided advanced and general training for graduates of Thawalib and Dinijah schools but also, more importantly, helped to minimize the gulf between the religious and Western educated persons. The college was an institution where graduates of religious schools could study together with those of the government schools and where the Islamic modernists from Al-Azhar could work together with Western-educated intellectuals. With the increased number of Cairo returnees, the growing participation of the Western-educated persons in the Kaum Muda educational movement, and the popularity of the colleges, the number of these teachers' training schools kept increasing. By 1940 there were already thirteen such colleges in Minangkabau. In order to accommodate their graduates, the first Islamic university was founded in Padang in 1940.

Into this situation of expansion of private schools, modernization of religious schools, emergence of Islamic colleges, and intense anti-government political activity, the central government introduced the Wild Schools Ordinance. Opposition to the ordinance soon created a common front for most of Minangkabau, as well as for other Indonesian political and educational organizations and increased the anti-government activities still further.

Campaign Against the Wild Schools Ordinance

On September 19, 1932, a "supervision ordinance for private schools'1 (*toezicht ordonnantie -particulier onderwijs*), popularly known as the Wild Schools Ordinance (*Wilde Scholen Ordonnantie*), was promulgated. The ordinance stipulated that those who wanted to teach in non-subsidized private schools should obtain written permission from the district office. Applicants should have a certificate from a government or subsidized school and should be able to convince the district officer that they would not violate colonial "rust en orde."[12] The ordinance was issued in order to protect the quality of the private schools, the so-called "wild schools," and to maintain a standardized school system. This ordinance was also designed to enable the government to prevent political influence in the private schools. The ordinance was felt to be necessary, because the existing ordinance (*Staatsblad 1923, no. 136*) only gave the government repressive powers; the new one was preventive and hopefully would allow enforcement of stricter controls on nationalist private schools.[13]

The ordinance soon aroused opposition from the majority of Islamic and nationalist organizations throughout Java and Minangkabau. Radical parties, such as the PNI Baru and Partindo, and loyal parties, such Budi Utomo, all opposed the ordinance. In Minangkabau, the opposition sealed the cooperation among the Kaum Muda organizations and created a common cause for Kaum Muda and Kaum Tua ulama.

Several factors contributed to the opposition. In the first place, the ordinance was issued at a time when the government itself was pursuing a retrenchment policy which had resulted in the suspension of school expansion. The Wild Schools Ordinance would sharply decrease the number of private schools, because many of their teachers had not graduated from a government or subsidized school. It would also impair the future of graduates from private schools whose diplomas were not recognized by the government. The ordinance, therefore, was seen as nothing less than a legal means to eliminate the rapidly expanding nationalist private

---

12 *Staatsblad* 1932, no. 494, September 1932.
13 Report of the Director of Education, B. J. O. Schrieke, in van der Wal, ed., *Onderwijsbeleid*, pp. 508-520.

schools. Ki Hadjar Dewantara, who emerged as the national leader of the opposition, predicted that the Wild Schools Ordinance could mean "the defeat of the national political movement" and "the death of the people's freedom."[14] It was also suspected that the ordinance might lead to arbitrary interpretation or misunderstanding by officials at the expense of the private schools. The ordinance's aim to achieve a standard school system was thought to foreshadow continuation of the "denationalizing process" of Indonesian youth.[15] The desire to develop a new educational system based on national culture had motivated the establishment of Taman Siswa and other nationalist private schools.

On October 1, 1932, Ki Hadjar Dewantara sent a telegram to the Governor-General, in which he stated that Taman Siswa rejected the ordinance and that it would, if necessary, "persistently conduct passive resistance" (*lijdelijk verzet*). In a very short time, his firm stand was followed by other political and educational organizations. They were determined to continue their schools at any cost.[16]

By the end of the year, almost all important organizations were participating in local opposition committees scattered throughout Java and West Sumatra. At the end of December, a national conference of the Committee to Help National Education was held in Jogjakarta. At the conference, Marah Sutan, a famous Minangkabau educator and the father of Sjafei, announced that the Minangkabau people would work closely with Ki Hadjar Dewantara in conducting "passive resistance." "There are more than 10,000 teachers and students in Minangkabau," he claimed, "who are determined to oppose the ordinance, even if they have to go to jail." In a mood of opposition, the conference also paid its respects to Rasuna Said, the first leader to be arrested as the result of the opposition movement.[17]

The Wild Schools Ordinance encountered the strongest opposition in Minangkabau. Every school organization, political parties, and a large number of adat leaders opposed the ordinance. Unlike the opposition to

---

14 *Ibid.*, p. 553.
15 In 1927, van der Plas wrote that there should be a "nationalizing process" in the government schools. See, *ibid.*, pp. 437-444.
16 On the reactions in various parts of Indonesia see Noer, "Rise and Development," pp. 291-297.
17 *Oetoesan Indonesia*, December 31 and January 3, 1933, in *Overzicht van de Inlandsch Pers*, 1/1933, p. 31.

the Guru Ordinance in 1928, opposition to the Wild Schools Ordinance was conducted by each organization separately, although they participated in the joint local committees. As in the case of the Guru Ordinance, the paramount impulse behind the opposition was religious.[18]

The opposition began to gain momentum in November 1932. Iljas Jacub, the head of Permi's department of education, argued that "the real origin of the Wild Schools Ordinance was the great difference between the government and the people."[19] He considered the ordinance even worse than the Guru Ordinance because it would affect the future of graduates from existing private schools.[20] The Dinijah schools' organization issued a resolution on November 19, 1932, stating that the Wild Schools Ordinance was an obstacle hindering the struggle of the Indonesian people to achieve educational progress. The Dinijah, therefore, was determined to work closely with other organizations in opposing the ordinance.[21] Students at the Islamic College announced that they were prepared to become substitute teachers if the present teachers at the private schools were arrested. The students secured the cooperation of their colleagues in the Normal Islam and other newly established Islamic teachers' training schools.[22] At the end of December, "10,000 students from Thawalib schools" were ready to back their teachers in opposition to the ordinance.[23] The PII, the newly transformed Kaum Tua organization, also joined the chorus of opposition. Not allowing themselves to be led by the Kaum Muda ulama, however, the Kaum Tua ulama sent a letter of protest directly to the government.[24] On December 18, the PSII, in accordance with the instruction of its central board, called simultaneous meetings of its branches. All meetings, however, were dispersed by the police. In order to dramatize its opposition, the party urged its members and other Minangkabau people to hold midnight prayers (*tahadjud*) individually or communally.[25]

---

18 van Heuven, "Memorie van Overgave," pp. 7-8.
19 *Tjaja Soematra*, November 19, 1932.
20 *Medan Rakjat*, October 1 and October 8, 1932, in *Overzicht van de Inlandsch Pers*, 42/1932, p. 268.
21 *Berita*, in *ibid.*, 49/1932, p. 377.
22 *Radio*, December 9, 1932.
23 Politieke Politioneel Overzicht, December 1932, *Mailrapport* 227x/'33.
24 *Ibid.*, January 1933, *Mailrapport* 357x/'33.
25 *Ibid.*, December 1932, *Mailrapport* 227x/'33; *Berita*, January 5, 1933.

In an emergency conference on December 15, Permi decided to coordinate the opposition movement of the Thawalib and Permi schools and to engage in concerted action with political parties in Java. On December 26-27, Permi conducted "simultaneous actions." During the two days, according to a government report, Permi held no less than 66 protest meetings throughout the West Coast of Sumatra. The majority of the meetings, however, were dispersed by the police. Some meetings were forced to adjourn before they started. In many places, Permi could not hold a meeting because the local authorities refused to grant permission.[26]

The Resident of the West Coast stated that the Wild Schools Ordinance provided "a practical front of political unity" and gave "something worthwhile for public meetings."[27] The ordinance was seen not simply as a legal hindrance to the development of secular private schools. The Permi statement of December 27 said that the ordinance would eventually "destroy the Indonesians1 cultural life at a time when they are struggling to fulfill their obligations according to Islam and [the law of] humanity."[28] The ordinance was a direct assault on Islamic doctrine, which emphasized the need for a continuing effort in search of knowledge. Kaum Muda ulama, under the leadership of Hadji Rasul, founded a committee of opposition in early December 1932. The committee was supported by the Muhammadijah and other Islamic organizations.[29] Shortly after its establishment, it urged the people to oppose the Wild Schools Ordinance and the Guru Ordinance, which was in force in areas outside Minangkabau. The committee appealed to the government to withdraw these ordinances. The resolution emphasized that the search

---

26 According to the Permi statement, "Only 32 of the 74 protest meetings planned could actually be held." The police re-fused permission for the rest. Loetan Gani, "Rintangan-Rintangan Pergerakan di Minangkabau," Berita, January 5, 1932.
27 van Heuven, "Memorie van Overgave," pp. 51-54.
28 Politieke Politioneel Overzicht, December 1932, *Mailrapport* 227x/'33.
29 A permanent board was installed in January 1933. The committee, known as the Comite Perloetjoetan "Goeroe Ordonnantie" dan "Ordonnantie Toezicht Particulier Scholen," included the following:

Chairman:	Dr. Hadji Abdul Karim Amrullah [Hadji Rasul]
Vice-Chairman:	Sjech M. Djamil Djambek
Secretary:	Hadji Abdul Malik
Treasurer:	Hadji Ibrahim Musa
Commissioners:	Sjech Abbas Abdullah
	Sjech Daud Rasjidi
	Hadji Adjhuri

Politieke Politioneel Overzicht, January 1933, *Mailrapport* 357x/'33.

for and the distribution of knowledge was a religious duty. The Prophet had instructed his followers "to seek knowledge from the cradle to the grave" and God had commanded mankind to discover "the secret of the universe." The government ordinance in effect tried to block Muslims from pursuing their religious obligations.

> The Indonesian people, who have become the humblest and the poorest nation in this world—because they are poor in knowledge—have been trying as best as they can to establish educational institutions, which are in accordance with their ideologies. [They are doing this] because it is a sacred right and a holy obligation that must be pursued by anyone of pure heart and of high morality. This should also be the attitude of the government if it really wants to improve the life of its subjects.[30]

The appeal of the Kaum Muda ulama, who had led the opposition to the Guru Ordinance, gave moral support to the political parties. Already by February 1933, 123 political and educational organizations in Minangkabau had joined the "ulama committee." In February, the committee held a conference in Padang Pandjang at which it decided, among other things: to intensify its opposition to the ordinance, to establish closer cooperation with all Indonesian organizations, and to establish a closer relationship with Islamic organizations abroad. On behalf of its supporting organizations, the committee repeated its appeal to the government for withdrawal of the Wild Schools Ordinance and the Guru Ordinance. In its resolution, the committee stated that it was prepared to obey government laws only if those laws did not violate their own religious law.

> After we have studied carefully our essential obligations to God, to Whom we must be responsible for our deeds, [we realize] that it is impossible to accept the two ordinances. If the government is determined to enforce such ordinances, [it would force us] to

---

30 "Makloemat Comite Perloetjoetan 'Goeroe Ordonnantie' dan 'Ordonnantie Toezicht Particulier Scholen,'" *Pembela Islam*, 57 (1933), pp. 42-43.

commit sin against our God. If we try to fulfill our obligation to God, we may have to betray the government.³¹

February, however, was the last month of the opposition movement. At the order of the Attorney-General, all public meetings for discussing the Wild Schools Ordinance were forbidden.³² Facing opposition from all major political parties, the central government suspended the enforcement of the ordinance.³³ The "passive resistance" of Ki Hadjar Dewantara and the religious appeal of the Kaum Muda ulama had ended in success. The government abandoned its idea of using preventive legal means to curb nationalist private schools. But the existing ordinance (*Staatsblad* 1923, no. 136) could still be a useful weapon to suppress undesirable influence in the private schools.

Government Campaign Against the Religious Schools

According to Resident van Heuven, there was a strong tendency among the Minangkabau to regard the religious schools as their special preserve and as a sphere where their "autonomy" should be inviolate. They expected the government to respect this privileged sphere, and they would not hesitate to act if the government encroached on it.³⁴ A similar conclusion was also reached by the Attorney-General during an investigation visit to the West Coast in July 1933. He realized that a new regulation concerning private schools was likely to incite political turmoil.³⁵ The best policy, therefore, was to implement effectively the legal sanctions already provided by the 1923 school ordinance.

In addition to suppressing radical political parties, the government wanted to eliminate political influence from religious schools. In the second half of 1933, several Kaum Muda schools were raided and a large

---

31 *Verbaal* March 23, 1933.
32 Politieke Politioneel Overzicht, February 1933, *Mailrapport* 590x/'33.
33 The opinions of various high officials is contained in van der Wal, ed., *Herinneringen*, pp. 151-153, and *Onderwijsbeleid*, pp 549-5557
34 Resident van Heuven, Letter to the Director of Education, Padang, April 12, 1933, no. 867x/P/ secret, *Mailrapport* 357x/'33; Letter of the Attorney-General to the Governor-General, Tarutung, July 17, 1933, *Mailrapport* 921x/'33.
35 Politieke Politioneel Overzicht, December 1932, *Mailrapport* 227x/'33.

amount of political literature was confiscated. In December, on the basis of evidence found during the raid, seven out of the twelve teachers at the Thawa-lib school of Padang Pandjang were forbidden to teach for "an unspecified time." This action was followed by the closing of two Permi schools, the Tsanawijah and the teachers' training school for girls. These schools were considered strongly anti-Dutch and their students thoroughly politicized.[36] In early 1934, the government forced the Dinijah Putri to expel two of its teachers who were former leaders of Permi. In Kerintji and Pariaman the Dutch local officials supported the adat authorities when they closed or took over schools established by Permi. In the meantime, the government continued its policy of preventing those who were former political leaders from teaching.

In the face of government repression, in December 1933, Permi dissolved its department of education and announced that each school was now an independent unit. The decision would weaken the party and the schools because it forced Permi leaders to choose between remaining in the party or becoming full-fledged teachers, but party leaders thought this was the only way to protect the schools from government action. Permi also reemphasized the independent character of its former boy scout organization, El-Hilaal, which had been under government surveillance.

It was feared, however, that dissolution of the department of education would endanger the success of the modernization program for religious schools. In January 1934, several teachers at the Thawalib schools who had had to resign from Permi formed a Council of Education which tried to function along the lines of Permi's department of education. Although the council could not successfully take the latter's place, it managed to consolidate the schools to some extent during the difficult process of "depoliticization" and modernization.

After the government enforced the vergaderverbod in August 1933, the Resident reported a strong tendency to shift the focus of activity from politics to schools. In spite of official suspicion, the modernization of religious schools continued. Without adequate organizational channels, however, the process was not even. There was no uniformity in programs

---

36 *Ibid.*, February 1934, *Mailrapport* 480x/'34.

or textbooks. This uneven development of religious schools continued until 1936, when a new milestone in the history of Minangkabau religious schools was reached. In that year a conference of all school organizations resulted in the standardization of Kaum Muda religious schools.

Conclusion

It took almost two decades for the religious schools to initiate a program that had been advocated by the pioneers of the Kaum Muda movement since the early 1910's. In the first Islamic journal, *Al-Moenir*, the Kaum Muda ulama had appealed for ilmu asjriah (knowledge which was in accordance with changing times), *ilmu akaliah* (knowledge which was based on intelligence) and European languages, needed for an understanding of new sciences. But these ulama, though they were modernists, were also orthodox reformers, and they made no substantial progress. They also could not make satisfactory improvements in their own schools. In 1915 Hadji Abdullah Ahmad, Kaum Muda leader in Padang, aided by several Western educated persons, established the HIS Adabijah, a Dutch-Native school where children were also given religious education. But soon after, the school received a subsidy from the government, and it hired a Dutch principal and Dutch-educated teachers. It was Zainuddin Labai, an able and dedicated former student of Hadji Rasul, who made a breakthrough in the madrasah tradition. In 1915 he founded the Dinijah school, which took the government school system as its model. The new graded system for religious schools was soon adopted by Hadji Rasul in the Sumatra Thawalib and by other Kaum Muda religious teachers. After 1915, the Kaum Muda religious schools continued to change. The system of instruction, the character of learning, the use of textbooks and the school organizations continued to change. The significance of the early 1930's is that it was a period when the majority of the Kaum Muda schools, their teachers, and many of their graduates, were involved in reform programs. It was a time when both Cairo returnees and Western-educated intellectuals were actively engaged in the modernization of religious schools.

The expansion of Kaum Muda religious schools and Kaum Muda sponsored "combined" schools contributed much to the group's predominance in Minangkabau political movements. The schools laid down a foundation for the spread and the continuity of the basic teachings of orthodox Islamic modernism. In this way, the Kaum Muda schools and preachers (muballigh) with their numerous organizations and publications confirmed more strongly the superiority of Islam over adat within the concept of alam Minangkabau. The Kaum Muda school system can be seen as the source of a number of observable tendencies in Minangkabau modern history, particularly those which were politically Islamic-oriented but intellectually open to Western influence.

The continuing process of modernization in the religious schools sometimes resulted in a conflict of generations, such as the conflict between the communist-oriented religious teachers and graduates and the Kaum Muda ulama, and the tension between the latter and the Islamic-nationalist Permi leaders. This process was also partly responsible for the internal dissension among the Kaum Muda educated group demonstrated by the conflict between the Muhammadijah and Permi. Since the early 1920's, the Kaum Muda schools had not only been the intellectual centers for the anti-colonial political movement but also had been the major motive force behind the intensifying political activities. Their close identification with the schools and their own ideals and professions had led the Kaum Muda ulama and their former students, despite differences on specific political and social issues, to form a common front in their opposition to the Guru Ordinance (1928) and the Wild Schools Ordinance (1932). This opposition itself contributed to a proliferation of religious and" combined" schools and encouraged the process of religious school modernization. Schools were also the institutions to which Islamic modernist leaders returned after political activities were suppressed and the political parties were paralyzed.

In September 1933, the government dealt a deathblow to Permi by arresting its important leaders and applying the vergader-verbod regulation to party meetings. In the middle of 1934, the party abandoned its political character and pledged to concentrate its activities solely in economic and educational fields. Permi, however, could not operate under government suspicion. It failed to revive its followers' enthusiasm because the government continued to stress rust en orde. In 1936, Permi, once the largest and most radical party in Sumatra, had to dissolve itself. Nevertheless, its Islamic College and the numerous Sumatra Thawalib schools it had helped to expand and modernize continued to develop. In

1936 a new major educational reform was begun, and in 1940 the Kaum Muda educated group with the cooperation of the Western educated intellectuals founded the first Islamic university in Indonesia.

IN RETROSPECT

Feelings of grievance, mounting anti-government sentiment, and a desire to create a new world "free from capitalist and kafir exploitation," contributed to the outbreak of rebellion in January 1927. The notion that the act of opposition itself was a kind of ibadah led some young Islamic modernists to participate in the so-called communist rebellion. The idea that rebellion was a way of purifying the social environment motivated several tarekat sjech, who led the rebellious movement. The daring attempt to gain independence, however, was harshly suppressed. The rebellion ended in despair, death or exile.

During the post-rebellion period, the Minangkabau attempted to recover from the psychological shock and tried to find new forms and a more solid foundation for social development. The ulama, whose prestige was gravely undermined in the three years of communist activities, recaptured the leadership from their former students, products of Kaum Muda schools. The Muhammadi-jah emerged as the first Kaum Muda organization designed to lead the ummat in the creation of a religiously based society and at the same time to utilize prevailing anti-government feelings in building its organization. The period from 1927 until the end of 1930, which included expansion of the Muhamma-dijah, the campaign against the Guru Ordinance, and the emergence of Permi and the PSII, was a time when the Kaum Muda educated group gradually spread its influence, taking the lead in the educational and political movements in West Sumatra. The period from 1931 to 1933, however, also exposed the various contradictory aspects in Minangkabau life. In this period, adat, the symbol of Minangkabau continuity and the traditional basis of legitimate political power, was put to the test. Should adat tolerate the existing colonial power, which was clearly not based on sakato alam (consensus of the people)? Or should adat be used to support and to cultivate new ideas brought by the Islamic modernists and Western educated intellectuals from the rantau? Tolerance of the foreign power meant nothing less than a betrayal of adat. On the other hand, complete acceptance of new ideas and trends might reduce the political power of the nagari authorities who represented adat. Both alternatives posed a threat to the continuity of the alam Minangkabau itself. The response to these questions resulted, on the one hand, in the participation of many penghulu in the political movement and, on the other, in a closer relationship between other adat authorities and the Dutch government. Tension inherent in Islamic thinking also came to the surface. The ideal of creating a right-guided society had to take into account the need to liberate the ummat from a kafir government. Islam, "the all-embracing and perfect religion" and the proper basis of uni-versal unity, had to cope with concepts of national unity based on secular instead of transcendental considerations. Both Is-lamic unity as well as kebangsaan unity challenged the idea of the ever-expanding world of Minangkabau and the traditional centripetal conception of its alam.

The period was one of political romanticism in Minangkabau, a time when political action for its own sake was most important and when a bold political speech might turn a leader into a hero. In spite of various examples which demonstrate the existential character of political activities, during this period there was also an intensive effort to modernize Minangkabau and to awaken the people to a realization of the tension between primordial attachments and the need for a new, enlarged conception of their world. For Minangkabau, the early 1930's were a period of political anxiety and ideological confusion on the one hand, and of the growing self-confidence in the ability to change the society on the other.

The preceding chapters have traced the emergence and growth of the influence of the second generation of the Islamic modern-ists. The expansion of religious doctrines beginning with the Kaum Muda ulama in the 1900's, the slackening doctrinal religious conflict, the rising popularity of schools as part of the consistent drive toward kemadjuan, and the growing anti-government feeling provided a favorable background for the predominance of the Kaum Muda educated group. Their divergent geographical origins and different social backgrounds and occupations helped this group dominate Minangkabau's social movements in the post-rebellion period. They managed to organize the most powerful pressure group, in spite of opposition from adat authorities, as represented by the nagari councils, and contempt from the Kaum Tua ulama who persisted in their traditional religious views of obedience to textual authorities and the Shafiite school of law. The rapid increase in the number of the Islamic modernists, as a result of the expansion of Kaum Muda schools, and their close identification with the populace made then unbeatable competitors for leadership of the popular movement. The Western educated persons, by contrast, were numerically weak and professionally had closer ties to the government. The influence of the nationalist Western-educated intellectuals, most of whom were perantau leaders, could only be effective through cooperation with the Islamic modernists. After the early 1930's, there was a trend toward minimizing the gap which existed between these two educated groups.

A common educational background and a similar outlook on religious matters proved the most important common denominators of the Kaum Muda educated group. Educated in the spirit of reform and trained to become religious teachers and muballigh, these young Islamic modernists saw the schools as the focus for their activities. The school was an institution which they used to expand their influence and to which they could return after their political activities were suppressed. As the focus of Islamic life, the religious schools were also the most sensitive political issue. Opposition to the Guru Ordinance and to the Wild Schools Ordinance and their immediate sequels, expressed through a proliferation of religious schools and the acceleration of anti-government political activity, showed the determination of the Kaum Muda ulama and their former students to protect their schools from outside interference. As in the past when the madrasah posed a potential challenge to the religious and adat establishment, new religious schools were also intellectual centers of the anti-government political movement. In the nineteenth and early twentieth centuries, madrasah, particularly the tarekat centers, provided the religious basis for the people's grievances. In the 1920's and the 1930's, new religious schools helped to formulate the ideological foundation of the independence movement.

The idea of returning to original Islamic doctrines, the need for the liberation of Islam from centuries of deviation, and the recognition of the inherent greatness of Islam brought appeals for an Islamic cultural renaissance as well as for political consciousness. In spite of the Kaum Muda ulama's rejection of direct participation in politics or any direct attack on the legitimacy of the present holders of power, their former students and organizations became deeply immersed in the political movement. The openly political character of the Kaum Muda educated group provoked the Dutch government to take an intolerant attitude. In the face of the rapid politicization of Islamic modernist followers, the government not only continued its traditional policy of supporting the adat authorities but also tried to incite the Kaum Tua ulama against the Kaum Muda followers.

Islamic modernism, which believed in the compatibility of religion with the modern world, provided a religious basis for social change. Its idea of the inherent greatness of Islamic civilization inspired self-confidence in meeting the outside world and strengthened the independence movement. The apologetic cultural appeal of Islamic modernism, however, also initiated the gradual trend toward the petrification of its doctrine. Islamic modernism, formulated at the turn of century when modern imperialism had attained the peak of its development and Islam was at the nadir of its history, laid the foundation for a new Islamic conservatism.

As a political appeal, Islamic modernism presented its followers with an ideological dilemma—the need to create a new "utopian" society based on moral victory and the importance of liberation from the kafir government. The conflict between the Muhammadijah, which was supported by the Kaum Muda ulama, and the political parties, such as Permi and the PSII, had its roots in this ideological ambiguity. Both the moral and political sides might converge in their basic rejection of the colonial government. Appeals for independence, which intensified the politicization of Minangkabau, forced the government to repress the Islamic political parties. The moral leadership of Hadji Rasul, who persistently opposed political solutions and who, according to the government, had rendered the administrative system entirely ineffective in the Danau region, provoked the central government to exile him in early 1940. Profound concern over political and moral questions and a lack of success in combining these two concerns became obvious after independence. The political frustration and moral sensitivity of the Islamic group can to some extent be seen as a reflection of the inner tension of its ideology.

Islamic doctrine was, undoubtedly, the main motivating force in the politicization of the Kaum Muda educated group. This trend was magnified by the Minangkabau political tradition, which also affected the political behavior of the Islamic modernists. Lacking a centralized and hierarchical authority, political life was focused in the nagari, where the political process was based on the proper use of established precedents and of the relevant hierarchy. The legitimacy of a decision which would have social significance required the deliberate use of mufakat. Failure to fulfill this requirement would result in a lack of support and in the disruption of social harmony. As a political institution, mufakat was also thought to symbolize the honor and pride of the rightful participants in the process. Attachment to this tradition, which was regarded as an essential part of Minangkabau life, was a factor in the rural rebellions and the spread of anti-government political movements.

Their attachment to the nagari political tradition caused the nagari authorities to oppose the movement of the Islamic modernists, who threatened their power, and made these authorities the bastion of Minangkabau conservatism. Change which was introduced by ignoring the established pattern would eventually disrupt the stability ahd harmony of the small world of the nagari. The adat authorities, after all, were traditionally not only the holders of political power, whose legitimacy was based on the sakato alam, but also the guardians of the ideals inherent in alam.

The continuing flow of new ideas and trends and the social conflict this caused were consequences of the Minangkabau concept of its alam. It was a world which recognized the existence of the rantau as a part of alam because it acknowledged the importance of the outside world as an area from which alam might receive stimuli to realize its own potentials. Rantau, the newly acquired or fringe territories, were of traditional political importance to the king, who did not have jurisdiction in the heartland. Economically, rantau was conceived as a region in which the Minangkabau adults made their living and accumulated money for the benefit of their matrilineal and nuclear families. As a cultural concept, rantau was an outlet to ease the internal tension in the small world of the nagari and a kind of rite of passage for the youth. In the rantau a young man was expected to prepare himself to become a full member of his community and to become a mature person. Experiences in the rantau were expected to secure the continuity of alam Minangkabau and to stimulate its historical goal of the attainment of a perfect and harmonious society. Nevertheless, cultural stimuli brought by the perantau, who had been influenced by their respective rantau regions, might also threaten alam itself.

The attempt to maintain a balance between the need for the elaboration of alam on the one hand and its continuity on the other is a major theme of Minangkabau history. The ambiguity of the rantau position in the Minangkabau world view is a factor that leads to social and generational conflict. It is also a basis of Minangkabau's dynamism as well as its conservatism. The latter aspect becomes more evident at a time when the drive toward change is strong. It is the time when rantau is thought to threaten the foundation of the Minangkabau world. Without rantau, however, alam is thought to be merely a potential, and the greatness of adat, which "neither rots in the rain nor cracks in the sun," cannot be tested.

The period from 1927 to 1933 was a time when ideas from the rantau, either in the form of Islamic modernism or anti-colonial nationalism, were expanding. The perantau, whether trained in Cairo, Java or Holland, assisted the expansion of private schools and the modernization of religious schools and continued the process of social change. At the same time, however, they captured the initiative from the nagari authorities. They exposed the incompatibility of the adat concept of the sakato alam with the existence of the colonial government and introduced and cultivated the idea of Indonesian unity based on the absorption of all ethnic loyalties into a new and enlarged world, the Indonesian nation. This idea of unity, however, challenged the traditional centripetal conception of alam and its notion of an ever expanding world. The conflicting yet complementary concepts of unity have continued to influence political development in West Sumatra before and after the independence and to exert their impact on the views and behavior of its political leaders.

By accepting Islam as an inseparable part of its world, Minangkabau had not only given a transcendental basis to its cultural moorings but had also made itself the object for changes originating far outside its geographical boundaries. Its acknowledgment of rantau as a kind of rite of passage contributed to the development of the Minangkabau social order largely by forcing it to fight for its continuity. Fascination with the ideals expressed in the adat sayings and the acceptance of the goals prescribed by Islam remain to dominate Minangkabau thinking. But its life is conditioned by its actual social system and by the recognition of political realities. These paradoxical forces and the inherent tensions in Islamic doctrine as well as in adat assumptions continue to characterize Minangkabau social behavior and historical development.

GLOSSARY

Adat	Local custom and traditional law. In the Minangkabau world view, adat and Islam are considered the two pillars of society.
Adat Djahilijah	Syncretic and unenlightened adat, i.e., not in accord with Islamic law.
Adat Islamijah	Adat in accord with Islamic law.
Akal, Akalijah	Intelligence, the faculty of reasoning in general.
Alam, Alam Minangkabau	The universe or world of the Minangkabau people.
Alamijah	Degree granted by the Al-Azhar University in Cairo to foreign students.
Anak Buah	Followers or dependents.
Aqidah	Article of faith or doctrinal statement in Islam.
Anak Nagari	The natives of a particular district or nagari.
Balai	The nagari council hall, traditionally used to refer to the council itself.
Bangsa	Ethnic group and, more recently, "nation."

Belahan	Believed blood relationship between the people of two nagari.
Beperkt Vergaderverbod	Dutch police regulation which limited holding of public meetings.
Bid'ah	Innovation in religious practice or views which leads to heresy.
Bilal	Adat religious functionary.
Bodi Tjaniago	One of two Minangkabau political traditions. It recognizes all penghulu in a nagari as equal.
Chatib	Adat religious functionary
Chilafijah	Differences in matters of doctrinal importance.
Controleur	Sub-regency head in the Dutch administrative hierarchy.
CSI	Central Sarekat Islam, Central Board of Sarekat Islam.
Datuk	Title of address for a penghulu.
Demang	Minangkabau head of a district in the Dutch administrative hierarchy.
Assistant Demang	Head of a sub-district.
Djaksa	Minangkabau public prosecutor in the Dutch administrative system.
Exorbitante Rechten	Extraordinary powers exercised by the Governor-General.
Fatwa	Religious judgments.
Fikh	Religious law, jurisprudence.
Friday Council	Prayer council held after the Friday service in the mosque.
Fukaha	Expert on religious law.
Guru	Teacher.

Guru Mengadji	Quranic recitation teacher in a traditional surau.
Hadith	The traditions of the Prophet Mohammad.
Hadji	Title of address for a person who com-pleted the religious pilgrimage to Mecca.
Halaqah	"Circle," refers to the system of instruction in traditional religious schools whereby the pupils sat around the teacher.
Haram	Forbidden according to Islamic religious law.
HIS	Hollandsch-Inlandsche School, Dutch-Native School, offering primary education in Dutch.
HPII	Himpunan Pemuda Islam Indonesia, Association of Indonesian Muslim Youth.
Ibadah	Ordinances of divine worship or religious duty.
Ibtidijah	Elementary religious school.
Idjitihad	Process of arriving at new religious judg-ments using reason and investigation of the Quran and the Hadith.
Idulfitri	Muslim Holy Day celebrating the end of the fasting month.
Ilmu	Knowledge, science.
Imam	Leader of prayer. Also the title of the spiritual leader of a Muslim community.

Iman	Proper religious belief and faith.
INS	Indonesisch-Nederlandsche School, Indonesian-Netherlands School, founded by Moh. Sjafei in Kaju Tanam.
Insulinde	Indies Nationalist Party.
Jawah	Indonesian/Malay community in the Middle East.
JIB	Jong Islamieten Bond, Young Islamic Union.
JSB	Jong Sumatranen Bond, Young Sumatran Union.
Kaba	Minangkabau traditional epic.
Kafir	Infidel, i.e., non-Muslim.
Kampung	Neighborhood.
Kaum	Group.
Kaum Hidjau	"Green" group, i.e., Muslims.
Kaum Intelek	Western-educated group.
Kaum Merah	"Red" group, i.e., communists.
Kaum Muda	"Young" group, i.e., progressives.
Kaum Tua	"Old" group, i.e., conservatives.
Kebangsaan	Nationalism.
Kebulatan	Resolution taken by the nagari council.
Kemadjuan	Progress and development, concept of "modernity."
Mendjadi Madju	Become "progressive," "modern."
Kemegahan	Glory.

Kemenakan (Kamanakan)	Kinship term in Minangkabau meaning nephew or niece. Also symbolizes the relationship of a person to his leader.
Kemerdekaan	Independence.
Kiai	Religious teacher.
KIM	Kepanduan Indonesia Muslim, Indonesian Muslim Boy Scouts.
Koto	In Minangkabau political terminology, a settlement which has not yet evolved into a nagari.
Koto Piliang	One of two Minangkabau political traditions. It recognizes the hierarchical ranking of penghulu within a nagari.
Kweekschool	Teachers' training institute.
Laras	Traditionally refers to the two political traditions in Minangkabau, Bodi Tjaniago and Koto Piliang. During the colonial period (up to 1914), laras also referred to the administrative unit above the nagari level.
Luhak	Traditional geographic division of the Minangkabau heartland.
Luhak nan Tigo	The three luhak: Tanah Datar, Agam, Lima Puluh Kota.
Mamak	A kinship term for maternal uncle. Also refers to the relationship of a lineage head to his followers.
Madrasah	Religious school.
Mazhab	School of jurisprudence in Islam.
Meisjesschool	Girls' school.

Merantau	Going to the rantau.
Minangkabau Raad	Regional council for Minangkabau under the Dutch.
Muballigh	Muslim propagandist or preacher.
Muda	Young, also progressive.
Mufakat	Consensus. In the Minangkabau adat context, it refers to the consensus of the penghulu in the nagari council.
MULO	Meer Uitgebreid Lagere Onderwijs, More Extended Lower Education, school offering advanced primary education in Dutch.
Mungkin	That which is logically possible.
Nafsu, Hawa Nafsu	Human natural desires.
Nagari	In Minangkabau political terminology, the most developed form of settlement, i.e., one having its own mosque and balai.
Naql	Established religious authorities.
NIP	Nationaal Indische Partij Indies National Party.
Parewa	Secular oriented, "individualists" in Minangkabau traditional society.
Parii	Partai Islam Indonesia, Indonesian Islamic Party.
Partindo	Partai Indonesia, Indonesian Party.
Patut	That which is morally proper.
Pemangku	Literally, the "holder." In the Minangkabau adat context, the person who represents the penghulu if the latter is ill or away.

Penghulu	The head of a matrilineal political unit, not to be confused with the penghulu in Java who is a religious official.
Penghulu Dagang	Dutch-appointed Minangkabau leader of dwellers in towns not native to them.
Perang Sabil	Holy War.
Permi	Persatuan Muslim Indonesia, Association of Indonesian Muslims, sometimes abbreviated PMI.
Perantau	One who leaves his nagari or the Minangkabau world to go to the rantau
Pergerakan	The political independence movement in Indonesia.
PGAI	Persatuan Guru Agama Islam, Association of Islamic Teachers.
PGHB	Perserikatan Guru Hindia Belanda, Union of Dutch East Indies Teachers.
PGSA	Persatuan Guru-Guru Sekolah Agama, Association of Religious School Teachers.
PI	Perhimpunan Indonesia, Indonesian Association.
PII	Pendidikan Islam Indonesia, Indonesian Islamic Education.
PKI	Partai Komunis Indonesia, Indonesian Communist Party.

Plakat Pandjang	The so-called Long Declaration issued by the Dutch in the early 1830's; it guaranteed the integrity of traditional Minangkabau society.
PMDS	Persatuan Murid-Murid Dinijah School, Association of Dinijah School Pupils.
PMM	Perhimpunan Muhammadijah Minangkabau, Union of Muhammadijah in Minangkabau.
PN	Pembela Negeri, Defenders of the Nation.
PNI	Partai Nasional Indonesia, Indonesian National Party.
PNI Baru	New PNI, also known as Pendidikan Nasional Indonesia, Indonesian National Education.
Pokrol Bambu	Unlicensed attorney.
PPPKI	Permufakatan Perhimpunan-Perhimpunan Kebang-saan Indonesia, Congress of Indonesian National Associations.
PSII	Partai Sarikat Islam Indonesia, Indonesian Islamic Union Party.
PTI	Persatuan Tarbijah Islamijah, Union of Islamic Students.
Radja	Representatives of the Minangkabau ruler who governed in the rantau districts.
Rantau	Fringe territories of the Minangkabau kingdom, also the non-Minangkabau world generally.

Reisregeling	Travel restriction imposed by the Dutch government on political leaders.
Riwak	Ethnic compound in the Al-Azhar University, Cairo.
Rodi, Rodi Kompeni	Corvée labor.
Rumah Gadang	Large Minangkabau family house.
Rust en Orde	Offical Dutch policy based on the maintenance of peace and order in the Indies.
SAAM	Sarekat Adat Alam Minangkabau, Adat Association of the Minangkabau World.
Sakato Alam	Consensus of the people, concept in Minangkabau political and social philosophy.
Santri	In Java, a Muslim who strives to fulfill all religious obligations.
Schakelschool	"Connecting" school, bridged the gap between the Indonesian vernacular schools and the European schools.
SCM	Sarekat Combinatie Minangkabau, Federation of Minangkabau Associations.
Sekolah Desa	Vernacular elementary school.
Setali Adat	Ties recognized by adat.
SI	Sarekat Islam, Islamic Union.
Sidang Djumat	Friday Council, prayer council held after the Friday service in the mosque.
Silat	Minangkabau art of unarmed combat.
Sjarak, Sjariah	Islamic law.

Sjech	Honorific title for a religious scholar, also leader of a tarekat brotherhood.
Spreekdelict	Sedition.
STOVIA	School tot Opleiding voor Indische Artsen, School for Training Indonesian Doctors.
Suku	Social unit in Minangkabau consisting of several matrilineal families.
Tabligh	Public religious gatherings.
Tambo	Traditional Minangkabau historical accounts.
Tanah Air	Homeland, fatherland.
Tanah Ulajat	Reserved communal land of a nagari.
Taqlid	Uncritical acceptance of the decision of textual authorities or teachers.
Tarekat	Literally, the "way" or "path," refers to the mystical brotherhoods in Islam.
Tasauf	Mysticism.
Tauhid	Doctrine of the absolute oneness of God.
Tjerdik Pandai	The "intelligentsia" of a nagari.
Tsanawijah	Secondary religious school.
Tua	Old, also conservative.
Tuanku Laras	Adat and administrative head of a nagari federation or laras, appointed by the Dutch government.
Ulama	Religious scholar.
Ummat, Ummat Islam	The community of believers in Islam.
Urang Asali	Original settlers of a nagari.

Urang Babangso	Original settlers of a nagari, also in the sense of the aristocracy of a nagari.
Urang Datang	New settlers in a nagari.
Urang Siak	Traveling religious student.
Vervolgschool	"Continuation" school, two-year program for graduates of vernacular elementary schools.
Volksschool	Three-year vernacular elementary school.
VSTP	Vereeniging van Spoor- en Tramwegpersoneel, Union of Railway and Tram Workers.
Wakaf	Religious endowment, usually land.

SELECTED BIBLIOGRAPHY

I. Archives in the Ministry of the Interior [The Hague, Holland]

A. Reports of Outgoing Residents and Governors [Memorie van Overgave]

Arends, P. C., September 2, 1927, *Mailrapport* 2592/'27.
Ballot, J., August 12, 1915, *Verbaal* April 5, 1916.
Gonggrijp, G. F. E., January 2, 1932, *Mailrapport* 360/'32.
Heckler, F., February 1910, *Verbaal* April 21, 1911.
Heuven, B. H. F. van, December 31, 1934, *Mailrapport* 254/'35.
LeFebvre, J. D. L., July 22, 1919, *Mailrapport* 2904/'19.
Spits, A. I., March 1937, *Mailrapport* 504/'37.
Whitlaw, W. A. C., April 1926, *Mailrapport* 2488/'26.

B. Official Correspondence on Particular Subjects

Abdul Muis' Activities: *Verbaal* January 30, 1919, no. 49; November 3, 1923, no C 16.
Guru Ordinance of 1925: *Verbaal* March 1921, no. 63/621; *Mailrapport* 214x/'27; 608x/'28; 870x/'28; 966x/'28; 1001x/'28; 1003x/'28; 64x/'29; 730x/'29.
Muhammadijah in Minangkabau: *Mailrapport* 523x/'27; 524x/'27; 1453x/'27; 431x/'30; 451x/'30; 538x/'30; 558x/'30; 712x/'30; 841x/'30; 1232x/'30.
Nagari Ordinance of 1914: *Verbaal* July 12, 1916, no. 47; March 4, 1919, no. 23.
Permi and PSII Leaders: *Mailrapport* 849x/'33; 930x/'33; 934x/'33;

1108x/'33; 1451x/'33; 327x/'34; 861x/'34.

Sarekat Islam in Minangkabau: *Mailrapport* 2357/'16; 291/' 17; 1351/'19.

Student Activities in Cairo and Mecca: *Mailrapport* 746x/'25; 1040x/'25; 1134x/'25; 281x/'28; 289x/'29;290x/'29; 490x/'29; 787x/'29; 1062x/'29; 1107x/'29.

C. Special Reports

Frijling and Cligneet. "De Sarekat Islam in Zuid Sumatra (Lam-pung, Palembang, Bengkulen en Djambi)," *Verbaal* November 27, 1915, no. 13.

Kern, R. "Politieke Toestand ter Sumatra's Westkust: Instelling Minangkabau Raad, Advies aan G.G., June 30, 1924," Kern Collection #145.

——— . "Voorstel om Natar Zainuddin en Hadji Datoeq Batoewah te Interneren, Advies ann G.G., July 23, 1924," Kern Collection #145.

Plas, Ch. 0. van der. "Gegevens Betreffende de Godsdienstige Stroomingen inhet Gewest Sumatra's Westkust," *Mailrapport* 527x/'29.

——— . "Neutraliseering en Bestrijding van Revolutionnaire Propaganda onder de Inheemsche Bevolking, in het Bijzonder van Java en Madoera," *Verbaal* May 1, 1929, C 9.

Roesad. "Het Modernisme in Penghoeloe Kringen, November 1933," in van Heuven, "Memorie van Overgave."

——— . "Nota over de Godsdienstig - Politieke Beweging ter Sumatra's Westkust, June 3, 1929," Mailrapport 1518x/'33.

——— . "Rapport over het Onderwijs aan Godsdienstscholen in Verband met de Ontdekkingen tijden de huiszoekingen in September 1933," *Mailrapport* 1518x/'33.

Ronkel, Ph. D. S. van. "Rapport Betreffende de Godsdienstige Verschijnselen ter Sumatra's Westkust," *Verbaal* April 4, 1916, no. 54.

Tumenggung, L. Datuk. "Geheim Nota voor de Adviseur voor Inlandsche Zaken over het Communisme ter Westkust van Sumatra, July 30, 1925," Kern Collection #46.

———. "Nota over de Toestanden ter Westkust van Sumatra, August 16, 1926," *Mailrapport* 934x/'26.

Vries, L. de. "Nota over Islamische Reacties in Nederlandsch-Indië Gedurende de Laatste Jaren, 1938," *Verbaal* September 30, 1938, no, 15.

II. Published Documents and Reports

Departement van Zaken Overzee. *Indisch Verslag.* 's-Gravenhage: n.p., 1931, 1932, 1933, 1934.

Handelingen van den Volksraad. Batavia: n.p., 1931-1934.

Kantoor voor Inlandsche Zaken. *Sarekat Islam Congres (le Nationaal Congres), 17-24 Juni 1916 te Bandoeng* (Behoort bij de geheime missieve van Wd. Adviseur voor Inlandsche Zaken, dd. 29 September 1916, No. 226). Batavia: Landsdruk-kerij, 1916-1919.

Volkstelling 1930, Vol. IV: *Inheemsche Bevolking van Sumatra.* Batavia: Dep. Landbouw, Nijverheid & Handel, 1935.

Wal, S. L. van der (ed.). *Het Onderwijsbeleid in Nederlands-Indië*, 1900-1940. Groningen: J. B. Wolters, 1963.

———. *De Volksraad en de Staatkundige Ontwikkeling van Nederlands-Indië*, Vol. I: 1891-1926. Groningen: J. B. Wolters, 1964.

III. Periodicals

A. Press Surveys

De Indische Gids, Monthly press reviews. 1900-1928.

Kantoor voor de Volkslectuur. *Overzicht van de Inlandsche en Maleisch-Chineesche Pers.* 1918-1928.

Koloniaal Tijdschrift, Press summaries. 1912-1919.

B. Newspapers

Berita dan Pewarta. Padang. 1933.

Bintang Tionghoa. Padang. 1914-1915.

Dagblad Radio. Padang. 1932-1935.

Neratja. Batavia. 1917-1924.

Oetoesan Melajoe. Padang. 1914-1923.

Oetoesan Melajoe - Perobahan. Padang. 1924.

Pertja Barat. Padang. 1911-1912.

Pewarta. Padang. 1934.

Pompai. Padang. 1929-1931.

Seng Po. Bukittinggi. 1927-1928.

Sinar Soematra. Padang. 1914-1935.

Soematra Tengah. Padang. 1914-1915.

Soeara Rakjat. Padang. 1914.

Sri Soematra. Padang. 1915-1917.

Tjaja Soematra. Padang. 1914-1933.

Warta Hindia. Padang. 1914-1928.

C. Journals

Al-Moenir. Padang. 1911-1915.

Al-Ittifaq Wal-iftiraq. Padang. 1919-1922.

Al-Ittiqan. Manindjau. 1920-1922.

Bintang Hindia. Bandung. 1904-1907.

Doenia Achirat. Bukittinggi. 1924-1926.

Jong Soematra. Batavia. 1918-1927.

Jong Soematra. Padang. 1925.

Kemadjoean Zaman. Padang Pandjang. 1928.

Het Koloniaal Weekblad. 1925-1933.

Locomotief (Sumatra issue). Semarang. 1925.

Medan Rakjat. Padang. 1931-1933.

Noeroelj aqin. Batu Sangkar. 1928.

Pahlawan Moeda. Bukittinggi. 1932, 1935.

Pandji Islam. Medan. 1936-1942.

Pedoman Masjarakat. Medan. 1936-1941.

Pembela Islam. Bandung. 1930-1934.

Perdamaian. Padang Pandjang. 1926.

Sinar Merdeka. Padang Sidempuan. 1919.

Soeara Kota Gedang. Bukittinggi. 1919-192 2.

Soeara Perempoean. Padang. 1918.

Soeloeh Melajoe. Padang. 1913.

Soematra Bergerak. Bukittinggi. 1923-1925.

Soenting Melajoe. Padang. 1912, 1917, 1919-1920.

IV. Books and Unpublished Manuscripts

Abdullah, Taufik. "Minangkabau 1900-1927: Preliminary Studies in Social Development." Master's thesis, Cornell University, 1967.

Achmad Chatib bin Abdul Latif. *Fatwa Tentang Tharikat Naqsja-bandijah*. Translated by A. Mn. Arief. Medan: Islamijah, 1965.

Adams, Charles Clarence. *Islam dan Dunia Modern di Mesir*. Translated by Ismail Djamil. Djakarta: Pustaka Rakjat, 1947.

Adatrechtbundels. 's-Gravenhage: Martinus Nijhoff. Vols. 1 (1911), 11 (1915), 27 (1928), 39 (1937).

Ahmad, Abdullah. *Ilmoe Sedjati*. 4 vols. Padang: Sjarikat Ilmoe, 1916.

——— . *Pemboeka Pintoe Sjoerga*. 2 vols. Padang: Al-Moenir, 1914/1915.

——— . *Titian Kesjorga: Kitab Oesoeloeddin*. Padang: Sjarikat Ilmoe, 1916.

Ahmed, Jamal Mohammed. *The Intellectual Origins of Egyptian Nationalism*. London: Oxford University Press, 1960.

Alfian. "Islamic Modernism in Indonesian Politics: The Muhammadijah during the Colonial Period, 1912-1940." Ph.D. Thesis, University of Wisconsin, 1969.

Amelz. *H.O.S. Tjokroaminoto: Hidup dan Perdjuangannja*. Djakarta: Bulan Bintang, [1952?].

Amir, Mohammad. *Boenga Rampai: Himpoenan Karangan jang Terbit Diantara Tahoen 1923 dan 1939*. Medan: Centrale Courant en Boekhandel, 1940.

Amrullah, A. Malik Karim [Hamka, pseud.]. *Adat Minangkabau Menghadapi Revolusi*. Djakarta: Tekad, 1965.

——— . *Ajahku: Riwajat Hidup Dr. H. Abd. Karim Amrullah dan*

Perdjuangan Kaum Agama di Sumatra. Djakarta: Djajamurni, 1967.

———. *Kenang-Kenangan Hidup.* 4 vols. Djakarta: Gapura, 1952/1953.

———. *Kjai Ahmad Dahlan.* Djakarta: Sinar Pudjangga, 1952.

———. *Pengaruh Muhammad Abduh di Indonesia.* Djakarta: Tintamas, 1959.

———. *Sedjarah Islam di Sumatera.* Medan: Pustaka Nasional, 1950.

———. *Sedjarah Minangkabau Dengan Agama Islam.* Fort de Kock: Tsamaratul Ichwan, 1929.

Anggaran Dasar dan Anggaran Tetangga dari Persatoean Moeslim Indonesia. Padang: PMI, 1930.

Aqidah Moehammadijah Bahagian Hizboel Wathan. Jogjakarta: n.p., 1927.

Batuah, A. M. Datuk Maruhum, and Dt. Bagindo Tanameh. *Hukum Adat dan Adat Minangkabau.* Djakarta: Pusaka Aseli, 1956.

Batuah, Ahmad Datuk, and A. Datuk Madjoindo. *Tambo Minangkabau.* Djakarta: Balai Pustaka, 1956.

Batuah Sango, Datuk. *Tambo Alam Minangkabau: Jaitu Asal Usul Minangkabau, Segala Peraturan Adat dan Undang-Undang Hukum Disegala Negeri jang Masuk Minangkabau.* Pajakumbuh: Limbago, n.d.

Benda, Harry J. *The Crescent and the Rising Sun: Indonesian Islam under the Japanese Occupation, 1942-1945.* The Hague: W. van Hoeve, 1958.

———. and Ruth T. McVey (eds.). *The Communist Uprisings of 1926-1927 in Indonesia: Key Documents.* Ithaca: Cornell Modern Indonesia Project, 1960.

Boekoe Peringatan 15 Tahoen Dinijah School Poeteri. Padang Pandjang: Dinijah School, 1938.

Bouman, Hendrik. *Enige Beschouwingen over de Ontwikkeling van het Indonesisch Nationalisme op Sumatra's Westkust*. Groningen: J. B. Wolters, 1949.

Brouwer, B. J. *De Houding van Idenburg en Colijn Tegenover de Indonesische Beweging*. Kampen: J.H. Kok, 1958.

Colijn, H. *Koloniale Vraagstukken van Heden en Morgen*. Amsterdam: Drukkerij de Standard, 1928.

Dahm, Bernhard. *Sukarno and the Struggle for Indonesian Independence*. Translated by Mary Somers Heidhues. Ithaca: Cornell University Press, 1969.

Diradjo, Datuk Sangguno. *Mustiko Adat Alam Minangkabau*. Djakarta: Kementerian P.P.& K., 1955.

Djaja, Tamar. "Pusaka Indonesia: Orang-Orang Besar Tanah Air." Vol. III, unpublished manuscript.

—————. "Islam di Indonesia." Unpublished manuscript.

Djedjak Langkah Hadji Agus Salim. Djakarta: Tintamas, 1954.

Federspiel, Howard M. *Persatuan Islam: Islamic Reform in Twentieth Century Indonesia*. Ithaca: Cornell Modern Indonesia Project, 1970.

Gedenkboek Samengesteld bij Gelegenheid van het 35 Jarig Bestaan der Kweekschool voor Inlandsche Onderwijzers te Fort de Kock (1873-1908). Arnhem: Threme, 1908.

Gobée, E., and C. Adriaanse. *Ambtelijke Adviezen van C. Snouck Hurgronje, 1889-1936*. Vol. 3. ' s -Gravenhage: Martinus Nijhoff, 1965.

Hamka, see Amrullah, A. Malik Karim.

Harahap, Parada. *Dari Pantai Kepantai: Perdjalanan ke Soematra*. 2 vols. Weltevreden: n.p., 1926.

—————. *Riwajat Dr. A. Rivai*. Medan: n.p., 1939.

Harris, Christina. *Nationalism and Revolution in Egypt: The Role of the Muslim Brotherhood*. The Hague: Mouton & Co., 1964.

Hatta, Mohammad. *Kumpulan Karangan*. Djakarta: Balai Ilmu, 1953. 4 vols.

Iskandar, Noer Sutan. *Pengalaman Masa Ketjil*. Djakarta: J. B. Wolters, 1949.

Josselin de Jong, P. E. de. *Minangkabau and Negri Sembilan: Socio-Political Structure in Indonesia*. Djakarta: Bhratara, 1960.

Joustra, M. *Minangkabau: Overzicht van het Land, Geschiedenis en Volk*. 's-Gravenhage: Martinus Nijhoff, 1923.

Junus, Mahmud. *Sedjarah Pendidikan Islam di Indonesia*. Pja-karta: Pustaka Mahmudiah, 1960.

Kerr, Malcolm H. *Islamic Reform: The Political and Legal Theories of Muhammad 'Abduh and Rashid Rida*. Berkeley: University of California Press, 1966.

Koch, P. M. G. *Menudju Kemerdekaan: Sedjarah Pergerakan Kebangsaan* Indonesia *sampai 1942*. Translated by Abdul Muis. Djakarta: Jajasan Pembangunan, 1951.

Maaruf, M. N. Sutan. *Riwajat X Koto, Manindjau*. Bukittinggi: Pembela Negeri, 1931.

McVey, Ruth T. *The Rise of Indonesian Communism*. Ithaca: Cornell University Press, 1965.

Mangkuto, Saalah Sutan. *Soeloeh Moeballigh Islam Indonesia*. Padang Pandjang: Boekhandel M. Thaib, 1929.

Meulen, D. van der. *Ik Stond er Bij Het Einde van Ons Koloniale Rijk*. Baarn: Bosch & Keuning, [196?].

Mukti Ali, Abdul. "The Muhammadijah Movement: A Bibliographical Introduction." Master's thesis, McGill University, 1957.

Nagazumi, Akira. "The Origin and the Earlier Years of the Budi Utomo, 1908-1918." Ph.D. thesis, Cornell University, 1967.

Nasroen, M. *Dasar Falsafah Adat Minangkabau.* Djakarta: Pasaman, 1957.

Noer, Deliar. "The Rise and Development of the Modernist Movement in Indonesia during the Dutch Colonial Period (1900-1942)." Ph.D. thesis, Cornell University, 1962.

Peringatan Congres Moehammadijah Minangkabau ke-XIX di Boekittinggi, 14-21 Maart 1930. Jogjakarta: n.p., 1931.

Peringatan (Verslag) dari "Madjelis Permoesjawaratan Oelama Minangkabau" membitjarakan "Goeroe Ordonnantie" pada tanggal T9 Agustus 1928 dan "Madjelis Permoesjawaratan Oelama" pada tanggal 4 Nopember 1928 menerima verslag perdjalanan oetoesan menghadap Toean Gouverneur-Generaal (Ali Emran Djamil and H. A. Karim Amrullah, eds.). Fort de Kock: n.p., 1928.

Petrus Blumberger, J. Th. *De Communistische Beweging in Nederlandsch-Indië.* Haarlem: Tjeenk Willink, 1935.

———. *De Nationalistische Beweging in Nederlandsch-Indië.* Haarlem: Tjeenk Willink, 1931.

Pijper, G. F. *Fragmenta Islamica: Studien over het Islamisme in Nederlandsch-*Indië. Leiden: E. J. Brill, 1934.

Pluvier, J. *Overzicht van de Ontwikkeling der Nationalistische Beweging in Indonesië in de Jaren 1930 tot 1942.* 's-Graven-hage: W. van Hoeve, 1953.

Pringgodigdo, A. Karim. *Sedjarah Pergerakan Rakjat Indonesia.* Djakarta: Pustaka Rakjat, 1950.

Prins, Jan. *Adat en Islamietische Plichtenleer in Indonesië.* Bandung: W. van Hoeve, 1954.

Pruys van der Hoeven, A. (ed.). *Een Woord over Sumatra in Brieven Verzameld.* 2 vols. Rotterdam: H. Nijgh, 1864.

Radjab, Muhammad. *Perang Paderi di Sumatera Barat, 1803-1838.* Djakarta: Kementerian P.P.& K., 1954.

Semasa Ketjil di Kampung (1913-1928): Autobiografi Seorang Anak Minangkabau. Djakarta: Balai Pustaka, 1950.

Raffles, Sophia. *Memoirs of the Life and Public Services, with Some of the Correspondence, of Sir Thomas Stamford Raffles*. London: John Murray, 1830.

Ridder de Stuers, H. J. J. L. *De Vestiging en Uitbreiding der Nederlanders ter Westkust van Sumatra*. 2 vols. Amsterdam: P. N. van Kampen, 1849/1850.

Roff, William R. *The Origins of Malay Nationalism*. Kuala Lumpur: Pustaka Ilmu, 1967.

Salam, Solichin. *Hadji Agus Salim: Hidup dan Perdjuangannja*. Djakarta: Djajamurni, 1961.

Sapija, M. *Sedjarah Pemberontakan di Kapal Tudjuh (Zeven Provinciën)*. Djakarta: n.p., 1960.

Schrieke, B. *Indonesian Sociological Studies*. 2 vols. The Hague: W. van Hoeve, 1955.

Schrieke, B. J. O. (ed.). *The Effect of Western Influence on Native Civilizations in the Malay Archipelago*. Batavia: G. Kolff, 1929.

Sedjarah Ringkas Sjech Abbas Abdullah Padang Djapang. Pajakumbuh: Wakaf Darul Funun Abbasiah, 1957.

Seperempat Abad Gerakan Wanita Indonesia di Sumatra Tengah. Bukittinggi: Panitia Kesatuan Wanita Indonesia Sumatra Tengah, 1953.

Sitorus, L. M. *Sedjarah Pergerakan Kebangsaan Indonesia*. Dja-karta: Pustaka Rakjat, 1951.

Sjafei, Mohammad. *Arah Aktif*. Djakarta: J. B. Wolters, 1953.

Sjahrir, Sutan. *Pikiran dan Perdjoeangan*. Djakarta: Poestaka Rakjat, 1947.

Snouck Hurgronje, C. *Mekka in the Latter Part of the Nineteenth Century*. Translated by J. H. Monahan. London: Luzac, 1931.

———. *Nederland en de Islam*. Leiden: E. J. Brill, 1915.

Sujono, Ag. *Aliran Baru dalam Pendidikan dan Pengadjaran*. Djakarta: Harapan Masa, 1965.

Sukarno. *Nationalism, Islam and Marxism*. With an introduction by Ruth T. McVey. Ithaca: Cornell Modern Indonesia Project, 1969.

———. *Negara Nasional dan Tjita-Tjita Islam*. Djakarta: Pustaka Endang, 1954.

Thaib, Aziz. *Hadji Djalaluddin Thaib Dt. Penghulu Besar*. Fort de Kock: n.p., 1934.

Van Niel, Robert. *The Emergence of the Modern Indonesian Elite*. The Hague: W. van Hoeve, 1960.

Von der Mehden, Fred R. "Islam and the Rise of Nationalism in Indonesia." Ph.D. thesis, University of California, Berkeley, 1957.

Wal, S. L. van der (ed.). *Herinneringen van Jhr. Mr. B. C. de Jonge: Met Brieven uit Zijn Nalatenschap*. Groningen: Wolters-Noordhoff, 1968.

V. Articles

Abbreviations

BKI	*Bijdragen tot de Taal-, Land- en Volkenkunde van Nederlandsch-Indië*
IG	*De Indische Gids*
JMBRAS	*Journal of the Royal Asiatic Society, Malayan Branch*
KS	*Koloniale Studien*
KT	*Koloniaal Tijdschrift*

TBG   Tijdschrift van het Bataviaasch Genootschap [also
           known as Tijdschrift voor Indische Taal-, Land- en
           Volkenkunde]

TBB   Tijdschrift voor het Binnenlandsch Bestuur

TNI   Tijdschrift voor Nederlandsch-Indië

Abdullah, Taufik. "Adat and Islam: An Examination of Conflict in Minangkabau," *Indonesia*, No. 2 (October 1966), 1-24.

―――――. "Some Notes on the *Kaba Tjindua Mato*: An Example of Minangkabau Traditional Literature," *Indonesia*, 9 (April 1970), pp. 1-23.

A.M.B.M. "Pada Menjatakan Pengadjaran Orang Boemi Poeteri di Padang Darat (Padangsche-Bovenlanden)," *TBB*, 9 (1894), 411-417.

Archer, Raymond L. "Muhammedan Mysticism in Sumatra," *JMBRAS*, 15, No. 2 (September 1937), 1-126.

Benda, Harry J. "The Communist Rebellions of 1926-1927 in Indonesia," *Pacific Historical Review*, 24 (February 1955), 139-152.

C.P. "Eene Beschouwing over den in den Nacht van 21 op 22 December 1915 Plaats Gehad Hebbenden Overval van Padang Pandjang," *KT*, 5, No. 2 (1916), 1209-1213.

Cuisinier, Jeanne. "La Guerre des Padri (1803-1838-1845)," *Archives de Sociologie des Religions*, 4 (1959), 70-88.

―――――. "Les Madrasah Féminines de Minangkabau," *Revue des Études Islamiques*, 23 (1955), 107-120.

Djaja, Tamar. "Rohana Kudus: Srikandi Islam Sebelum Kartini," *Hikmah*, 9, No. 13 (April 7, 1956), 16-18.

"Godsdienstige Rechtspraak ter Sumatra's Westkust: Penghulus en Adatrechtspraak in het District Padang," *Adatrechtbundels*, 39 (1931), 212-228.

H., v. d. "Oorsprong der Padaries (Eene Sect op de Westkust van Sumatra)," *TNI*, 1, No. 1 (1838), 113-132.

"De Inlandsche Beweging: Politieke Situatie, Onrust ter Sumatra's Westkust," *Koloniaal Weekblad* (1932), 607.

James, K. A. "Indië Weerbaar, te Fort de Kock in 1914," *KT*, 2 (1916), 1599-1603.

———. "De Nagari Kota Gedang," *TBB*, 49 (1915), 185-195.

———. "De Opleiding der Inlandsche Hoofden op de Buitenbezittingen," *IG*, 30, No. 1 (1908), 16-21.

Junus, Umar. "Some Remarks on Minangkabau Social Structure," *BKI*, 120, No. 3 (1964), 293-326.

Kroesen, Th. A. L. "Het Inlandsch Bestuur ter Sumatra's Westkust," *TNI*, 2 (4th S), No. 2 (1873), 81-109, 208-230.

Kroon, W. J. "De Invoering van Belastingen op Sumatra's Westkust," *TBB*, 51 (1917), 342-351; 52 (1917), 170-179.

"Legende van de Afkomst der Sumatranen en van Hunne Instellingen," *TNI*, 30, No. 1 (1859), 378-389.

Lekkerkerker, C. "Meisjesonderwijs, Coëducatie en Meisjesscholen voor de Inlandsche Bevolking in Nederlandsch-Indië" *KT*, 3 (1914), 865-884.

Leyds, J. W. J. "Larassen in Minangkabau," *KS*, 10, No. 1 (1926), 387-416.

Maretin, J. V. "Disappearance of Matriclan Survivals in Minangkabau Family and Marriage Relations," *BKI*, 117 (1961), 168-195.

Mendelaar, J. J. "Bestuur en Besturen in de Menangkabau," *IG*, 62 (1940), 529-549.

"Het Moehammedansch Lyceum te Loeboek Sikaping," *Koloniaal Weekblad*, No. 4 (1926), 8.

Moresco, E. "The New Constitution of the Netherlands Indies," *Asiatic Review*, 23 (1927), pp. 216-224.

Nieuwenhuis, A. W. "De Onrust in Indie en Hare Oorzaken," *Tropisch Nederland*, 1 (1928/1929).

"Organisatie van Volksonderwijs in Kerintji (Fragment uit een Rapport van J. E. Edie)," *TBB*, 47 (1914), 342-344.

Plas, Ch. O. van der. "Mededeelingen over de Stroomingen in de Moslimsche Gemeenschap in Nederlandsch-Indië en der Neder-landsche Islam-Politiek," *Verslagen der Vergadering van het Indisch Genootschap*, February 16, 1934, pp. 253-272.

Prins, Jan. "Adat Law and Muslim Religious Law in Modern Indonesia: An Introduction," *Die Welt des Islams*, 1 (NS) (1951), 283-300.

———. "Rondom de Oude Strijdvraag van Minangkabau," *Indonesië*, 7 (1960-1961), 117-129.

R., W. W. van. "Midden-Sumatraansche Problemen," *Indische Post*, 31 (June 28 and July 3, 5, 1924).

Roesad. "Minangkabausche Toestanden," *Orgaan van den Nederlandsch- Indischen Politiek-Ekonomischen Bond*, 4 (1923), 587-590, 645-647.

Roff, William R. "Indonesian and Malay Students in Cairo in the 1920Ts," *Indonesia*, 9 (April 1970), 73-87.

Ronkel, Ph. S. van. "Het Heiligdom te Oelakan," *TBG*, 56 (1914), 281-316.

———— "Inlandsche Getuigenissen Aangaande de Padri-Oorlog," *IG*, 17 (NS), No. 2 (1915), 1099-1119.

————. "Een Maleisch Getuigenis over den Weg des Islams in Sumatra," *BKI*, 75 (1919), 363-378.

————. "De Twee Moskeeen en de Adat," *KT*, 6, No. 2 (1917), 1589-1599.

Rooij, J. F. A. de. "De Positie der Volkshoofden in een Gedeelte der Padangsche Bovenlanden; Hunne Ethnografische en Hunne Politieke Beteekenis," *IG*, 12, No. 1 (1890), 634-681.

Scheltema de Heere, G. A. N. "De Belastinginvoering op Sumatras Westkust," *IG*, 45 (1923), 122-156.

Schrieke, B. "Bijdrage tot de Bibliografie van Huidige Godsdien-stige Beweging ter Sumatra's Westkust," *TBG*, 59 (1920), 249-325.

————. "De Islam op Sumatra," *Koloniaal Weekblad*, 25, No. 53 (December 31, 1925), 4-6.

————. "Het Probleem der Bestuursorganisatie ter Sumatra's Westkust," KS,.ll, No. 1 (1927), 57-106.

Snouck Hurgronje, C. "Een en Ander over het Inlandsche Onderwijs in de Padangsche Bovenlanden (1883)," in Snouck Hurgronje, *Verspreide Geschriften* (Leiden: E. J. Brill, 1924), Vol. 4, pp. 49 ff.

Stap, H. W. "De Nagarie-Ordonnantie ter Sumatra's Westkust," *TBB*, 53 (1917), 699-765.

————. "Een Statistiek in de Onderafdeeling Oud Agam, Afdeeling Agam, Sumatra's Westkust," *TBB*, 52 (1917), 141-169.

Stapel, F. W. "Een Verhandeling over het Ontstaan van het Menangkabausche Rijk en Zijn Adat," *BKI*, 92 (1935), 459-470.

Steijn Parvé, H. A. "De Secte der Padaries (Padries) in de Bovenlanden van Sumatra," *TBG*, 3 (1855), 249-278.

Tanner, Nancy. "Disputing and Dispute Settlement Among the Minangkabau of Indonesia," *Indonesia*, 8 (October 1969), pp. 21-67.

Verkerk Pistorius, A. W. P. "Iets over de Slaven en Afstamme-lingen van Slaven in de Padangsche Bovenlanden," *TNI*, 2 (3rd S), No. 1 (1868), 434-443

"De Priester en Zijn Invloed op de Samenleving in de Padangsche Bovenlanden," TNI, (3rd S), No. 2 (1869), 423-452.

Wal van Anckeveen, G. de. "Maleische Democratie en Padangsche Toestanden," *Adatrechtbundels*, 1 (1911), 114-128.

Wall, A. F. von de. "Kort Begrijp der Beteekenis van de Tarekat, naar het Maleisch van Sajid Oesman Ibn Abdoellah Ibn Akil Ibn Jahja," *TBG*, 35 (1893), 223-277.

Westenenk, L. C. "De Inlandsche Bestuurshoofden ter Sumatra's Westkust," *KT*, 2 (1913), 673-693, 828-846.

X.Y. "Het Inlandsch Onderwijs ter Sumatra's Westkust," *KT*, 2 (1913), 390-408.

www.ingramcontent.com/pod-product-compliance
Lightning Source LLC
Chambersburg PA
CBHW020640230426
43665CB00008B/252